The Soviet Union

cond edition

The World's Landscapes
Edited by Dr. J. M. Houston

The Soviet Union

Second edition

W. H. Parker,
M.A., M.Sc., D. Phil.

with a Foreword by

J. M. Houston
Chancellor of Regent College, Vancouver

Longman
London and New York

Longman Group Limited
Longman House, Burnt Mill, Harlow
Essex CM20 2JE, England
Associated companies throughout the world

*Published in the United States of America
by Longman Inc., New York*

First published 1969
Second edition 1983

British Library Cataloguing in Publication Data

Parker, W. H.
The Soviet Union. – 2nd ed. – (The World's
landscapes)
1. Soviet Union – Description and travel – 1970–
I. Title   II. Series
914.7   DK29
ISBN 0-582-30111-4

Library of Congress Cataloging in Publication Data

Parker, W. H. (William Henry), 1912–
The Soviet Union.
(The World's landscapes; no.   )
Bibliography: p.
Includes index.
1. Soviet Union – Description and travel – 1970–
2. Man – Influence on nature – Soviet Union. I. Title.
II. Series.
DK29.P38 1983   914.7   82-20360
ISBN 0-582-30111-4

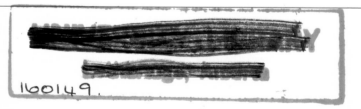
Printed in Singapore by
Huntsmen Offset Printing Pte Ltd.

Contents

List of illustrations

Acknowledgements

We are grateful to Novosti Press Agency for permission to reproduce figs. 5, 7, 10, 11, 13, 14, 17, 20, 22, 24, 26, 27, 29, 31, 34, 37, 38, 40, 44, 46, 47, 50, 51, 53, 54, 55, 59, 61, 62 and 63. Figs 6, 12, 23, 32 are from photographs by Richard Parker. Fig. 35 is by courtesy of Bronwen Hoare.

We are grateful to the following for permission to use copyright material:

The Clarendon Press for two extracts from *Herodotus*, translated by J. E. Powell; Constable and Company Limited for two extracts from *Through Siberia* by J. Stradling, edited by F. H. H. Guillemard.

Foreword

by Dr J. M. Houston, Chancellor of Regent College, Vancouver, BC

Despite the multitude of geographical books that deal with differing areas of the world, no series has before attempted to explain man's role in moulding and changing its diverse landscapes. At the most there are books that study individual areas in detail, but usually in language too technical for the general reader. It is the purpose of this series to take regional geographical studies to the frontiers of contemporary research on the making of the world's landscapes. This is being done by specialists, each in his own area, yet in non-technical language that should appeal to both the general reader and to the discerning student.

We are leaving behind us an age that has viewed nature as an objective reality. Today, we are living in a more pragmatic, less idealistic age. The nouns of previous thought forms are the verbs of a new outlook. Pure thought is being replaced by the use of knowledge for a technological society, busily engaged in changing the face of the earth. It is an age of operational thinking. The very functions of nature are being threatened by scientific take-overs, and it is not too fanciful to predict that the daily weather, the biological cycles of life processes, as well as the energy of the atom will become harnessed to human corporations. Thus it becomes imperative that all thoughtful citizens of our world today should know something of the changes man has already wrought in his physical habitat, and which he is now modifying with accelerating power.

Studies of man's impact on the landscapes of the earth are expanding rapidly. They involve diverse disciplines such as Quaternary sciences, archaeology, history and anthropology, with subjects that range from pollen analysis, to plant domestication, field systems, settlement patterns and industrial land use. But with his sense of place, and his sympathy for synthesis, the geographer is well placed to handle this diversity of data in a meaningful manner. The appraisal of landscape changes, how and when man has altered and remoulded the surface of the earth, is both pragmatic and interesting to a wide range of readers.

The concept of 'landscape' is of course both concrete and elusive. In its Anglo-Saxon origin, *landscipe* referred to some unit of area that was a natural entity, such as the lands of a tribe or of a feudal lord. It was only at the end of the sixteenth century that through the influence of Dutch landscape painters, the word also acquired the idea of a unit of visual perceptions, of a view. In the

German *landschaft*, both definitions have been maintained, a source of confusion and uncertainty in the use of the term. However, despite scholarly analysis of its ambiguity, the concept of landscape has increasing currency precisely because of its ambiguity. It refers to the total man–land complex in place and time, suggesting spatial interactions, and indicative of visual features that we can select, such as field and settlement patterns, set in the mosaics of relief, soils and vegetation. Thus the 'landscape' is the point of reference in the selection of widely ranging data. It is the tangible context of man's association with the earth. It is the documentary evidence of the power of human perception to mould the resources of nature into human usage, a perception as varied as his cultures. Today the ideological attitudes of man are being more dramatically imprinted on the earth than ever before, owing to technological capabilities.

In a book of this modest length, yet covering so extensive and intricate data, much could have been said that has necessarily been omitted. And as it is a pioneer work the author has touched only in some fields that still await more research. Enough has been said in this work, however, to indicate the powerful realities of the geographical zones of the Soviet Union, as a recurrent context of Russian society, and of the follies of human arrogance that defy this context. Today, Soviet scientists are more fully aware of the untoward consequences that may result from changing the natural landscapes of their country.

In this second edition, Dr Parker has added new material. He gives a vivid picture of the bureaucracy of Soviet industry to-day. He adds interesting data on environmental pollution, whose effects upon the biosphere are still unknown. He notes that the ideals of environmental laws are not matched with reality. There is still no public perception of some forms of pollution, such as the dangers of nuclear power. Perhaps the most powerful way in which the Soviet state has affected the natural environment, is the interference with the natural flow of surface water. But nowhere is the distinctive policy of the Soviet Union seen more than in its townscapes; 1200 of them are newly created, and there has been a post-war rise of the urban population by nearly 150 millions.

J. M. Houston

Preface

At a time when fissiparist tendencies are pulling geography apart, integrated landscape studies are of supreme value. They serve as a reminder that both naturally-caused and man-introduced features exist together on the earth's surface, mutually interacting, and forming distinctive patterns which vary areally according to the physical nature of the environment and the type of human culture which occupies it.

I have grouped the landscapes of the USSR into five 'belts', based mainly on natural vegetation, following the example of Soviet physical geographers. After travelling many thousands of miles in the USSR by sea, air, rail, road, river and canal, experience has convinced me that the natural environment remains the determining influence in shaping the Soviet countryside, despite the increasing number and size of innovations due to human activity. For further clarification the belts have been divided into zones – and where the subject matter has demanded or space allowed – the zones have been split up into subzones or subdivided into regions. Ideally the whole country would thus have been reduced to regions, but this would have required a much larger book. I am all too conscious of having at times been too summary and at others too selective, and that my style is terser than it would have been had I had more pages at my disposal.

In this second edition the economic information in the regional chapters has been brought up to date, and the final chapter has been expanded to take account of various recent developments and special features.

W. H. Parker
Stowe Grange,
St Briavels,
Gloucestershire.

Notes to the Reader

In this book, tons = metric tons (tonnes), and billions = thousands of millions (milliards); Russia = the land between the Carpathians to the west and the Urals to the east, between the Baltic and White Seas to the north, the Black and Caspian Seas to the south; Siberia = the territory of the RSFSR from the Urals to the Pacific.

A capital initial 'R' is used to distinguish the fifteen full Union Republics (Armenian, Azerbaydzhanian, Belorussian, Estonian, Georgian, Kazakh, Kirgiz, Latvian, Lithuanian, Moldavian, Russian, Tadzhik, Turkmen, Ukrainian, Uzbek SSRs) from the subordinate autonomous republics (ASSRs).

In the transliteration of the names of towns, the soft sign ('), a second consecutive 'y', or an 'i' before 'y', are omitted: thus 'Gorky' for 'Gor'kiy', 'Vostochny' for 'Vostochnyy'.

Both imperial and metric measurements have been used, a bimensuralism in keeping with the present coexistence of the two systems in Britain and America.

The numbers appearing in parentheses after the names of towns are the 1981 population estimates.

Naberezhnye Chelny/Brezhnev. On 23 November 1982 *Pravda* announced that the name of the truck- and diesel-engine-manufacturing city of Naberezhnye Chelny (Chelny-on-the-bank – i.e. of the River Kama) was to be changed to Brezhnev. There are references to Chelny on pp. xiii, 39, 108, 191, and it is shown on Figs 41 and 65.

Abbreviations and glossary

a.s.l.	Above sea level.
ASSR	autonomous soviet socialist republic: these are based on a minority nationality within a Union Republic (SSR) to which they are subordinate.
BAM	Baykal–Amur Railway (*Baykalo–Amurskaya Magistral'*).
CMEA	Council for Mutual Economic Assistance, also abbreviated COMECON.
CPSU	Communist Party of the Soviet Union.
GNP	Gross national product.

izba	Russian log house.
KamAZ	Kama motor works, the giant truck-building plant at Naberezhnye Chelny (*Kamskiy avtozavod*).
khata	Ukrainian thatched cottage.
KMA	Kursk Magnetic Anomaly, a large ironfield in south-central Russia.
kolkhoz	Collective farm (*kollektivnoye khozyaystvo*).
kray	Province, territory.
Min-	Ministry of –, in compound contractions (*ministerstvo*).
MW	Megawatts (thousands of kilowatts).
oblast	County, province.
pop.	Population.
RSFSR	Russian Soviet Federal Socialist Republic.
SSR	Soviet Socialist Republic, i.e. one of the fifteen Union Republics that make up the USSR.
SSSR	Union of Soviet Socialist Republics (*Soyuz Sovetskikh Sotsialisticheskikh Respublik*).
TPK	Territorial production complex (*territorialno-proizvodstvennyy kompleks*).
TSR	Trans-Siberian Railway.

1
The making of the landscapes

Natural landscapes

Russia has long been renowned for the uniformity of its relief and for its lack of really mountainous territory, and this generalization applies also to much of Siberia and Central Asia. The reasons for this relative monotony lie in the geological structure of the country. The western and central areas consist of two stable parts of the earth's crust which have undergone relatively little disturbance as far back as geological knowledge extends. These large stable blocks or platforms are basically composed of ancient and highly resistant crystalline formations. Where they have dipped beneath the sea, they have gathered a covering of sedimentary rocks, but in places the ancient rocks appear at the surface to form what are known as 'shields'.

The western platform, which extends from the White Sea to the Black and Caspian Seas, and from the Carpathians to the Urals, is known as the Russian platform. It finds surface expression as the Russian lowland, being wholly without mountainous relief. Its extent corresponds quite closely to the political area sometimes known as Russia-in-Europe. The eastern or Siberian platform extends from the Urals to the river Lena, where it forms the physiographic regions of the West Siberian plain, the central Siberian plateau and the lowlands and plateaux of Soviet Central Asia.

Along the southern and eastern margins of these platforms, there are, by contrast, areas of instability. Here, there has at times been 'sagging', leading to the creation of deep seas in which vast quantities of sediment were deposited by rivers draining from the uplifted continental areas. This accumulation of enormous thicknesses of sediment, transformed by age into such familiar rocks as clays, shales, sandstones and limestones, has subsequently undergone lateral compression. The stable platforms on both sides of it have moved together, possibly as a result of the flow of subterranean molten material. The accumulated masses of sedimentary rock have been forced to fold upwards, taking with them chunks of the 'floor' of ancient crystalline rock upon which they were laid down. These earth movements were accompanied by the penetration of the unstable area by masses of igneous or molten magma from the heated interior of the earth. In places, this forced its way through to the surface, but cooled and solidified slowly within the layers of sedimentary rock, metamorphosing those within reach into metamorphic rocks which, as a result, usually became crystalline and harder than before their contact with the magma. Such mountain-building processes are known as orogeneses and there have been at least four of them in the geological history of the Soviet Union. They are the Caledonian (early Palaeozoic), Hercynian (later Palaeozoic), Secondary (Mesozoic) and Alpine (Tertiary). Generally, the older ones are the lowest and closest to the edge of the platforms, while the newer, outer ones are the highest.

Each orogenesis had its effect on the mountains created by the previous ones. These mountains had usually been worn down, providing fresh material for the building of their successors. Their remains, consisting of rocks now hard, old, highly intruded and metamorphosed, were cracked or faulted by the renewed pressure, and sections of them were re-elevated along the fault lines. The pressures against them affected even the stable blocks beyond, causing them also to warp and crack, though not so dramatically as within the unstable belt. Thus, in the Russian platform, uplands like the Valday Hills and Donets Heights were elevated; in Central Asia the Kazakh upland was formed, and the whole eastern section of the Siberian platform was lifted several thousand feet. Between the two platforms themselves, the Ural Mountains (Hercynian) were ridged up. As a result of these processes, mountains of varying height, composition and complexity border the Russian and Siberian platforms along their southern and eastern sides: Carpathian, Crimean, Caucasus, Kopet Dag, Alai, Pamir, Tyan Shan, Altay, Sayan, Transbaykalian, East and Northeast Siberian, Sikhote Alin, Sakhalin and Kamchatka. Their lofty height and mountainous relief contrast sharply with the plains and plateaux of the platforms.

The absence of strong relief, combined with continental position, is reflected in a relatively simple climatic pattern. In most parts of the world, climatic conditions are greatly affected by the influence of seas, hills and mountains. But the Russian and Siberian platforms constitute a large part of the earth's land surface which is not only without mountainous relief, but insulated to an unusual degree from oceanic influence. The effect of the northern ocean is largely nullified by its frozen condition; the influence of the southern and eastern seas is kept out by the mountain rim. Marine influence enters unimpeded only from the west, between the mountains of Scandinavia and the Carpathians, but its effect has already been tempered by distance when it reaches the Soviet frontier, and is increasingly weakened as it travels eastwards. Direct oceanic influence is actually greatest in the far northwest of the country, where warm Gulf Stream water gives the Murman coast some of the mildest winter weather to be found in the whole country.

The climate is therefore strongly continental, with very cold winters and warm summers. Most precipitation falls in summer, but the winter share comes as snow. Brief springs intervene between the cold winter and summer heat, but autumns are more protracted. The cold winters become colder east-wards, the warm summers hotter southwards. Precipitation declines both northwards and southwards from a central belt, and within this belt it falls off towards the east.

Climate makes its own direct contribution to the landscape. According to the quantity and condition of the moisture held in the air, it shades the sky above and marks the ground beneath, leaving it wet, dry or hidden beneath water or snow; it often fills the air between with mist droplets, raindrops or snowflakes. When the air moves in wind, the clouds race, trees bend, ripples arise on the rivers and lakes, dust flies and sand stirs in the deserts. Snow is the dominant element in almost all Soviet winter landscapes. The snow-cover map does not, however, resemble the annual precipitation map, nor even the map of winter precipitation. It lacks the concentration in the west which characterizes both these maps. Instead, it shows a compactly shaped area with a thick snow cover of over 28 inches in the very centre of the country. From this central core, which is over a thousand miles across and bisected by the river Yenisey, the depth of snow falls off in each direction, the only exception being the Ural mountains (Fig. 1).

Climates change, and past climates have left behind land forms which deter-mine the relief of much of lowland Russia. Successive ice ages in the Pleistocene period not only witnessed intensive glacial activity on mountain tops and the valleys leading down from them, but saw large continental ice sheets move across the lowlands. These came southwards across the whole northwestern

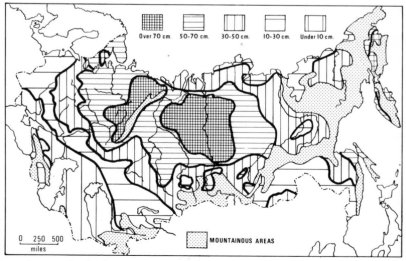

1. Average depth of snow cover

part of the country, carving, scraping, polishing and gouging the rocks over which they passed. The resulting hollows are now filled with innumerable lakes, the more resistant rocks standing up amidst the tundra or forest as great rounded humps. Such a glacially-eroded landscape is typical of Karelia. When the ice melted away, the rock debris borne along on, in and under it was dropped, scattering boulders, gravel, sands and clay, usually in a haphazard mixture. These dumps impeded the normal drainage channels, creating lakes and swamps. The farther the ice sheet had come, the more of this morainic material it carried, culminating in a maximum accumulation along its forward margin. Hence the farthest extent of the last ice sheet is marked by the deposition of a long line of terminal morainic hills. These run from Poland via Minsk, Smolensk, Vyazma and Mozhaysk, north of Moscow to the Volga at Yaroslavl and beyond. Because they rise above the ill-drained country so common in western Russia, these hills carry the main road and railway from Warsaw to Moscow, and they provided the main route taken by the armies of both Napoleon and Hitler.

South of the terminal moraine, melt water from the ice sheet spread alluvial material over the countryside. But whereas the melting ice dropped its moraine haphazardly, the running water in this fluvioglacial zone distributed it in an orderly fashion according to size and weight. For, as running water slows down, so it drops first the heavier material, and last, the lightest. The large watercourses needed to carry the immense quantities of melt water developed broad, open valleys. Often temporary lakes formed and collected level expanses of alluvial deposit on their beds. The present relief of this fluvioglacial zone, with its gentler outlines and wide valleys, is very different from the hummocky and swampy boulder-strewn landscape of the morainic zone to the north.

Farther south still, in southern Russia and the Ukraine, and in parts of Central Asia and southern Siberia, material fine enough to be lifted from the moraines as dust by the wind, during a succeeding dry phase in the climate, was dropped to form immense thicknesses of loess. This fine-grained but remarkably coherent deposit, by covering inequalities in the ground, gave rise to level country in which deep gullies and ravines form sharp gashes.

The landscape-forming processes sketched above were complicated by the superimposition, upon the first, of three more glaciations, although it is naturally the latest which has left the most pronounced imprint. Although the climate has generally been getting warmer since the ice ages, there was a period about 4,000 years ago (the sub-Boreal or xerothermal), when the climate of Russia was hotter and drier. As a result, the latitudinal vegetation zones and the accompanying wild life lay farther north—the northern boundary of the arid lands lay in the present steppe zone, the northern boundary of the steppe zone lay in the present forest belt. The present soils still retain many of the characteristics which they developed as a result of this earlier climate and vegetation, but these characteristics have been modified by the increase of moisture and the consequent shift of vegetation that has occurred since.

According to Sauer, 'the resemblance or contrast between natural landscapes in the large is primarily a matter of climate. We may go farther and assert that under a given climate a distinctive landscape will develop in time, the climate ultimately cancelling the geognostic factor in many cases.'[1]

In the platform part of the USSR, forming three-quarters of its area, the absence of strong relief and marine influence has allowed climate to draw broad latitudinal belts of natural vegetation across it. To them must be added the belt of mountains in which strong relief rather than vegetation type dominates the landscape. The central belt of higher rainfall and snowfall is forested, but the nature of the forest changes from the wetter, milder, western to the drier and (in winter) colder eastern end. Northwards of this central and axial belt, the forest falls away and, in the absence of a true summer, tundra takes its place. Southwards the forest declines also, making way for steppe grassland, which in turn, with greater heat and aridity, yields to desert (Fig. 2).

Soil does not normally form part of the visible natural landscape, except where exposed in gullies and ravines, or left incompletely covered in regions too dry to afford a full vegetal cover. It is, none the less, a most important factor in determining the nature of a landscape. Berg went as far as to say that 'every landscape expresses a certain soil type'.[2] Indeed, over much of the USSR, a poor sandy soil will almost inevitably support a pine forest, and the

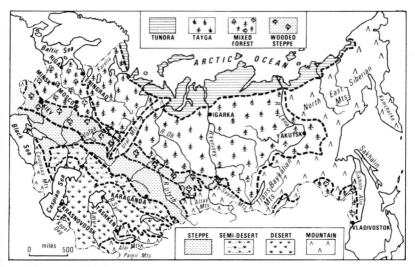

2. *Vegetation–landscape zones*

heavy clays and marls will develop bogs. In man-modified landscapes, soil is often a dominant element, especially between the time of ploughing and the growth of the crop. And it has had overwhelming importance in determining the direction in which man has attempted to alter the landscape through agriculture.

Cultural landscapes

The cultural landscape includes elements of a widely differing kind. There are those which, though resulting from man's interference, remain subject to physical laws: the birch forest that grows up when the natural forest of conifers is destroyed, and the cultivated plants substituted for natural vegetation. On the other hand, there are new elements of landscape resulting from the complete transformation of natural materials, such as buildings and railways. The former may be known as modified-natural landscapes and the latter as artificial elements. Some aspects of landscape have been much more greatly changed by man's presence than others: natural vegetation and wild life have been drastically affected, but the relief, the atmosphere and the seas relatively little.

The ability of man to influence the landscape will be determined by his culture. This may be considered as both social and technical. The social side includes his organization into economic, political, religious and other groupings, while the technical aspect embraces his knowledge of the natural environment, and the skills and tools he possesses to exploit this knowledge. The technical culture will decide what impact he can make on his geographical environment, but the social culture will determine the purpose and direction of this impact.

Cultures may evolve slowly or they may be changed abruptly, either by internal revolution or foreign conquest. Examples of all three processes are to be found in the history of the territory that is now the Soviet Union. A traditional indigenous culture will not only be a means of modifying the geographical environment. It will itself have developed largely in response to it – to its opportunities, its challenges, its restrictions, its prohibitions. But a revolutionary or alien culture, resulting from an accident of history, will not be in such harmony with the geographical environment. It is more likely to enter into conflict with it. But with time, man and nature must come to terms, and the relationship revert to one of mutual interaction rather than unilateral impact.

The great material advances made by the USSR doubtless owe much to the Soviet culture in both its aspects – the socialist organization of society and the application of modern technology. But they could not have been made without the resources contained in the natural environment (Fig. 3). This holds stupendous reserves of coal, petroleum, natural gas and hydroelectric

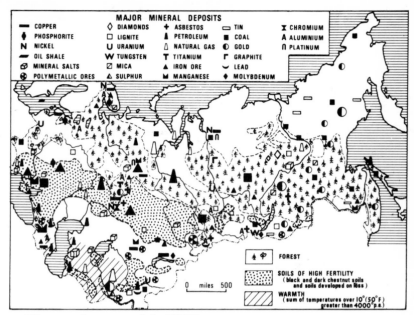

MAJOR MINERAL DEPOSITS

— COPPER	◇ DIAMONDS	+ ASBESTOS	▭ TIN	𝕏 CHROMIUM
◆ PHOSPHORITE	▢ LIGNITE	▲ PETROLEUM	■ COAL	A ALUMINIUM
N NICKEL	U URANIUM	△ NATURAL GAS	◑ GOLD	∩ PLATINUM
⌐ OIL SHALE	W TUNGSTEN	T TITANIUM	Γ GRAPHITE	
⊘ MINERAL SALTS	⊠ MICA	▲ IRON ORE	⌣ LEAD	
⊕ POLYMETALLIC ORES	△ SULPHUR	⋈ MANGANESE	◆ MOLYBDENUM	

0   miles   500

✿ 𝜑   FOREST

SOILS OF HIGH FERTILITY
(black and dark chestnut soils
and soils developed on loss)

WARMTH
(sum of temperatures over 10°(50°F)
greater than 4000°p.a.)

3. The natural resources of the USSR

power; it contains stores of all the metals and other minerals required for economic development; its forests are immense and its waters abound in fish. Although not so well endowed in possibilities for agriculture, it was until recently able to feed its population – now nearly 280 million – without appreciable imports of foodstuffs. It is the effective exploitation by the human culture of the natural environment that has produced the modified-natural and artificial elements in the landscape – the cultivated land, the sown pastures and the plantations, the buildings, plant, railways, roads, dams and reservoirs. Thus, a rich natural environment has made possible an advanced cultural environment, and the two are combined in the unique geographical environment of the USSR.

The natural environment does not act merely as a passive vehicle for natural resources. It presents also what may be called 'anti-resources' – obstacles and hindrances to the development of resources (Fig. 4). Although the natural environment of the USSR, taken as a whole, is in many respects the richest on earth, its anti-resources are also powerful. They include limited access to the oceans, immense distances without benefit of sea transport, a far northerly position producing long, severely cold winters and permanently frozen ground, a large proportion of mountainous terrain, much arid land and saline soil, and immense tracts of bog. It is not, in this environment, sufficient for a culture to

7

be able to exploit the natural wealth. It must also be capable of overcoming the natural obstacles.

Pre-Soviet cultures, whether tribal, feudal or capitalist, were less able to exploit the natural resources and to conquer the natural anti-resources. They had, of course, a much less advanced technology. But it is also arguable that, because the natural difficulties were so great, the organization of the whole of the nation's energies into a single force, and its direction by zealots who viewed the conquest of nature as a challenge to be accepted or a mission to be fulfilled, was a necessary prerequisite for success.

Impressive though the Soviet development of the geographical environment has been, the natural vegetation zones retain their validity as the major divisions of landscape geography in the USSR. So vast and strongly drawn are they, that the most awe-inspiring of man's works appear, more often than not, as local interruptions of the natural landscape rather than forming new landscapes of their own. Even where the natural plant cover has been destroyed, the climate which produced it remains to limit what can be grown instead. And certain climatic phenomena are so immutable, so strong, so emphatic, that man can do little more than mitigate their harsh landscape-determining quality. Examples are the long winter night in the tundra, the heavy snowfall and permanently frozen subsoil (permafrost) of much of the forest belt, the snow-melt

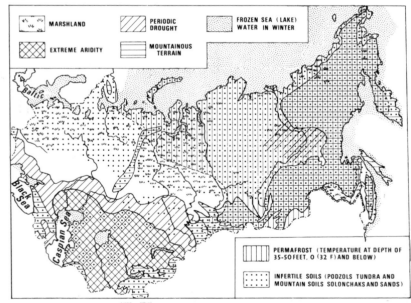

4. *The 'anti-resources' of the USSR*

erosion, dust storms and crippling droughts of the steppe, and the scorching heat and dearth of water in the deserts.

The landscape belts, zones and regions of the USSR, as described in this book, are listed below:

TUNDRA BELT. Distinguished by a covering of diminutive plants and shrubs. The *tundra zone* is treeless, but in the *wooded tundra* zone there are some trees, usually of poor growth. Soils are tundra, tundra-glei, and peat-marshy.

FOREST BELT. Vast expanses remain covered with forest, large-scale clearing being limited to the southern areas. Soils are podsolic and peat-marshy. The *tayga* zone consists chiefly of needle-leaved coniferous and small-leaved deciduous trees and subdivides into three regions:

1. The North Russian spruce tayga, with moderately severe winters.
2. The West Siberian swamp tayga, with severe winters and permafrost.
3. The Central Siberian larch tayga, with very severe winters and permafrost.

The *mixed forest* zone consists of a mixture of needle-leaved coniferous, small-leaved and broad-leaved deciduous trees. About 40 per cent of the area remains forested, despite a long history of human occupation and agricultural and industrial development. This zone includes the Baltic and White Russian republics, the northern Ukraine, as well as the Industrial Centre around Moscow.

STEPPE BELT. Needle-leaved coniferous trees, other than the pine, drop out, and steppe grassland – now almost entirely converted to arable – is typical. The northern zone of *wooded steppe* (*lesostep*) has islands of forest, and is the only zone in the USSR to combine fertile soils with an adequate supply of warmth and moisture for crops. It subdivides into:

1. *The western or Ukraino-Russian lesostep*, where broad-leaved trees like oak constitute the islands of wood, now sadly diminished, and where soils are grey forest or degraded black earths; and,
2. *The Siberian lesostep*, where the forest islands are of birch, and the soils black earth or saline.

In the southern or *steppe* zone, forest is confined to the river valleys or to shelter-belt plantations. It is subject to periodic drought, especially in the east. It subdivides into:

1. The western steppe as far east as the Volga, with rich black earth soils; and
2. The eastern steppe, mainly in Kazakhstan, where the climate is drier and more extreme, and where dark chestnut-coloured and saline soils predominate.

ARID BELT. Summers are hotter, longer and drier than in the other belts, although winter is still cold. A continuous cover of vegetation is not maintained, and desert shrubs appear. In the northern or *semi-desert* zone, steppe

10

TABLE I. *Area, population and climate*

	AREA %	POPULATION %	POPULATION DENSITY (PER SQ. MILE)	MEAN TEMPERATURE OF WARMEST MONTH °C (°F in brackets)	MEAN TEMPERATURE OF COLDEST MONTH °C (°F in brackets)	AVERAGE ANNUAL PRECIPITATION (INCHES)	AVERAGE DURATION OF SNOWFALL (MONTHS)
TUNDRA BELT	10	0*	1	0–14 (32) (58)	−10—−34 (14) (−30)	19–4	7–10
FOREST BELT	34	31					
Tayga zone	29	7					
North Russian	7	5	22	10–18 (50) (64)	−8—−20 (18) (−4)	22–15	5–7
West Siberian	7	1	3	10–19 (50) (66)	−19—−28 (−2) (−19)	20–18	6–8
Central Siberian	15	1	2	10–20 (50) (68)	−20—−45 (−4) (−49)	18–5	6–9
Mixed forest zone	5	24	151	17–20 (63) (68)	−3—−12 (27) (10)	26–18	3–6
STEPPE BELT	15	44					
Wooded steppe zone	7	27					
Ukraino-Russian	4	21	175	19–22 (67) (72)	−3—−12 (27) (10)	25–18	3–5
Siberian	3	6	64	18–20 (65) (68)	−18—−20 (−1) (−4)	19–13	6–7

Grass steppe zone	8	17					
Western steppe	3	12	125	21–23 (70) (74)	−10 — −18 (14) (0)	26–14	1–5
Eastern steppe	5	5	30	20–22 (68) (72)	−15 — −17·5 (5) (0)	16–10	5–6
ARID BELT	15	10					
Semi-desert zone	4	1	10	24–26 (75) (79)	−6 — −17 (21) (1)	12–5	3–4
Desert zone	11	9	25	25–32 (77) (90)	2 — −6 (36) (21)	10–2	0–2
MOUNTAIN BELT	26	15	16				
USSR	100	100	31				

* less than 0·5 per cent.

The population data given above relate to 1980 when the total population was 266 million.

grasses are also found and the soils are light chestnut-coloured or saline. The remainder of the belt is made up of the *desert* zone, where sands, grey-brown and grey desert soils, or saline soils predominate; there are significant areas of irrigation.

MOUNTAIN BELT. There is vertical zoning of vegetation. Human settlement and communications are concentrated in the valleys. Mining and hydroelectric developments are increasingly important.

Some statistical information about the area, population and climate of these belts, zones and regions is given in Table 1.

2
Pre-revolutionary cultures and the landscape

The forest belt

The forests of Russia, before they were penetrated by the East Slavs, were the domain of Lithuanian, Estonian, Finnish and other tribes, who were then in a primitive state. Tacitus gives this description of the Finns (Fenni) at about A.D. 100:

> The Finns are extremely ferocious and miserably poor. They have no weapons, no horses and no household goods. They eat herbs, dress in skins and live in holes in the ground. They depend for hunting on arrows tipped with bone, for they have no iron. Both men and women live by hunting: the women accompany the men and seek out their share of the prey. Their children have no other protection from wild beasts and from the weather than a framework of boughs woven together. (*Germania* 46.3–4.)

By the ninth century, the East Slavs had colonized the mixed forest region and the adjoining forest steppe, subduing the Finnish and other primitive inhabitants or driving them into the tayga forest to the north. Although they became sedentary farmers, their culture remained closely allied to the forests in which they lived. To obtain clearings in which to grow crops, they felled and burned the trees, thus giving a temporary boost to the fertility of the poor podsolic soils. Here they grew rye for food and flax for clothing. From the beginning, their farming showed an expansive tendency that has characterized Russian agriculture down to the present time. As their population grew, and as the fertility of the clearings declined, so they made fresh ones, abandoning the old to livestock. From these they produced hides, tallow and hog's bristles for trade. Three other forest commodities also figured prominently in their commerce: furs, beeswax and honey.

In this forest culture all buildings were of wood. Herodotus writes of a town that its wall was 'high and all of wood; and their houses and their temples are of wood also' (IV.105.9). The Russian log house or *izba* (Fig. 5), found in town and village alike, remained little changed for centuries. It was thus described in 1778:

> The cottages . . . are of a square shape; formed of whole trees, piled upon one another, and secured at the four corners with mortices and tenons. The interstices between these piles are filled with moss. Within, the timbers are

5. Traditional log houses or izbas *are still built in rural districts. These are being put up in the Vyatka area of the North Russian tayga*

smoothed with the axe, so as to form the appearance of wainscot; but without are left with the bark in their rude state. The roofs are in a penthouse form, and generally composed of the bark of trees or shingles, which are sometimes covered with mould or turf. The peasants usually construct the whole house solely with the assistance of the hatchet, and cut the planks of the floor with the same instrument, in many parts being unacquainted with the use of the saw . . .[1]

Only the brick stove, a large massive object, on the top of which beds were made, was not of timber; but it was wood fuel that burned inside it and that caused smoke to hang, thick and heavy, over every village the winter long, and which frequently caused disastrous fires. The rest of the furniture was all of wood.

Timber was also laid down in streets and roads to make them passable during the spring thaw and autumn rains. Bridges, sledges, carts, canoes and barges were all of wood or bark. The wooden bath-house was an old East Slavic institution, in which huge quantities of wood were burned to heat the water, and in which the bathers whipped each other with fir branches and poured water over each other from wooden pails. The practice was described in the eleventh century thus:

6. Kabikha, a village near Yaroslavl: sledges are still used in rural districts

I saw the land of the Slavs, and while I was among them I noticed their wooden bath-houses. They warm them to extreme heat, then undress, and after anointing themselves with tallow, they take young reeds and lash their bodies. They actually lash themselves so violently that they barely escape alive. Then they drench themselves with cold water and thus are revived.[2]

And in the eighteenth century:

There are benches all round, at some distance one above another, differing in the degrees of heat, so that everyone chooses the temperature that best suits him: upon one of those benches they lay themselves down at full length, quite naked, and having sweated as long as they think proper, they are well washed with warm water, and well rubbed with handfulls of herbs. But what is most admirable is, when they find the heat too intense, both men and women will run out of the stove, naked as they are, plunge into the river, and swim about for some time; if it is in the winter, they will roll in the snow.[3]

Not only pails, but almost every utensil was made of wood, articles of iron and copper being exceedingly rare. The dominance of wood as a fuel lasted until late in the nineteenth century. Steamers and railways used it until the Revolution, and the great charcoal-burning iron industry, established in the Urals by Peter the Great, was not overtaken by the coal-using Ukraine until the 1890s.

When the Russians settled in Siberia, whether in the tayga zone or in the wooded steppe, as Cossacks, exiles, farmers or administrators, they found timber in plenty and were thus able to reproduce their wood-using culture without difficulty. But even in the steppe and semi-desert zones, they built

15

towns of wood, floating the timber down the rivers. Samara, Saratov and Astrakhan on the Volga were all predominantly wooden towns.

Because felling the trees, clearing the ground of glacially deposited rocks, and ploughing the poor soils required a concerted effort, communal organization was strongly developed in the forest belt, and the village commune survived into the twentieth century. Because arrangements made with a few elders were binding upon the whole village, the system lent itself to the spread of serfdom, and the two institutions went hand in hand during the eighteenth and much of the nineteenth century. The commune necessitated settlement in large villages, rather than in isolated farmsteads, and it involved the annual allotment of the arable land amongst the peasant households, each of which had strips, averaging in width about ten yards, in the various fields. Until the 'collectivization' of the 1930s, the fields bore a medieval striped appearance.

The wood culture of old Russia remains an important though fast-diminishing element in the Soviet landscape. Old villages composed of izbas are still common, especially in Siberia, and new houses are often built in the same way. Large areas of the towns consist of old wooden houses.

Scandinavian influence
The East Slavs were not able to develop their culture free from interference and influence from outside. This came first from the northwest, from Swedish Vikings or Varangians. These subjugated the various Finnish and Slavic tribes and hammered them together into one relatively unified state to which the name Rus was given, in much the same way as the Normans forced cohesion and organization upon the peoples of England. The Vikings were waterborne plunderers and merchants, trading with the booty that arose from their raids. They found forested Slavic Russia especially fruitful. From its central area navigable rivers, linked with each other by easy portages, flowed in all directions, making it possible to establish an all-water route between northern and southern Europe by way of the Baltic and Black Seas, and with the east by way of the Caspian. The native inhabitants could be forced to part with their wax, honey, linen and skins, and were themselves excellent material for the slave trade. They even manufactured the boats the Varangians needed for their river traffic:

> Their Slav allies . . . in their hills in winter time, hollow out the boats, and when they have finished them and the ice melts with the warmer weather, they bring them down to the nearest streams. And since these flow into the river Dnieper, they descend this river, draw up the boats, and hand them over to the Russes.[4]

The Russes constructed many large wooden stockaded forts at strategic points on the waterway routes, adding to those already built by the Slavs. Many of these had grown into very large and important trading towns by the time the Mongols overthrew the Russian state in 1237–38; for example, Kiev, Novgorod, Smolensk, Pskov, Polotsk and Pinsk.

This involvement in trade was a major contribution to the Slavic culture. The forest zone produced goods for trade rather than for food, and therefore trade was essential if its inhabitants were to make material progress. Trade required organization and protective strength and these the Vikings introduced into Russia. It also required access to the sea – the great theme of Russian history. The Russians did not struggle with other peoples for an outlet to the seas to which their rivers led merely because they were avid for power and glory, but because of their dependence on trade. When, in the sixteenth century, the Swedes closed the outlet to the Baltic, and the Poles blocked the overland route to western Europe, the growth of flax and hemp, on which many districts depended, fell off sharply, causing great distress. Peter the Great (1689–1725) realized that if Russia was to catch up the advanced nations of Europe she must gain and secure access to the Baltic. He therefore wrested control of Livonia from Sweden, and sought to establish himself on the Azov Sea. Ivan the Terrible (1533–84) had already, by his conquest of Astrakhan, made contact with Persia and the East via the Volga, which subsequently became a very busy trade artery in the navigable season. Strahlenberg (1730) speaks of

> large flat-bottomed vessels in which they bring goods to Nizhniy Novgorod; they carry back in them, on their return, grain, vodka, timber and other Russian commodities. These vessels are very strongly built, and carry one mast and a large sail; but as they can only sail before the wind, they generally have three or four hundred men on board who, if the wind is contrary, are compelled to tow them.[5]

The so-called 'Volga boatmen' or *burlaki*, who drew these vessels along by human power, have been made famous in song and by Repin's paintings.

Trade was not wholly carried by the rivers. Overland caravans crossed Siberia to China:

> The caravan leaves Moscow in the winter and returns after three years bringing back silks and cottons, gold, precious stones, china and other goods, to the great advantage of Russia. The merchants benefit also in this, that on the way out they can trade with the towns of Siberia under Russian dominion, and on the way back, with the Tartars, with whom they exchange Chinese tobacco for furs and other articles.[6]

Moscow itself was, above all, a great trading town. Its commercial quarter of Kitaygorod was a vast and permanent fair displaying goods from many lands. It shared the moated centre of the city with the Kremlin, the seat of military and political power.

7. Twelfth-century monastery churches near Yaroslavl

Trade did not affect the landscape only by the creation of commercial towns, of traffic on the rivers and overland, and by the cutting of canals to link the rivers. The sale of Russian tallow, furs, wax, honey, bristles, hides, etc., abroad was used for the import of many goods that became part of the Russian scene, whether used to adorn palaces, mansions and churches or to dress the wealthier classes.

Byzantine influence

Christianity was established in Russia in the second half of the tenth century, and the formal conversion took place in 989 when Grand Prince Vladimir I accepted missionaries from Constantinople. This opened the way for powerful Byzantine influences and Kievan Russia soon became a cultural province of Constantinople. The most important effect upon the landscape was the appearance in increasing numbers, over the whole country, of churches in the Byzantine style (Fig. 7). Many of these have been carefully preserved by the Soviet authorities.

Churches and monastic buildings were at first of wood and continued to be so built throughout the forest zone until recent times. But with Byzantine influence came the art of building in brick and stone, and where the necessary resources and skills could be had, these materials were increasingly used for town churches. There were various styles, all with the typical bulbous cupolas. Some had tall, severe white perpendicular-style walls, surmounted by arches and crowned by towers culminating in these bulbs, as at Novgorod. Occasionally the walls were ornately decorated, as at St Dmitry, Vladimir, and sometimes recessed, with arched outer wall panels carrying paintings, as at the St Sergius monastery at Zagorsk. Often the architect concentrated on the towers. These were usually octagonal, broken by arched openings, and constructed in sections, the smaller upon the larger. Occasionally, there would be an elaborate confusion, with octagonal, cylindrical and pyramidical towers and cupolas at different levels, and with triangles and semicircles striving for mastery in the external design, as at St Basil's, Moscow.

The contrast between the white-walled stone or brick churches, their gilded cupolas aglint in the sun, and the collection of wooden izbas that surrounded them showed, almost everywhere in Russia, the strange impact of Byzantium upon the native forest culture. The mixture could be deceptive from afar. Coxe's words on approaching Vyazma were repeated by many other travellers when catching their first glimpse of a Russian town:

> At some distance the number of spires and domes rising above the trees, which conceal the contiguous hovels, would lead a traveller unacquainted with the country to expect a large city, when he will find only a collection of wooden huts.[7]

Mongol influence

In the year 1237 a great horde of Mongols crossed the Volga and fell upon central Russia, burning the towns, killing the men and enslaving the women. In 1239 they attacked the Dnieper region, sacking Kiev and neighbouring towns. Although the immediate effect in burned cities and untilled fields was catastrophic, little direct result of the Mongol invasion remains, except the existence of Tartar quarters in such towns as Kazan. Indirect influence has been more significant. The disaster of the Mongol invasion helped to produce a highly autocratic form of government in Russia. For centuries people lived in terror of raids by Tartars who could be bought off only by the regular payment of tribute. To ensure the safety of the state, it became essential that the prince should have the power to take away all he needed to effect payment, even if it meant taking everything. There was no room for constitutional checks and no time for parliamentary debate. The princes of Moscow won respect and allegiance above their rivals largely because of their greater ability to keep the terrible Tartar at bay. They emerged from the struggle unbridled despots, as was morbidly illustrated by the reign of Ivan IV, the Terrible. As Fletcher[8] wrote in 1590, 'the state and form of their government is plain tyrannical, as applying all to the behoof of the prince, and that after a most barbarous manner'.

The concentration of political power and the distribution of economic wealth are in themselves important geographical factors. Given two similar natural environments, if one is inhabited by a people among whom the wealth is fairly well distributed, implying that they have retained considerable political power in their own hands, then the general prosperity will be reflected in the well-kept houses and farms of the population as a whole. But if the other is occupied by a people living under unrestrained tyranny, then misery and poverty will be evident in the countryside with, by contrast, a remarkable concentration of wealth, in the form of palaces, churches and mansions, in and around the autocrat's capital city. This latter was the case of Russia. The mass of the people lived in wooden hovels grouped in primitive villages. But the tsar and his nobles possessed ornate palaces and costly mansions in which treasures of immense value were housed.

Autocracy, by stamping out the expression of individual genius, encouraged uniformity in the human landscape, for few had the heart, the will or the means to make an individualistic contribution by putting their talents to work. Unable to call anything their own, they had little inclination to improve their houses and farm buildings, to beautify their towns, or to embellish their surroundings. Nor were they able to obtain inspiration from abroad:

> They excel in no kind of common art, much less in any learning or literal kind of knowledge: which they are kept from of purpose . . . that they may be fitter for the servile condition wherein now they are, and have neither reason nor valour to attempt innovation. For this purpose also they are kept from travelling, that they may learn nothing, nor see the fashions of other countries abroad. You shall seldom see a Russ traveller, except he be with some ambassador, or that he make a scape out of his country.[9]

The great streams of exiles that made their way annually to harsh and distant parts of Siberia drained away many of the most enterprising and able. It was not, as so often supposed, the climate or want of native ability that made Russian culture seem so poverty-stricken to the foreigner, but the fact that under the autocracy, ingeniousness found no encouragement. Coxe was one of the very few to perceive this:

> Some authors, in considering the small advances made by the Russians in the arts and sciences, when compared with the progress of the more enlightened

nations in Europe, have erroneously attributed this deficiency to the effects of climate, or to an innate want of genius . . .

Many impediments arise from the government, religion, and particularly from the vassalage of the peasants, which tend to check the diffusion of the arts and sciences, without the necessity of having recourse to a supposed want of genius, or to the effect of climate.[10]

The Russian claim to have been the first with many inventions later made in the West is a justifiable one. But there were no forces in society interested enough to seize upon these early scientific discoveries and apply them – they remained mere curiosities.

Western influence

From the seventeenth century onwards, the dominating influences brought to bear on Russia came from the West, from Europe. The greatest single expression of this influence was the city of Petersburg (Leningrad), founded by Peter I in 1703, with the avowed intention of giving his country a capital comparable architecturally to Paris or Vienna. His successors, the tsarinas who reigned for most of the eighteenth century, brought in great foreign architects who assembled, on what had before been the swampy deltaic islands of the Neva, a magnificent arrangement of churches, palaces and other large buildings erected in classical style.

The pressure upon the higher nobility to live in the new town resulted in the building of many elegant streets of town houses. In the latter part of the century, Catherine II succeeded in outdoing Versailles. She concentrated in one spot almost the whole wealth of a country even more effectively than the French kings had been able to do. Catherine did not limit herself to further embellishing Petersburg, but encouraged the erection of more substantial buildings than the normal izba in the older towns of Muscovy. At Tver (Kalinin): 'she raised at her own expense, the governor's house, the bishop's palace, courts of justice, the new exchange, prison, and other public edifices; and offered to every person who would build a brick house a loan.'[11]

Western influence early made its impact felt in Moscow. Ivan III (1462–1505) brought in Italian architects who not only designed the Kremlin Wall and Towers, but the Granovitaya and Teremnoy Palaces and the Arkhanglesky and Uspensky cathedrals inside. But the Italian style of a few buildings in the city centre scarcely gave Moscow a western appearance, the mass of the city being composed of narrow, filthy streets of wooden houses. It was cleansed and renovated periodically by fire, the worst conflagrations being in 1737 and 1812. In the latter, many old noblemen's town seats were destroyed and, as the century wore on, their place was taken by workshops, warehouses and factories built in wood or brick. Steam engines were installed in many of these and chimneys belched forth smoke, while appalling slums grew up around.

In the first years of the twentieth century, a new dose of westernization came to the large cities in the form of tramlines, gas and electric light. Increasingly also, shops in the western style were beginning to line the streets. But as late as the Revolution the average Russian town was still remarkably free of western influence, except in the very centre where a few brick or stone buildings shared with the church the distinction of a cultural origin outside of the country.

Out in the countryside, westernization found expression in the landowner's mansion. Under foreign influence, the gentry ceased to be satisfied with the 'old Muscovite manor-house of logs or plaster-finished brick'. Instead, they must now needs build

> colonnaded mansions, sometimes of considerable size with a great columned reception hall and long, low wings, half circling a broad forecourt of honour. With their stately porticos, their chapels and their theatres, their gardens, lakes and parks, their swarming retinues of servants, some of these mansions, in their borrowed European style, were very tolerable miniatures of Versailles.[12]

Some landlords also began to apply western improvements in agriculture to their farms: hay crops appeared here and machinery there, and in the fifty years before the Revolution such innovations greatly modified the landscape in certain areas.

The most widespread and far-reaching of western introductions, full of implications for the landscape, was the railway. The first major lines to be built inside Russia were Petersburg–Moscow (1851), and Petersburg–Warsaw (1862), after which progress was rapid. By the Revolution, there were nearly 50,000 miles of railway, laid down on a broad gauge of 1·524 metres.

The steppe belt

While the East Slavs were colonizing Russia and developing into the Russian nation, nomadic peoples roamed at will over the steppe, often levying tribute upon the settled agricultural peoples to the north. Herodotus, writing in the fifth century B.C. about the Scythians, tells that they 'have established neither cities nor walled places, but all carry their houses about with them, riding on horses and shooting with the bow, and their sustenance is not from ploughing but from their herds, and their dwellings are on waggons.'[13]

There was little change in the nomadic culture for over two thousand years and its long reign had little revolutionary effect upon the landscape. But the nomads left behind their 'kurgans', earth burial mounds, usually conical in shape, which are very numerous in some districts and break the flat, monotonous expanse. And they may have been instrumental in pushing the boundary of the grassland northwards at the expense of the forest.

The culture of the ancient Greeks touched the steppes when colonies were founded on the north shore of the Black Sea: notably Tyras at the Dniester mouth, Olbia on the Bug estuary and Theodosia near Kerch. Olbia was built in a steepsided valley and ringed by a thick stone wall with turrets. Inside were the temples and characteristic buildings of a classical Greek town. Outside were the wheatfields of the colonists. For a time these cities flourished on the exchange of grain, timber, furs, honey and wax brought across the Scythian-held steppes, for wines, textiles and olive oil from Mediterranean regions. But their position was precarious and repeated attacks by the nomads brought about their decay.

The remarkable Greek colony of Heraclean Chersonesus was rather different. It was founded on a flattish-topped promontory at the western end of the Crimean Mountains in the sixth century B.C., and lay a little to the west of the site of the present town of Sevastopol. Its geographical advantages lay in the excellent harbours which the deep inlets of the north coast of its peninsular promontory gave it, and in its defensibility, which gave it a relative immunity from nomadic intrusion.

The town itself, with its temples, public and private buildings, aqueducts, walls, towers and gates, survived for nearly two thousand years. It was mistress, not only of its promontory, which was mainly devoted to vineyards, but of the whole west coast of the Crimea. It lived by exporting wine, grain and salted fish in return for pottery and textiles, although as time went on, it developed its own handicraft industries. Later, as an outpost of the Byzantine Empire, it added Christian churches to its old Greek temples. It was taken by Vladimir, Grand Prince of Kievan Russia, in 988, and he is said to have embraced Christianity here. It was again taken and sacked by Orderd of Lithuania in the fourteenth century, and by the Crimean Tartars and Turks in the fifteenth. Its finest marbles were taken by the Turks to Constantinople. Thereafter, its ruins remained undisturbed until the 1780s, when the Russians raided the site for stone with which to build Sevastopol, and very little of this ancient Greek town was left standing. Its promontory formed the scene of the main operations of the Crimean War in 1854–6.

For a time, Kievan Russia, the mercantile state established on the Dnieper by Vikings and East Slavs in the ninth and tenth centuries, controlled the lower courses of the Dniester and Bug across the western steppe, and was thus able to trade directly with Constantinople. This hold of the Russians on the western steppes was subject to continual harassment from nomadic tribes, and it was utterly broken by the Mongol Tartar onslaught of 1238–9. For 500 years the nomads were to control the Black Sea steppes, preventing their colonization, and challenged only by the Cossacks (Fig. 8).

The Cossacks were Ukrainians and Russians who had escaped from the oppressive life of the forest belt, and had adapted themselves to conditions on the steppe. Their headquarters were on the main rivers, where they lived a free life as raiders, hunters, fishermen and, later, as farmers. Eventually they lost their political liberty, coming under the control of the tsars, but they remained socially free and became prosperous economically. The Don Cossack city of Cherkassk, on an island in the river, resembled Venice: 'The entrance is by broad canals, which intersect it in all parts. On either side, wooden houses, built on piles, appear to float upon the water . . . There is not, I believe, a single spot in the whole town which is not annually inundated.'[14]

Early in the nineteenth century, the Don Cossacks abandoned this uncomfortably watery and regularly flooded site for a new capital on dry land – Novocherkassk. Cossacks were used by the tsars to protect newly won or settled Russian territory and, in consequence, they and their customs came to be found along the foot of the Caucasus, and right across Siberia as far as the Pacific.

When, in the last decades of the eighteenth century, the Turkish hold on the steppes was broken, large numbers of colonists began to enter the steppe. Besides Russians and Ukrainians, there were numerous groups of foreigners invited by Catherine II (1762–96). They included Serbs, Montenegrins, Bulgarians, Moldavians, Swiss, Germans, French, Greeks and Armenians,

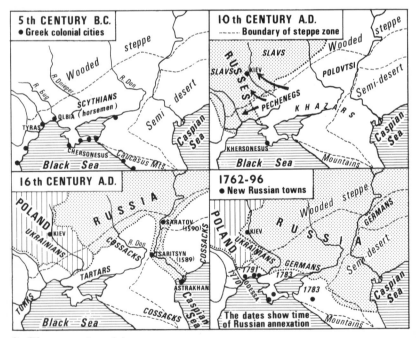

8. *The occupation of the western steppe*

each with a different culture and each leaving its distinct imprint on the landscape. The German Mennonites won high praise for their ordered cleanliness and efficient agriculture. They 'planted extensive orchards, and laid out great gardens, possessing the finest breed of cows in the country, and growing a great abundance of corn'.[15]

The French introduced merino sheep on to the steppe. The Greeks were fishermen along the Sea of Azov coast near Kerch, while on land they grew tobacco, which, after 'pulling', was 'strung, or tied singly, by the stalk of the leaf on long threads, and hung up under sheds, exposed to the air and sun, but kept from rain, until it be thoroughly dried'.[16] In the towns, they were found as 'respectable merchants' and shopkeepers. The Armenians specialized in business and commerce. At their town of Nakhichevan-on-Don they held a great fair, where there were to be found 'slippers, sandals and boots . . . tobacconists, pipe-makers, clothiers, linen-drapers, grocers, butchers, bakers, blacksmiths, silk mercers, dealers in India shawls, etc.' They lived in 'comfortable houses, many of which are limestone, and covered with tiles, in the manufacture of which, as well as of pottery, the inhabitants are skilful'.[17] But not all the wiles of the clever Armenians could prevent their town from being displaced as the commercial centre of the lower Don district by the nearby and better-placed Rostov.

During the seventeenth and eighteenth centuries, Ukrainians from the west and Russians from the north began to re-enter the steppe, colonizing its northern margins behind an advancing shield of wooden fortifications and fortresses, many of which grew into large market towns when their military function became obsolete. The Ukrainians were better adapted than the Russians to the steppe environment, their typical house or *khata* using less wood than the Russian *izba*, but making more use of reeds, thatch and clay:

> Their method of building cottages is both cheap and expeditious and very warm and comfortable when well finished. The corner posts are of wood, proportioned to the size of the house to be built, with light rafters and beams, and spars at regular distances for the walls, over which is laid, both within and without, a covering of reeds; the roof is of reeds also. When the plastering is dry, they are whitewashed and the windows and frames and doors painted, which renders them the neatest cottages I have seen. In this manner the sheep-sheds, barns and outhouses . . . are erected.[18]

Russian colonists on the steppe often found themselves in dire straits, lacking wood and inexperienced in khata-building. Clarke saw several Russian villages along the banks of the Don, but they were 'wretched hovels, constructed of the reeds and flags which grow in the shallows'.

Once the Russian power was established on the southern coasts, a vigorous traffic, by land and water, began to cross the steppes. Long caravans of

Ukrainian waggons, drawn by oxen, carried grain to the ports, bringing back raisins, figs, wines, dried fish and salt. In the drier eastern steppes, camels were used. On the Don, in 1800, 'barges, laden with corn were seen moving with its current towards the Sea of Azov'.

Catherine II established several seaports on the newly won Black Sea coast, planning them spaciously and erecting splendid buildings of local white limestone in classical style along the broad streets. At Nikolayev, the public buildings were constructed of 'a fine white calcareous stone full of shells', and Odessa was built 'with the same calcareous stone . . . which gives a very showy appearance to the buildings'.[19]

The arid belt

In the arid lands of Central Asia, irrigated oases have contrasted with the surrounding desert for many centuries. As long ago as the fourth millennium B.C., men were using small dams and ditches to direct water to their farms in the piedmont region. Later, when techniques had improved sufficiently to cope with more powerful streams, farmers began to use the waters of the Syr in the Fergana valley, and of the Amu. It has been estimated that between the fourth century B.C. and the second century A.D., when irrigation reached its zenith, about 9 million acres were irrigated in the deltas and lower courses of the Amu and Syr, supporting a population density of from 60 to 125 per acre.[20] Wheat, barley, sesame, millet, cotton and fruit (apricots, peaches, plums, grapes, melons) appear to have been grown. The Zeravshan valley was also an important area of early irrigation.

The irrigation farmers had to struggle both with the caprices of the rivers and the raids of enemies. They could usually cope with the former, if left in peace by the latter. Numerous ancient fortifications testify to the efforts they made to protect themselves, but they were particularly vulnerable because their livelihood depended on works which could be easily disrupted but not so easily repaired. For a time they formed part of the Persian Empire and a passage in Herodotus's *History* (*c.* 420 B.C.) illustrates their predicament:

> Now in Asia there is a plain enclosed on every hand by a mountain, and in the mountain there are five clefts. . . . In this mountain that encloseth the plain riseth a great river; and the name of the river is Aces.* This river formerly watered the lands of the said nations, being divided into five streams and flowing to each nation through a different cleft.
>
> But since they have been subject to the Persian king, they have fared worse; for the king built walls across the clefts in the mountain and set sluices at each cleft; and so, when the water was prevented from issuing

* Oxus, or the Amu river.

forth, the plain within the mountains became a deep lake, because the river flowed thereinto but had no issue. These nations, therefore, which were wont to use the water aforetime, are now in great trouble continually, because they have not the use thereof. For in winter God raineth upon them even as on other men; but they need the water in summer, when they sow millet and sesame.

When therefore no water is vouchsafed them, they go to Persia, they and their wives, and stand outside the king's gates and cry and howl. Then the king commandeth to open the sluices which lead to the nation whose need is sorest. And when their land hath drunk the water and is satisfied, these sluices are shut up, and the king commandeth to open others for whichsoever of the other nations is most in need. And as I have heard, he exacteth much money besides the tribute for opening the sluices.[21]

A sharp decline in the amount of irrigated land seems to have accompanied the inroads of the Huns from Mongolia about A.D. 500, but thereafter the oases recovered their prosperity. In the eighth century, they became part of the Mohammedan culture and took on the distinctive appearance which mosques, minarets and madrasah colleges bestow. Bukhara's Great Minaret, dating from the twelfth century, still stands.

Irrigated agriculture became, along with commerce and artisan industry, the basis of the flourishing Central Asian state of Khorezm, with splendid towns protected by walls and citadels: Urgench, Khiva, Bukhara, Samarkand, etc. Caravans from China, India, Persia, Tartary and the Greek Empire met here, and their busy bazaars offered the products of a growing number of skilled craftsmen. Remarkable contributions to mathematics, astronomy, geography and philosophy were made by such scholars of Khorezm as Al Khoresm (780–847), Al Biruni (973–1048) and Ibn Sind (980–1037).

In the early thirteenth century, great Khorezm was overthrown by the Mongol hordes of Chingiz Khan, and its wonderful cities were razed to the ground. However, after the initial catastrophe, irrigation works were repaired, trade returned and towns were rebuilt, and the region benefited from the establishment of a *pax Mongolica* from the Dnieper to the Pacific. Then, in the late fourteenth century, the great conqueror, Tamberlaine (Timur) made Samarkand capital of his vast empire. It was transformed by Tamberlaine and his grandson, Ulugbek, becoming resplendent with magnificent palaces, mosques, mausoleums and madrasahs, and surrounded by beautiful parks and well-watered gardens. Samarkand was exceptional, however, reflecting not merely the local culture, but the best that could be culled from the realms of India, Persia, Mesopotamia and Transcaucasia. The fifteenth century saw handicrafts and artisan industries flourishing once again. Samarkand paper was reckoned the best in the world, and its crimson velvet was sent to distant parts. The city was crowded with bazaars, one for each trade. Locally produced cotton and silk provided the population with gaily-coloured garments and the merchants with valuable export staples.

During the sixteenth and seventeenth centuries, the towns of what were now the Khiva and Bukhara khanates continued to grow and to accumulate new buildings, distinguished by their vaulted cupola roofs. But the splendour was departing. The Abdulaziz-khan mosque in Bukhara, built in 1652, was the last noteworthy building. Trade was falling off with the rise of ocean sea routes, and the feudal khanates tended to stagnate. The Russian conquest of 1864–84 made little difference. The feudal rulers were strengthened in their hold over their peoples, Russian quarters were built alongside the ancient towns, and there was a considerable increase in the growth of cotton and rice by irrigation.

The mountain belt

For 350 years – from 1427 to 1783 – the Crimean Mountains, along with the rest of the peninsula, were occupied by the Crimean Tartars. They presented a striking contrast to their predecessors, the Greeks of Chersonesus and other colonies. Instead of living in massive buildings of squared limestone, the Tartars were semi-nomadic shepherds, bringing from the east a culture in which dwellings were skin *yurts* or adobe huts. They built their towns and villages in valleys in the mountains. Bakhchisaray, the Tartar capital, was thus described in 1825:

> The numerous minarets of mosques, the ancient palace with the adjoining mausoleums, and a profusion of white chimneys rising amidst the richest foliage, produce a peculiarly beautiful and picturesque effect . . .
>
> Though the town does not contain one magnificent object, yet there is a singularity and beauty in the *tout-ensemble* which cannot fail to yield much pleasure. . . . The streets are narrow, winding and dirty. The houses are generally small.[22]

The Tartar villages along the cliffed Crimean coast were

> generally built on the declivity of the hills, and the houses are arranged, sometimes like terraces, rising one above another, sometimes more like steps of a single stair, and sometimes irregularly scattered. In some places they are almost entirely formed by natural hollows in the rock, and in others by making excavations; so that the natives have little more to do than to add a front and a roof to their huts. Few of them are of wood; they are almost all constructed of stone and clay, in the rudest manner. . . . Their roofs, made of strong planks, and flat, like a floor, are covered with argillaceous earth, which hardens in the sun, and becomes impenetrable to water.[23]

The mountain peoples of the Caucasus often lived in a similar manner.

As the nineteenth century progressed, Russian quarters developed alongside the Tartar habitations, and large white villas began to be built by the wealthy on the Crimean mountain slopes looking out to sea. Of the destructive aspect of the Russian conquest, Lyall wrote:

> We have heard much of the forbearance, kindness and toleration of Russia towards her conquered provinces, and she often deserves that praise; but, assuredly, for many years, the Tartars were treated with much severity, which led to great emigration. They have also suffered the most violent insults: their mosques, their minarets, their palaces, their baths, their water-conduits, their fountains, and even their tombs, have been thrown down, ruined and rased.[24]

The most remarkable Russian contribution to the Crimean landscape was the new resort town of Yalta, which by 1850 had become

> the great rendez-vous of the tourists, who flock in great numbers to the Crimea during the summer season. The quay then presents an animated scene, and small craft from all parts lie at anchor in the little bay. Nothing then can be more pleasing than the effect of the white town placed at the extremity of the bay, surrounded by rich scenery, with the high crests of the hills behind, also covered with verdure. The elegant buildings, the handsome hotels, and the general appearance of the population, all announce it as a town favoured by the rich and pleasure-seeking.[25]

3
The Soviet culture and the landscape

Marxist–Leninism

In March of 1917 the tsarist régime, manifestly unable to govern the country or to carry on the war with Germany with any hope of success, collapsed. Among the various disparate groups which had combined to meet this emergency, only one had the skill of leadership and the firmness of purpose necessary to establish itself in power. Lenin's Bolsheviks controlled the 'soviets', or works councils, into which the most politically minded of the Petrograd workers were organized. They were, besides, activated by an irresistible zeal which arose from their fanatical belief in Marxism. On 7 November (25 October, old style), the Bolsheviks seized power from the provisional government, and the Soviet state was set up. Henceforth the doctrines expounded in the writings of Marx and Engels, and elaborated by Lenin, were to form the official creed of the new régime and to provide the philosophical basis for all its activities.

The relationship between man and his environment is a fundamental aspect of Marxism. The total environment encompassing man consists of the human environment – his fellow men or society, and the geographical environment, which is partly man-made or man-modified and partly natural. Marxist–Leninists emphasize the contrast between 'nature' on the one hand, governed as it is by physical laws, and 'society', which develops according to social laws. But there has been some disagreement among them as to the relationship between these two aspects of environment. There are those who regard society as capable of evolution unaffected by nature, though increasingly able to alter it. On the other hand, there is the view of the majority that nature and society cannot be divorced, and that even though they operate according to different laws, each deeply penetrates the other with its influence.

Geographers have sometimes been divided into two groups: 'determinists' who maintain that man's progress is determined by the natural or geographical environment which surrounds him; and 'possibilists' who say that the environment allows him various possibilities from which he can choose. Marxists rightly regard this grouping as oversimplified and unscientific. They reject determinism on the grounds that society evolves according to its own laws, although some admit that changes in the pace and direction of that evolution may be due to the nature of the geographical environment. But they cannot accept possibilism either, as they believe the form of society, not mere chance or choice, will decide how far man makes use of the opportunities to be found in the natural environment.

Although Marxists may argue about the influence of nature upon society, they are more agreed about and more interested in the impact of socially organized man upon nature. This is summed up in the slogan: 'Nature influences society; society transforms nature.' Basic to the creed of Marxism is the belief that reason will triumph over nature – including human nature. It is maintained that a more purposeful impact can be made upon nature by a society in which all productive activity is planned, coordinated and controlled by the state than in a feudal or capitalist society.

Marxism offered more hope to Russia than either the geographical doctrines of determinism or possibilism. The natural environment in northern Eurasia is difficult and hostile. The country is isolated from the rest of the world by ice, by mountain and by swamp. For a thousand years the Russians fought to gain a foothold on the shores of their surrounding seas, only to find that these seas were landlocked antechambers to the great oceans whose freedom they could never aspire to enjoy. The country is vast, but when the extent of land covered by Arctic waste, tayga forest, rugged mountains and arid desert is subtracted, the amount of farmland is relatively small and much of this has poor boulder-strewn, ill-drained and washed-out soils. The growing season is perilously short and the best lands are never free from the threat of drought. For a large part of the year almost the whole Soviet state is gripped with frost, making many forms of economic activity difficult if not impossible. Even the stupendous mineral wealth is made hard and expensive to exploit because so much of it lies beneath vast swamps, in permanently frozen ground or on the flanks of mountains.

For a Russian to accept any form of determinism would be to resign himself, in deep pessimism, to a permanent back seat among the nations. Possibilism offers little more, because the possibilities inherent in the natural environment are harsh or exacting or costly. Given a free choice, and without benefit of socialist enthusiasm, compulsion or persuasion, man in this environment would tend to take the line of least resistance, abandon the struggle, conforming as best he might to the necessities of his situation and remaining forever backward. Such appeared to be the destiny of Russia under tsarism. It is no wonder that Marxist ideas, promising that man, suitably organized, could triumph over nature, should find a warmer welcome in Russia than in countries where the natural environment is more propitious.

Although the Marxist approach to environmental problems accords with sound geographical doctrine in that it discards both determinism and possibilism, it is open to criticism in that too much emphasis is put upon the nature of society and too little on other aspects of culture. The result is overemphasis on social and political factors. If for 'society' we substitute 'culture', including in that term scientific knowledge and technology as well as social and political organization, we are on stronger ground. It can then be asserted that the impact of man upon nature, and nature's influence upon man, will be governed by his culture.

The transformation of a river valley into a vast artificial lake terminating in a giant dam, beneath which a powerful force of electrical energy is generated, is distinguished from more primitive attempts to use water power by the advanced technology employed and not by the social system under which it was constructed. There are both capitalist and communist achievements of this kind, and a communist dam is not to be differentiated technically from a capitalist dam. It could be argued that one kind of society facilitates advances in technology more than another, but it is not yet clear whether capitalism or communism has the advantage in this respect. It seems reasonable, therefore, to criticize the Marxist approach on the ground that it exaggerates the importance of society as the determining factor in the mutual relationship of man and his natural environment.

The social and political organization of a people is but part, and not neces-

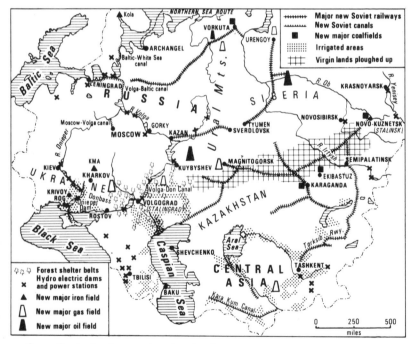

9. *Some Soviet landscape-changing developments*

sarily the most important part, of its culture. Some observers have even suggested that, under the drive of a common technology, capitalism and communism are moving towards similar economic and social forms. Certainly, as landscape-changing agents, advanced capitalist countries will have more effect than underdeveloped communist ones and vice versa. In theory, the Marxist state has the advantage that the landscape is being remodelled with a regard to the wellbeing of both man and nature, rather than to private profit and national expediency, but this is not always borne out in practice.

Probably the main landscape-shaping effect of Marxist–Leninism has stemmed from its concern with the location of economic activity, and, therefore, of human settlement. Marx himself condemned economic specialization, whereby industrialized countries created in their dependencies one-product economies to satisfy their own needs. In this way, the exploitation of man by master in industry was paralleled by the exploitation of the backward regions of the world by the more advanced. All countries should have balanced economies and a measure of self-sufficiency, but as this ran counter to the needs of capitalism, communism would be an essential prerequisite. On these grounds, Lenin condemned the economic organization of the tsarist empire as the exploitation of the outer colonial regions to the advantage of metropolitan Russia.

In conformity with this attitude, the new Soviet state was organized into nationalistic rather than geographical or economic regions, and from the beginning support was given to the idea of diversified economies for those regions. Marxist philosophy, in this respect also, accorded closely with the needs of Russia. The very inadequate transport system which the Bolsheviks had inherited had been run down almost to a complete standstill by the troublous years of war, revolution and civil war (1914–21). Economic regions aiming at self-sufficiency, with their industries located close to sources of energy and raw materials, and forced to develop whatever agricultural potential they possessed, would minimize the need for transport. Furthermore, as Soviet Russia was threatened by the hostility of the powerful capitalist world, the dispersal of economic activity resulting from such a policy would be a safeguard against military conquest.

Such a policy, according both with the tenets of Marxist–Leninism and the interest of Russia, if put into effect, would have obvious significance for the country's economic geography and therefore for its landscape. It would result in the many-sided development of a continental interior. Hitherto, such interiors had been exploited for raw materials and foodstuffs which were handled in great port cities where the bulk of the population was concentrated. This was true – and, broadly speaking, still is – even of the North American continent. The application of Marxist principles to the heartland of Eurasia would mean the establishment of industrial areas, not only thousands of miles from the sea, but independent of seaports and world commerce. This would be a unique development in the economic geography of the world.

Thus the establishment in Russia of a government pledged to implement the doctrines of Marxist–Leninism over the vast extent of the former Russian Empire was fraught with possibilities for altering the natural and geographical environments.

Industrialization

It has been noted that the Bolsheviks were more interested in the socio-political side of culture than in technology, as their main aim was the establishment of a new society in which it should be impossible for men to exploit others for private gain. It was obvious from the start, however, that if the new society was to survive the hostile international atmosphere which greeted its birth, and if it was to provide a better life than the old, then technical progress was essential. This was, however, particularly difficult for the infant Soviet state to achieve. It was to take four more years of conflict – until 1921 – to establish its authority, and by then all was confusion and the factories and railways of the country had almost ceased to function. The new government had to retreat temporarily from its principles and allow private enterprise to re-establish industry, transport and commerce. Even so, by 1925, when the state took management back into its hands, gross industrial output was only 73 per cent of the 1913 level.

Lenin, who died in 1924, did not neglect the technological side, but stressed the importance of electrification and it was therefore in that field that most progress was made before 1928: thirty stations were erected with a total capacity of 1·75 million kW. In 1928 the decision was made to push ahead with all possible speed and vigour with the planned industrialization of the country. This decision, after years of fruitless argument as to what should be done, was the result of the emergence of Stalin as the dominant personality in the Communist party. The three five-year plans, 1928–32, 1933–37 and 1938–41, converted the country from a chaotic backward state, in which 78 per cent of the population were peasants, into a foremost industrial power, capable of defeating Nazi Germany in war.

During the first five-year plan alone, industrial output rose to 2·7 times that of 1913, and labour employment in industry doubled from 3 to 6 million: 1,500 new factories and works were built and many others reconstructed or repaired. To provide a supply of iron and steel, three large up-to-date integrated works were erected at Krivoy Rog in the Ukraine, at Magnitogorsk in the Urals and at Stalinsk (Kuznetsk) in Siberia. Gorky, Sverdlovsk and many other towns received engineering plant in which the mining machinery and transport equipment essential for industrial expansion were produced. At Kharkov, Kiev, Voronezh, Rostov and Stalingrad giant tractor works to aid the trans-

*10. **This new synthetic-fibre plant at Barnaul illustrates the present emphasis on the expansion of the chemical industry***

formation of agriculture were established. The chemical industry was introduced. A large new hydroelectric power station was built on the Dnieper, its reservoir drowning the rapids and making the river wholly navigable. New railways, notably the Turksib (Semipalatinsk–Tashkent), were laid down, and thousands of miles were re-laid and double-tracked. The Baltic–White Sea (1933) and Moscow–Volga (1937) canals were cut, and new modern vessels introduced on the waterways. Irrigation works doubled the production of cotton in Central Asia.

The success of these prewar plans was largely a result of the zeal and devotion of the Party organizers and of the enthusiasm and pride in achievement of millions of ordinary Russians who, for the first time for many centuries, were given a chance to demonstrate their skill in industry. It was due also to the sheer physical stamina of a people inured to hardship and sacrifice, the people of whom Richard Chancellor, the first Englishman to come into contact with them, had written, 'I believe they be such men for hard living as are not under the sun; for no cold will hurt them. . . . If they knew their strength no man were able to make match with them.' Much of the initial work had to be done with bare hands in blizzard or frost, without proper tools, let alone machinery. The materials for the great Dnieper dam were carried in hundreds of peasant carts and much of the concrete was mixed manually. Thousands of young workers arrived on the barren, wintry site of what was to become the great metallurgical city of Magnitogorsk, with nothing but tents to sleep in and nothing but axes and wheelbarrows to build with.

Not all the hardship and sacrifice was voluntary. Much of it was endured by the inmates of forced labour camps in which political prisoners and others lived and died in the harshest conditions. Success undoubtedly owed much also to the resolute leadership and iron-willed ruthlessness of Stalin, and the introduction, by every means of publicity available, of an element of personal devotion – not to mention fear – into the labour of the masses.

There was foreign help. Like Peter the Great, Stalin recruited foreign experts in the western world. An American, Colonel Hugh Cooper, supervised the construction of the Dnieper dam, and was awarded the Order of the Red Banner for doing so. British and other foreign engineers took care of the machine-tool and machine-building industries, and Germans helped with the introduction of chemicals. Stalin was fortunate in that his first two five-year plans coincided with a depression of unparalleled severity in the capitalist world, as a result of which an unusually large amount of foreign skill was unemployed. But unlike Peter, Stalin saw to it that dependence on outside help was shortlived, and the foreigners were soon sent packing.

The aim was economic self-sufficiency in the basic requirements of heavy industry. This involved the denial to the population of all but the bare necessities, and even these were often lacking in the early years. At first, expensive imports of foreign machine tools were inevitable, and these had to be paid for, partly by the export of timber felled by forced labour, and partly by the export of grain, which the population as a whole, often on the verge of famine, could ill afford to spare.

The collectivization and mechanization of agriculture

Agriculture and the countryside constituted the chief problem of the new government, which in 1917 had handed over the ownership of all farmland to the peasants. But when, ten years later, Stalin set the country on the path towards economic self-sufficiency, he found the peasants a strongly entrenched class controlling the country's food supply. He needed food to feed the growing industrial towns, but he had nothing to offer in return: industry was almost entirely devoted to providing heavy industrial goods. He needed export grain to pay for the essential imports of skills and machinery, but the peasants, with the land under their own control, and no profitable market available for the crops they grew, had no spur to greater productivity.

A struggle between the government and the peasants ensued. At first this took the form of compulsory state requisitioning of food supplies, a difficult operation in a country made up largely of peasants whose long experience of oppression had made them past masters in the arts of concealing, deceiving and evading. The state next risked everything on an attempt to merge the peasant holdings into large collective farms which would have to be worked by machinery, and would therefore be dependent upon the state for its provision and for the oil to drive it. Some form of communal organization was, in any case, desirable on Marxist ideological grounds. The fact that peasants could be divided into three groups, the rich 'kulaks', the 'middle peasants' and the 'poor peasants', gave some scope to the Party, since the operation could be made to look like an attack upon the 'kulaks' in the interest of the poor peasants. Many in the Party opposed forced collectivization, but the need for a solution to the food problem was desperate. For a time, when local Party authorities overdid compulsion, it was touch and go whether a peasant revolt would overthrow the Soviets. But famine, a result of the turmoil that now existed in the countryside, weakened the resistance of the peasants, and Stalin made enough concessions to save the day. By 1933 most of the land was collectivized, and machinery, flowing from the new factories, was assembled in local stations under Party control.

The countryside, though still smouldering with discontent, was now subjugated to the needs of the state and compulsory deliveries of food began to move into the towns, while droves of uncooperative peasants were sent off to labour camps. Cultivating the land in large farms with machinery soon liberated large quantities of surplus labour which moved to the towns, and the 1939 census showed the percentage of peasants to have fallen from 78 to 54. Whether the total human suffering was greater than that occasioned by the Enclosure Acts in England is open to question, but the concentration of the Soviet agricultural and industrial revolution within the space of a few years made its horror the more dramatic.

War, reconstruction and technological progress

The German invasion of 1941 meant that the Soviet peoples had to endure a period of even more intense suffering and even greater toil. But landscape change was accelerated. While the western occupied districts of Russia were being devastated, the economic development of the Urals, Siberia, Central Asia and the Caucasus was speeded up. When the war was over in 1945, twenty million lives had been lost and the most productive part of the country ravaged. One thousand seven hundred and ten urban settlements and 70,000 villages had been burned to the ground. Yet another supreme effort was called for in the 1946–50 plan of reconstruction. Whereas the United States had emerged from the war with enormous industrial capacity, a relatively small loss of life, no physical damage, and possession of nuclear weapons, the Soviet Union lay devastated and defenceless against the new bomb.

Stalin lived to see the reconstruction completed and the rapid pace of industrialization resumed. But by the time he died (1953), his rule had degenerated into a tyranny accompanied by excesses and abuses of all kinds. He had, however, provided the iron determination necessary for the rapid transformation of the country. Since Stalin's death, the combination of state power and modern technology has produced a succession of great advances in the

Soviet economy, giving it world leadership in many spheres. In the production of the basic materials, progress has been unabated (Table 2). Oil and gas have

TABLE 2. *Total annual production of various commodities (millions of tons)*

	COAL	PETROLEUM	NATURAL GAS*	ELEC-TRICITY†	IRON ORE	STEEL	CEMENT
1928	36	12	0.3	3	6	4	2
1940	166	31	3	32	30	18	6
1950	261	38	6	90	40	27	10
1960	513	148	45	292	106	65	45
1970	624	353	198	741	197	116	95
1980	716	603	435	1,295	245	148	125

*billions of cubic metres   † billions of kWh

taken over the preponderant role in satisfying the country's energy needs (Table 3). Soviet output of electricity has risen from 27 per cent of the United States

TABLE 3. *Percentage of energy provided by various sources*

	COAL	OIL	GAS	NUCLEAR & HYDRO	OTHERS
1940	69	22	2	2	5
1960	56	32	8	3	1
1980	24	44	26	4	2
1985 plan	21	39	32	6	2

total in 1955 to over 50 per cent in 1980, notwithstanding a great increase in American production. Hydroelectric dams have created vast reservoir lakes on many rivers, and the hydro stations at Sayanogorsk (installed capacity 6,400 MW) and Krasnoyarsk (6,000 MW), both on the Yenisey, are rivalled only by the American Grand Coulee (6,180 MW). The world's largest thermal stations are now being built on the Ekibastuz and Kansk–Achinsk lignite fields, and a nuclear programme is under way. The electrification of the countryside continues – agriculture consumed nearly four times as much current in 1982 as in 1965. This, together with the formation of a national grid, has landscape impact as more and more pylon-borne transmission lines stride across the land.

11. Stalingrad (now Volgograd) in 1943, after its destruction in the Battle of 1942–43

More canals have been cut since the war: two important navigational waterways, the Volga–Don (1953) and Volga–Baltic (1964) facilitate the penetration of Russia by sea-going river vessels; two major irrigation canals, the Kakhovka and the Kara Kum, water the south Ukrainian steppe and the Turkmen desert respectively. The rail route length has more than doubled during the Soviet period, and one-third of it has been electrified. Recent achievements have been the 800-mile West Siberian line from Tyumen to the gasfield at Urengoy and the 2,000-mile-long BAM. Both were built across extraordinarily difficult terrain. Only the United States has a comparable development of civil aviation and space research. In 1957 the first artificial earth satellite was put into orbit, and in 1961 Yury Gagarin became the first man to travel in space.

Great industrial projects recently completed or under construction include the Kama truck plant at Chelny, the direct-reduction steelworks at Oskol on the KMA, the Orenburg gas-chemical complex, giant petrochemical works at Tobolsk and Tomsk in West Siberia, and the wood-chemical complex at Ust Ilimsk.

The growth of cities

The Soviet period has seen a remarkable increase in the urban population, from 18 per cent of a total of 147 million at the 1926 census to 48 per cent of a

12. Ancient and modern in Kalinin Avenue in the centre of Moscow

total of 262 million at the 1979 census. During the 1980s it has risen further to almost 65 per cent of a population of 270 million. This means that Soviet towns have had to accommodate an increase of 150 million inhabitants in little over fifty years, a period which included a war in which many of the country's larger towns were razed to the ground. In view of this, the wonder is, not that urban living space is so restricted in Soviet cities, but that the problem of housing has been tackled so effectively.

In the main this has been done by building large estates of tall blocks of flats, using a steel framework and prefabricated concrete slabs. In the early days these blocks tended to be plain and gaunt, but for most of them the drabness of standardization is relieved by the use of balconies. The uniformity arising from standardization has been criticized, but it was dictated by the need to provide large quantities of accommodation speedily. In any case, the array of similar blocks, aided by wide spacing and tree planting, is often more pleasing than a conglomeration of buildings of discordant individual styles. Latterly, local authorities have been encouraged to widen their choice of designs.

Over a thousand new towns have been founded in the Soviet period. About half of them were already the sites of villages or hamlets; the rest sprang up on empty land. Some of them – Magnitogorsk, Novokuznetsk, Karaganda – have already become large cities with several hundred thousand people, while many others exceed 100,000. Town planners are able to try out new ideas in the design of the latest towns, many of which excite admiration for their beauty of design, their attention to health and recreation in the provision of playgrounds and gardens, and their isolation of pedestrians from traffic and of industry from dwellings. Especially interesting are the *akademgorodoki* (academic townships) attached to some of the larger cities. These are devoted wholly to scientific research, and composed of institutes, laboratories, libraries, housing and services.

The emphasis on education and culture in Soviet life is reflected in the large number of buildings devoted to them. These, along with administrative buildings, usually dominate the town centre, and are often erected in a neoclassical style in contrast to the housing blocks. Although the authorities display undue haste in their desire to clear away the wooden houses of the northern and the adobe dwellings of the southern towns, often destroying much that is historic and picturesque, if not beautiful, they show a laudable determination to preserve old churches, mosques and palaces.

The streets of new or reconstructed Soviet cities are invariably broad tree-lined avenues, with trolley-buses, buses, taxis and lorries forming the bulk of the traffic, and with donkey carts and hand barrows surviving in the eastern towns. But already the tide of motor-cars is rising. The general cleanliness, the absence of litter, the paucity of advertisements and neon signs, the more regular architecture, all combine to give Soviet towns distinctiveness.

4
The tundra belt

Natural landscapes

The tundra zone, which fringes the northern shores of the Soviet Union and includes the off-lying islands, occupies an area of about 835,000 square miles, or 10 per cent of that of the whole USSR. Most of it was affected by one or other of the great ice sheets of the Quaternary ice ages. These scraped, polished, grooved, crushed or sheared the rocks on their advance, and dropped boulders and stones haphazardly on their retreat.

During the period that has elapsed since – a very brief interval geologically – running water, the prime agent of erosion in more temperate climes, has had little time in which to mould the landscape. It is stayed for the greater part of each year by the icy grip of frost. Hence, although the great rivers which enter the zone from the south make their way across it as adult streams, the inter-vening land has been unable to develop any maturity of form, and the drainage system is chaotic. With running water almost paralysed as a sculptor of relief and a moderator of slope, frost weathering becomes the most important physical process affecting the landscape. Wherever the surface rocks can be permeated by water, its freezing has a shattering effect and produces tons of debris which skirt the summits, litter the plateaux, screen the slopes and clutter up the valley bottoms.

The contrast between winter and summer is another feature of the tundra zone. As it lies almost wholly within the Arctic Circle, it is totally deprived of daylight in midwinter. At this season, a sombre cloud cover may result in nearly total darkness, or the whole land may lie shrouded in fog, or a blizzard fill the air with whirling snowflakes. But if the skies are clear, as they often are in the east, moonlight will reveal a still and silent scene of snow and ice. There is little sign of life except for wild reindeer in the far north, the occasional appearance of a shambling polar bear or stealthy polar fox – scarcely distinguishable in their white coats from the ubiquitous snow – and the emergence, now and again, of little lemmings from their holes.

Lengthening days, while better illuminating this frigid landscape, will do little to soften its harshness until the approach of midsummer. In June the sun circles the horizon and there is no night. Monotony gives way to variety. The snow and ice melt away to reveal contrasts of surface. Freshly thawed stretches of squelchy, peaty, moss-covered soil turn suddenly from brown to green and,

13. The tundra city of Norilsk (pop. 184,000) in the mid-winter polar night, when there is no daylight

after a few more days, diminutive plants burst into flower. Streams run again and rapids and falls resume noisy activity. A myriad lakes and ponds and large expanses of swamp cover much of the ground which, thawed out on the surface only and permanently frozen beneath, does not drain easily. Bare surfaces of ice-polished, glacier-scratched rock reveal, on closer inspection, tiny plants growing in every crevice, while elsewhere chaotic masses of boulders and stones are strewn over wide areas. But slopes and hollows never visited by the sun remain clad in snow and ice.

The brightly coloured flowers provide the most delightful and refreshing aspect of the summer scene. They are borne by small plants that cling to the rock on southward-facing slopes, or grow interspersed amongst the mosses. The blossoms are large in proportion to their tiny stalks, and of many colours: violets, blue gentians, forget-me-nots, yellow violas and buttercups, pink catchflies, multi-coloured pansies and Arctic poppies – and many others.

Animal, bird and insect life, so absent in the long winter, abounds in the brief summer. The ground swarms with lemmings upon which the larger animals feed. The wild reindeer has, alas, been virtually exterminated during this century, but cast antlers, skeletons and bones are still part of the tundra scene. Polar bear and polar fox, the white coat of the latter now brown for summer wear, frequent the coastal areas, and the seal suns itself on the spring ice offshore. The Alpine hare darts amongst the bushes in the valleys. Wolves

43

enter the tundra from the forest in search of prey. And, every summer, wild-fowl – swans, geese, ducks, snipe – flock into the area. The coastal cliffs and offshore islands, and the waters of the inland lakes, are alive with birds. Even on the northern island of Novaya Zemlya over thirty species have been observed, and well over forty on the south island. The damp summer air is thick with flies and mosquitoes.

A tundra climate is usually defined as one in which the warmest month has an average mean temperature of between 0° C (32° F) and 10° C (50° F). This permits the growth of small plants, but not trees. Chilling winds off the sea which, with its melting masses of ice, is always cold, keep average temperatures down, but warm spells occur occasionally, and readings of 30° C (86° F) and over in the shade are not uncommon.

If all solar radiation were allowed to reach the surface, the polar regions, in their nightless summer, would receive as much as the tropics, but although there is much daylight, there is very little sunshine. Cloud, mist and fog commonly obscure the sun and much of the heat energy is spent on evaporating moisture instead of warming the ground. For although total annual precipitation is small, most of it falls in summer. The absence of a developed natural drainage system impedes run-off, and the permafrost underground prevents downward percolation. Furthermore, even the summer precipitation often comes as snow, and this has to be melted before the air temperature can be raised much above freezing point.

In the west cyclonic disturbances are common and produce very changeable weather, with a rapid alternation of sunshine, rain, sleet and fog. The Gulf Stream, though moderating the severity of winter along the Murmansk coast, does little for it in the summer, when mean temperatures stay in the region of 10° C (50° F). But the period of surface thaw is longer in the west; it decreases eastwards from a maximum of about four months to less than two on the north coast of eastern Siberia. In September the loss of heat through the lengthening nights rapidly overtakes the dwindling amount gained during the shrinking days. Snow and ice, once formed, no longer thaw and the tundra is soon shrouded once more in white before it is lost in the darkness of the Arctic night.

The term 'tundra belt' is a useful one to distinguish the northernmost lands of the Soviet Union; and the uniform mantle of snow, ice and darkness which clothes them in winter gives them unity for most of the year. But the brief summer uncovers a variety of landscapes distinguished by their peculiar vegetation cover or relief.

There is a latitudinal zoning. The northernmost of the Arctic islands are perpetually covered by ice and snow, and so is most of Novaya Zemlya which straddles the 75th parallel. High plateaux and mountains confront the sea with rocky and precipitous cliffs through which glaciers have carved steepsided fiords and these are now filled with rock rubble. On the southern island the

14. The 'midnight sun' of the tundra summer near Norilsk

highlands are snow-covered, but the northern island is capped with ice from which glaciers descend the fiords to the sea. Here and there, high ice-sharpened peaks protrude above the icecap, notably Peak Sedov, which reaches 3,300 feet above sea-level. Yet even round the coasts of the Frants Iosif Islands and of North Island, Novaya Zemlya, there are areas free of snow to which a scanty vegetation of moss and lichen clings. The mean July temperature of such areas averages between 0° C (32° F) and 5° C (41° F), yet thirty-seven species of flowering plant have been recognized in the Frants Iosif group, where the polar bear and polar fox, together with a few migrant birds in summer, form the only wild life. On northern Novaya Zemlya, there are also wild reindeer and lemmings, while the coastal cliffs house many birds. Great masses of driftwood beat against the shores.

Moving southwards, the arctic desert is succeeded by arctic tundra, which is found on southernmost Novaya Zemlya, on Vaygach Island, on the New Siberian Islands and along the mainland coast from the Yamal peninsula to the Lena delta (Figs. 15 and 16). Beyond, it occurs less continuously as far as the Kolyma river mouth. It is interspersed with large stretches of swamp. Arctic tundra is predominantly a poor thin covering of moss and lichens, with shrubs confined to the watercourses and well-sheltered spots. But the number of species of minuscule flowering plants may rise to 200. Mean July temperatures are about 5° C (41° F) or 6° C (43° F), but temperature is not the only control. This landscape is developed on flattish expanses which are relatively dry, because the strong winds sweep away the snow. 'Spot tundra', in which roundish patches of ground 2 or 3 feet in diameter are left bare, is common. This may be caused by frost-heaving, the elevated portions of the surface being dried out by the wind so as to be unable to sustain plant life. Very low ground temperatures certainly occur in the Arctic tundra zone owing to the thinness of the snow cover and consequently the frost is hard and deep.

Relief adds further variety to some of the Arctic tundra areas. Thus, on Vaygach Island the old Palaeozoic slates have been so severely folded that the strata stand up on end, and on the western side, form steep, ledged and broken cliffs. In summer these hold the nests of innumerable birds. On the lower eastern side, masses of soft sand cover the old rocks and form low cliffs. The low elevations of Vaygach Island are continued across the Kara Strait in the southern part of Novaya Zemlya's south island. Here too, masses of sand, gravel and rock debris form mounds up to a hundred feet high.

The arctic tundra is followed southwards by the tundra proper or 'typical' tundra, in which the ground is carpeted with mosses and lichens, while many shrubs, such as blackberry, crowberry and cowberry, have also established themselves. Bushes and even trees mark the watercourses. A variety of tiny plants, characterized by their few leaves and short stems, blossom into flower. During the short vegetative season this landscape can be very attractive to the eye: the greens, greys and browns of the mosses and lichens blend harmoniously together and contrast with the black peat soil, while the flowers provide splashes of bright colour. But swarms of flies and mosquitoes plague man and beast alike.

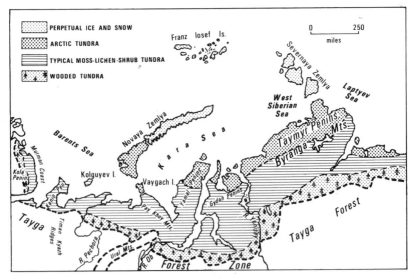

15. The western tundra: subzones

In wetter parts of the Kola and the Kanin peninsulas, the shrubs are in some areas far more extensive than in 'typical' tundra, and form a shrub tundra. Elsewhere in the wetter west, especially along the Murman coast, a bush tundra, in which the ground is covered by compact, impenetrable and extensive thickets of dwarf birch and dwarf willow, is encountered.

The monotony of the 'typical' tundra is also varied by relief. The main interruptions to the generally low-lying land in the Russian sector are the crystalline plateau which runs across the Kanin peninsula, and the Timan Kryazh ridges of folded Palaeozoic rocks which run out to the Barents Sea in rocky promontories. But these are hills rather than mountains and are equalled in height by the great glacial moraine which parallels the coast. The Russian sector of the tundra is separated from the Siberian by the Pay Khoy range. This continues the Urals northwestwards towards the islands of Vaygach and Novaya Zemlya, and its folded Palaeozoic rocks, though well below the average height of the Urals, none the less stand up boldly from the surrounding swamp. In the Siberian sector the main relief is given by the range of dislocated Palaeozoic rocks that cross the Taymyr peninsula from west to east at heights of between 1,000 and 1,500 feet.

Finally comes the wooded tundra, which, as it contains trees, is not properly a tundra landscape at all, but a zone of transition to the tayga forest. It forms an almost continuous but narrow belt from the Pechora in the west to the Kolyma in the east. The trees are often dwarfed, deformed and untidy in appearance, and much of the ground is taken up by sphagnum bog, characterized by the whitish spongy leaves of the sphagnum moss.

In the west the wooded tundra usually consists of individual birch and spruce trees rising above dense thickets of willow scrub. Eastwards, the ground becomes more open and the trees are grouped in islands which stand out amidst broad expanses of swamp and tundra proper. Sometimes the occurrence of these wooded patches is a matter of shelter, sometimes of drainage and often of soil: where soils are rich in lime, for instance, the tundra gives way to wood if climatic conditions allow. Larch is the commonest tree in the wooded tundra of eastern Siberia.

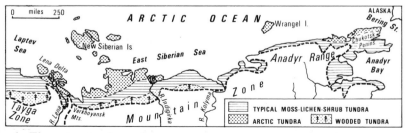

16. The eastern tundra: subzones

A phenomenon found in wetter situations, both in the 'typical' tundra and in the wooded tundra, is the peat hill. This is a mound of frozen peat up to 75 feet long and 12 or 15 feet high, the surface of which is thickly coated with mosses and lichens. Bushes, such as the bog whortleberry and dwarf birches, also grow on these mounds, but the prevalence of bog moss gives them a greyish or whitish appearance. The surrounding ground is usually swampy with waterlogged hollows, or is scrub covered, so that the peat hills offer islands of reindeer pasture in otherwise useless land. Another distinctive tundra is that in which the peat surface carries little hillocks, about a foot high, composed of the accumulated stalks of lichens, mosses and grasses. This has a whitish appearance and occurs in the Pechora region of northern Russia.

In the postglacial epoch the tundra zone lay much farther south than it does now, and survivals of tundra vegetation have been observed near Vyazma at latitude 55° 10′ N. Its present boundary with the forest is not stationary: earlier in this century it was thought to be advancing on the tayga forest, but 'observations of the last two decades show that the forest is gaining on the tundra, not just locally, but all along the line'.[1]

The great Siberian rivers cross the tundra belt and divide it up into sections. The long estuaries of the Ob and Yenisey are flanked by vast swamps, but the Lena comes close up to the Verkhoyansk range before entering its vast delta which covers over 10,000 square miles.

Cultural landscapes

Landscape change is largely the result of man's use of natural resources. In the tundra these are limited to animals, sources of energy (coal, oil, gas, wind and tide) and to metals (nickel, copper, cobalt, tin and gold). The 'anti-resources' militating against their exploitation are formidable in the extreme. They are so inimical to human life that, until the sixteenth century, the tundra was inhabited only by a few primitive peoples: the Lapps in the west, the Samoyeds or Nenets in the centre, and the Chukchi and Eskimo in the east. Together, these probably never amounted to more than thirty or forty thousand souls and their numbers decreased when contact with the Russians brought new diseases and the partial dissolution of their economic and social organization. The reindeer, along with a wide variety of fish, eggs and fowl, could have provided sustenance for a larger population. The reindeer was also an excellent source of clothing, shelter and transport, and its skin possessed the invaluable quality of remaining flexible in extreme cold. But the low temperatures, the blizzards, the absence of essential vitamins from the diet and the long dark months without sunlight ensured that life would be nasty, brutish and short.

These primitive peoples left little mark upon the landscape. Viewed against the natural environment as a whole, their migrations, southwards into the

17. Exploitation of the tundra gasfield on the Yamal peninsula

forest in autumn and back again into the tundra in spring, were fleeting and insignificant, as was the occasional intrusion of driftwood huts, reindeer-skin tents and the smoke issuing therefrom. No doubt their presence had some effect upon the balance of wild life, but this was probably small until contact was made with Europeans. Then the natives began to hunt and trap to a far greater degree than before. They no longer merely satisfied their own modest needs, but had to find tribute for their new masters. The possibility of acquiring firearms, alcohol and other goods gave them an irresistible incentive to extort the greatest possible booty from the animal world about them. Firearms facilitated this intensified onslaught upon the wild life of the belt.

Russians from Novgorod reached the Murman and White Sea coasts in the thirteenth century, if not before, but it was not until the sixteenth century that they became really active. By the end of that century, they were not only trading with the natives for furs and fish, but taking part themselves in the destruction of seals for train oil. During the seventeenth and eighteenth centuries they explored and mastered the remainder of the tundra belt to the east, meeting little opposition from the natives, apart from the Chukchi of the far northeast. Tribute, normally in the form of furs, was levied upon the whole indigenous population. Meanwhile the Russians had planted garrisons, established trading posts, and settled in numerous places as traders, fishers, hunters, trappers and exiles.

The relatively well-built Russian log house now appeared alongside the shabby wooden shacks of the Lapps and the reindeer-skin or birch-bark tents of the Nenets and Chukchi. In larger settlements there might be also a church and a storehouse. Many natives, previously wholly nomadic, joined the Russian settlements, though still living in tents or shacks. As such settlements grew, their surroundings became increasingly disfigured, not only by accumulations of reindeer bones and antlers, but by heaps of refuse of all kinds.

The coasts of the Kola peninsula and the lower estuaries of the great rivers were the more densely settled areas, where Russians could be counted in hundreds or even thousands. Elsewhere they were in isolated groups of two or three families, supporting themselves by fishing, trapping or hunting. Such settlers were often exiles or their descendants. The traders usually lived in the larger settlements that grew up round the fortified trading posts. The total number of Russians was, however, never large during the tsarist period, perhaps between ten and twenty thousand.

An early Russian town was Obdorsk (now Salekhard), founded on the lower Ob in 1595. It retained its garrison of Cossacks until the end of the eighteenth century, and continued throughout the nineteenth to support a population of about a thousand. Farflung Nizhnekolymsk, founded on the Kolyma in 1644, soon became a centre for the eastward-moving fur trade, and survived throughout the eighteenth and nineteenth centuries, its Russian population being reinforced from time to time by government-despatched exiles.

The chief tsarist centre on the Yenisey, Dudinka, was of much later growth. Only forty inhabitants were attributed to it in 1868, but in 1914 Nansen described it as 'the Moscow of the north' and 'the most important place in the whole district'.[2] Its houses stood out unmistakably along the top of the high eastern bank of the great river. Although it was in the wooded tundra zone, Nansen saw in its vicinity 'nothing much in the way of trees, only a few stunted larches scattered here and there with long intervals between'. Dudinka's growth resulted from the introduction of regular steamboat services on the Yenisey. It was the lower terminus for these and consequently became an important river port and collection/distribution centre.

As the Russian settlers, permanent or temporary, were accustomed to a broader diet than the fish and reindeer meat of the natives, attempts were made, wherever possible, to practise some form of agriculture. Such attempts were limited to the southernmost of the tundra zones – the wooded tundra. In the Siberian districts, they amounted to no more than collecting hay from the riverside meadows. But in the west, in the Kola and White Sea districts, some settlements managed to grow potatoes and even a little barley. With the development of regular steamboat services on the main rivers, which brought north supplies of flour and other foodstuffs in return for fish and furs, the need for locally-grown produce became less urgent.

The half-century of Soviet power has witnessed a striking increase in the population of the tundra region from a possible 40,000 inhabitants to a figure that may well exceed a million if labour camps and military personnel are included. This dramatic rise is the result of the energetic development of the region's natural resources in the face of formidable environmental difficulties by government planning and investment, by forced and convict labour, and by the zeal of those dedicated to 'building communism' in the more remote parts of the country.

A large proportion of the population – perhaps as much as three-quarters – is urban; the larger agglomerations are shown in Table 4.

TABLE 4. *Population of urban agglomerations in the tundra belt (thousands)*

	LATITUDE	1959	1981
Murmansk	69°	222	394
Pechora coalfield	68°	170	218
Norilsk	69°	118	184

During the tsarist period, many of the Russian inhabitants of this region were exiles and convicts or their descendants. Stalin used compulsion on a much larger and a more highly organized scale, and during the 1930s there was a mass movement of forced labour to camps and construction sites in all parts of the Arctic. In the 1940s this labour force, mainly Russian and Ukrainian, was reinforced by droves of German prisoners of war, Poles, and others who had fallen foul of the ruthless dictatorship. Since Stalin's death, recruitment to the labour camps has been limited to convicted criminals. Financial and other incentives have been used to attract Russians to the north, but there has been some retreat of Russian population from the north in recent years.

This great increase in population and the developments which have caused it have left their mark on the landscape, but as they have been largely concentrated in the intensively-developed urban areas, there has been no transformation of the region as a whole. The larger towns, such as Murmansk and Norilsk, have central streets of apartment blocks of the standard design found elsewhere in the USSR. Being newly built, they lack the styles of architecture found in older Russian towns, and their distinctiveness lies in their climatic environment – midwinter night, midsummer sun and a long period of snow-slush cover.

Murmansk, the largest city of the Far North, depends mainly on fishing and fish-processing, in which occupation it is the leading Soviet centre. The other urban agglomerations are mostly connected with mining enterprises. The equipment associated with these often forms a feature of the local scene, its prominence heightened by the absence of tree cover. The chief mining activities are shown on Figs 18 and 19.

Coal-mining on the Pechora coalfield began in 1933 with forced labour and, owing to the shortage of coal caused by the German occupation of the Ukraine, was greatly expanded during the war years, using prisoner-of-war labour. Despite the difficulties of mining in permafrost, production around Vorkuta has been expanded to about 25 million tons a year, because of the shortage of good coking coal in northwestern and central Russia.

The Norilsk mining area is remarkable for a variety of mining and smelting activities, as well as for the size and growth of the urban area. The district has its own coalfield, and the glow of its furnaces in winter, the smoke from its giant stacks in summer, make the presence of its nickel, copper and cobalt smelters

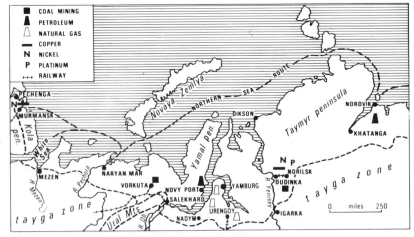

18. The western tundra: economic development

visible for miles around. A pipeline, laid along the Yenisey bed from a field 150 miles away now brings natural gas to the city. This has set free thousands of coalminers for other work. Although forced labour was the rule in the city's infancy, the town is now large and well-planned enough to provide urban amenities of a kind likely to retain population under a freer system. But there is no daylight for forty-seven days and snow lies on the ground for 250 days of each year.

Vast deposits of natural gas have been discovered near the Ob estuary, and the two fields around Nadym and Urengoy produce 200 billion cubic metres a year. A third field is being developed near Yamburg. Pipelines run from Urengoy to Central Russia and to the Urals, and a new railway links the gasfield with the south. The previously virgin tundra has had to accommodate hundreds of test boreholes, along with gas-pumping stations, new roads, pylons carrying electric transmission lines, the expanded settlement of Nadym and the new town of Urengoy. Conditions are appalling, with work impossible on at least a tenth of the days of the year because of extreme cold or wind, and difficult at all times because of permafrost. Winter freezing with all its problems, does at least offer a firm surface for the movement of heavy equipment, but in summer many areas become swampy, and flies and mosquitoes give acute discomfort. Fog is common at all seasons. Despite countermeasures, widespread damage to the environment in the form of pollution of the air by gases and of the ground and water by waste and effluent, inevitably results. The permafrost prevents seepage into the ground, and low temperatures delay decomposition. Petroleum also was discovered in 1967 near Novy Port. Other modern intrusions into the previously uninhabited and desolate tundra are connected with tin mining and gold extraction along the Arctic coastlands of eastern Siberia.

Increasing economic activity has created a growing demand for power, and the Kola nuclear power station has been built near Murmansk in the west. A thermal station at Norilsk provides electricity and hot water for the Dudinka-Norilsk area with its population of a quarter million, and this is supplemented by a small hydro station (Ust Khantayskaya). Floating power stations supply

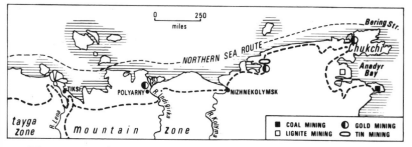

19. The eastern tundra: economic development

isolated mining ventures near the Arctic coast: one, anchored at the mouth of the Indigirka river sends current by a 60-mile transmission line to the gold-mining centre of Polyarny. There are tidal power stations in Kola Bay near Murmansk and at Mezen Bay in the White Sea.

The movement into the tundra of hundreds of thousands of Russians – miners, factory workers, professional men and administrators, fishermen and seamen, military forces – has many times increased the need for foodstuffs in this non-agricultural region. To reduce the consequent demand upon transport in an area almost entirely without railways and roads, and where water transport is available for a brief season only each year, every effort has been made, despite the high cost, to produce food locally. Besides attempting to put the traditional reindeer-breeding and herding on a less haphazard and more scientific basis than before, hothouses and soil-heating apparatus have been installed near many settlements, and large expanses of heated glasshouses are therefore a feature of many tundra landscapes. Experimental farms are constantly looking for new ways of overcoming the formidable climatic and soil impediments to food production. The farthest northern agricultural districts, lying at 71 to 72° N, are near Khatanga and Tiksi, where potatoes and vegetables are grown in the open. There are now said to be 200 state farms in the Far North growing vegetables and breeding livestock. The Pechora coalfield organization, Vorku-tugol, with over 200,000 mouths to feed, runs its own state farms, and these include reindeer farms, vegetable plots, hothouses and apiaries.

While the Soviet period has seen the creation of towns for the Russians, it has also witnessed the building of villages for the native peoples who were previously wholly nomadic. Groups of new wooden cottages have made their appearance along with storehouses, Party administrative huts and boarding schools. As the economy of these peoples is still based on reindeer herding and sea-animal hunting, it is impossible for all parents to live continuously in their villages. The children, however, remain in the boarding schools, learning to read and write both their own language and Russian. Here, too, they are made aware of the nature, achievements and aims of the state of which they are citizens, thus facilitating their eventual assimilation to modern Soviet culture.

Fish-processing plants, fat-rendering furnaces and motor-vessel stations have revitalized the native fishing industry and brought increased populations to shore-based settlements. This is true not only of the Murman coast, but also of the Pechora, Ob and Yenisey estuaries, and especially of the Chukotka peninsula. Here there is an annual catch of between 40,000 and 70,000 seals and between 4,000 and 6,000 walruses. The natives are thus enabled to develop handicrafts using seal leather, furs and bone, and to obtain fats for traditional methods of heating and lighting.

Improved conditions and medical care have arrested the decline in the numbers of the native peoples which resulted from contacts with the Russians

20. Tiksi, a Northern Sea Route port and tundra settlement, in winter

before the Revolution, but Russians in the tundra zone now form the vast majority of the population, whereas previously they were a minority. The burden carried by Russian immigrants in the Far North, and the strain upon an inadequate labour force would be greatly lessened if local labour could be enlisted for mining and industry. For a long time it seemed that all attempts in this direction had failed, but now more recruits are being found among the non-Russian peoples.

Another important factor in the use and modification of the natural environment has been the establishment of the northern sea route. After exploratory and preliminary work in the early 1930's the Arctic coast of Russia and Siberia began to be systematically navigated by cargo vessels convoyed by icebreakers in 1935. During the war, when the normal supply routes became hazardous, the northern sea route was used to enable American goods to be brought along the Arctic coast and up the various rivers. The navigational season has been progressively lengthened by the use of ever more powerful icebreakers, aided by air survey of ice conditions. The first nuclear-powered icebreaker, the *Lenin*, launched in 1959, has been succeeded by the more modern and powerful *Arktika* and *Sibir*. A passage is now kept open throughout the winter in the western section between Murmansk and Dudinka, enabling the Kola non-ferrous metallurgical centre of Monchegorsk to receive an uninterrupted supply of Norilsk nickel and copper concentrates. Heavy equipment for the tundra gasfields also comes by the sea route, and West German steel pipe is delivered by this means to Novy Port. The generating units installed in the great Siberian power stations are too large to travel overland, but proceed from the Elektrosila works in Leningrad by water via the Baltic–White Sea canal, the northern sea route and the Yenisey river.

The development of the sea route has been accompanied by the construction of some eighty ports and stations on the Arctic coasts and estuaries to give facilities not only for handling vessels and their cargoes, but also to provide the meteorological and hydrological information necessary for successful ice navigation. Many of the stations have become centres of Arctic research generally, beyond the immediate needs of the sea route. As a result, several places, previously insignificant or non-existent, have grown into small towns of between one and twenty thousand people. Their wooden buildings, the stacks of coal, timber and other goods, the meteorological and other equipment and the wind-powered generating towers are characteristic of these places. Strong winds over long periods favour the generation of electricity by this means.

Until almost the very end of the tsarist period, the tundra was quite without railways. But in 1915–16 the line from Leningrad to Murmansk was built to circumvent the German blockade of Allied supplies to Russia. In 1960 this line was extended into former Finnish territory to serve the nickel-mining towns of Pechenga and Nikel-Murm. Another branch from Murmansk runs twenty-five miles down the east bank of the Kola estuary to the outport of Vayenga. In the 1930s a line was brought to Vorkuta to make coal-mining possible on the Pechora field, and in the 1950s this line was carried across the Urals to Labytnangi on the Ob. In 1937 Norilsk was linked to the Yenisey river port of Dudinka, and in the 1960s a new line was built northwards from Norilsk to the new mining town of Talnakh.

The traditional methods of transport evolved by the native peoples – the reindeer or dog sleigh – are still used over those vast stretches which are not accessible to railway, navigable river or sea route. They have the advantage over water transport that they are not interrupted by the eight- or nine-month period of frost, but only by the brief summer. Aircraft, especially helicopters, are a common sight over the gasfields.

The Soviet tundra has high strategic value, as it confronts the North American continent across the frozen ocean. Highly-trained northern forces with specialized equipment form an important part of the Soviet army, navy and air force, and military bases are attached to many of the sea route stations. White fur-coated soldiers and snowmobiles, with criss-crossing tracks on the snow and vapour trails in the sky, must be a common sight in many parts of the region.

5
The forest belt

The forest belt is nearly 4,000 miles long from west to east, and varies in north–south extent from 600 to 1,200 miles. Its area of nearly three million square miles is equal to that of the United States. The northern boundary approximates to the mean July isotherm of 10° C (50° F), while the southern coincides with the southernmost limit of the spruce and is characterized by the change from washed-out podsolized soils to dark-coloured fertile soils.

Natural landscapes

Throughout most of the belt, coniferous species predominate – spruce, pine, fir, larch and cedar. The small surface area of their needle leaves so reduces transpiration in winter that, except for the larch, they alone are able to remain in leaf throughout the year. This enables them to start growing immediately spring is warm enough, a great advantage over deciduous trees in a short-summered climate. The shape of both tree and leaf enables them effortlessly to shake off excess amounts of snow such as would irreparably damage the upward-held branches of broadleaved deciduous trees, if they were in leaf. Some small-leaved deciduous trees are associated with the evergreens, notably the birch, aspen and alder. In the southwest, the presence of broadleaved species such as oak, maple, ash and linden, gives rise to a distinct forest type traditionally known as the Mixed Forest. But the remainder of the great forest belt, in which broadleaved trees are absent, is known as boreal forest or *tayga*.

Climate and soil both affect the nature of the tayga forest. The spruce flourishes on the richer loamy soils, the pine on the poorer sandy ones. Birch and larch, both deciduous, are found where the winter is too severe for ever-green trees to survive. Alder and cedar frequent the less well-drained land, while many extensive bogs and occasional meadows break the continuity of the forest.

The impact of climate upon the landscape is not so dramatic as in the tundra. Only a relatively small part of the belt experiences an unbroken winter night. There are two main landscape seasons: winter, when there is a snow covering and all water is frozen, and summer. Where there are deciduous woods, the distinction between the two seasons is heightened by the contrast between the bare forlorn silhouettes of trees in winter and their full summer foliage.

But, over most of the zone, the unchanged appearance of the evergreen needle-leaved forest gives a dominant aspect to the landscape which is common to all seasons.

Before large-scale interference by man, the forest zone was rich in wild life. Amongst the larger mammals, there were elk, aurochs, reindeer, wolves, bear and lynx in plenty, with enormous numbers of the smaller animals: squirrels, marten, beaver, sable, red fox, ermine, etc.; their thick fur kept them warm in the severe winter. Of smaller creatures, hedgehogs, voles and mice are numerous. A few birds, chiefly owls and varieties of grouse and partridge, remain all winter, and many of the migrants are away only during the coldest months. Varieties of woodpecker, crossbill and nutcracker are common, and play a part in landscape formation by distributing seeds. The population of birds and animals declines sharply northwards.

Within the forest belt, four landscape regions can be distinguished. These are the North Russian spruce tayga, the West Siberian swamp tayga, the Central Siberian larch tayga and the Mixed Forest.

The North Russian spruce tayga

This section of the boreal forest extends from the Soviet frontier on the west to the Urals. Its total area is about 590,000 square miles – more than twice the size of Texas.

The typical tayga vegetation, prevalent in the central part of the region, is a dense spruce forest with an undergrowth of bilberry and similar bushes, and the ground is floored with mosses. The spruce has a tall, straight, tapering stem. Its numerous short branches form a delicate spire, and in the light of a sunny day, the needle leaves are bright green. As it needs a relatively well-drained and nourishing soil, its place is often taken by the pine, by the deciduous birch – its white stem conspicuous in the otherwise dark forest – and by the alder. There are vast stretches of bog, especially in the north and west. The continuity of the great expanses of spruce forest is also interrupted by the larger rivers, which have drawn winding ribbons of treeless flood plain, sometimes supporting natural meadows, across it. From the air, previous river courses can be clearly seen, weaving their way from side to side in the alluvial valleys.

Northwards, as the wooded tundra is approached, the trees become shorter and sparser and the proportion of birches rises. Eastwards the number of species increases as the European spruce is joined by the Siberian variety, and by fir, larch and cedar. Southwards, with the longer, warmer summers, deciduous species such as aspen, linden, elm, alder, oak and hazel, form a vigorous undergrowth. North of the Volga, large expanses of sandy ground, sometimes blown into dunes, are covered with pine forest. In the west also, where morainic deposits from the last glaciation give a mainly coarse and sandy soil, the pine predominates. This tree is altogether different from the shapely spruce: it has a stouter trunk, the branches are thicker and the outline more irregular, often with a flattish top. It is more open and allows more light to penetrate.

In winter the ground carries a snow cover whose average depth increases from 20 inches in the west to 35 inches in the east. The cold season becomes both severer and longer eastwards: in the southwest the January mean temperature is $-8°$ C ($18°$ F) and the snow lasts an average of 160 days; in the northeast these figures become $-20°$ C ($-4°$ F) and 220 days respectively. There is much cyclonic activity and summers are cloudy and rainy, with a July mean temperature ranging from $10°$ C ($50°$ F) in the extreme north to $18°$ C ($64°$ F) along the southern margins. Total precipitation declines from over 22 inches in the southwest to under 15 in the northeast. Thus, although there is more snow in the east, there is more summer rain in the west.

Relief is seldom striking, and flattish watershed areas of moderate height separate broad swampy depressions. Even the Timan Mountains, which rise in places well over a thousand feet, have large, level, boggy expanses between their parallel ridges. Here and there, however, pineclad hillocks of glacial moraine, and karstic phenomena caused by the solution of limestone diversify the dull relief of the interfluves.

The strongest relief is found along the western margins in Kola and Karelia, where the hard crystalline rocks resisted erosion more than the horizontal sedimentary rocks of the Russian lowland to the east. They have, furthermore, experienced a vigorous and recent glaciation. The advancing ice sheet has sculptured the granites into bold forms, polished and scratched the bare rock, and carved numerous lake-filled hollows. On its retreat it has left behind long winding ridges of sandy stony material (eskers), conical heaps of sand and gravel (kames), and many other haphazard hummocky deposits, all clad with pines. These features have frustrated the orderly development of a drainage

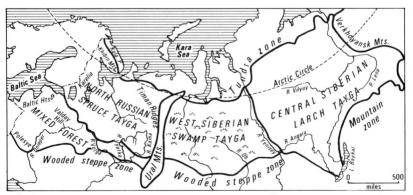

21. The forest belt: zones and regions

system, so that picturesque lakes nestle amongst the forested hills, and water-falls and rapids mark the often precipitate descent of the streams.

In the Kola peninsula, crystalline igneous masses have been elevated to heights of up to 4,000 feet, notably in the Khibin Mountains. They rise abruptly out of a boggy plain. Only the lower slopes are forested, and tundra takes over above 1,500 feet. Much of the relief consists of bald rounded masses, but in the summit areas there are precipices and rock fields. Snow falls at any time in the year.

Relatively strong relief is also found in the watershed upland between the Kama and the Vyatka. Here, besides morainic hills and water-filled solution hollows, there is much ravine development and the incised rivers have spruce-forested banks rising steeply from the water's edge.

The West Siberian swamp tayga

This region, which has an area of about 630,000 square miles, occupies the greater part of the West Siberian plain, a vast flat expanse extending from the Urals to the Yenisey and from the Arctic Circle to the 52nd parallel, a distance of almost a thousand miles in each direction. It is drained mostly by the Ob to the Kara Sea. But so slight is the gradient (1 in 33,000) that the river falls less than 300 feet in its 1,800-mile journey through the forest zone, and its average speed is less than one mile per hour. As outlet to the northern sea is hampered by the freezing of the lower course for nine months of the year, vast floods form in spring.

Over half the region is peat bog, and the peat layer is sometimes as much as 10 feet thick. This swampiness is due to several factors. The plain has almost no relief, and a generally concave shape. Precipitation greatly exceeds evaporation. The ground is frozen, and therefore impermeable, for most of the year, and the subsoil is permanently frozen in the north. Swamps are most widespread on the broad interfluves. The valleys are better drained because their sides have some slope – those of the great rivers Ob and Yenisey are surprisingly steep.

Forest is found mainly on these valley slopes, on sandy ridges which stand above the floods and extend across the swamps, and on other isolated, drier stretches of land. In the north, where the swamp is underlain by permafrost, trees are sparse and low, and consist of flat-rooted species of Siberian spruce and larch. In the central section about half the area is forested with fir, spruce, pine and birch. Birch increases southwards until it predominates along the southern margins, giving way here and there to pine woods and small groupings of cedar, fir and aspen.

The seasonal climatic change strongly affects the landscape. Snow covers the ground, and water is frozen for five months in the south and up to eight months in the north, and the January mean temperature ranges from $-19°$ C $(-2°$ F$)$

22. This oil rig moves across the swamps of the West Siberian oilfield like a hovercraft

in the southwest to $-28°$ C ($-19°$ F) in the northeast. In summer the thaw reveals the great peat bogs, evaporation from which keeps the atmosphere humid, and swarms of mosquitoes and flies fill the air. The July mean temperatures differ little over the region, ranging from $10°$ C ($50°$ F) in the north to $19°$ C ($66°$ F) in the south.

The Central Siberian larch tayga
This covers a vast territory extending from the Yenisey river to the Verkhoyansk mountain range beyond the river Lena – $1\frac{1}{4}$ million square miles. The tayga

forest here extends both farther north (to $72\frac{1}{2}°$ N) and farther south (to 52° N) than in the other regions. Relief is here a more important factor in the landscape, for although the old sedimentary rocks remain, for the most part, nearly horizontal, they have been elevated to heights of between 1,000 and 3,000 feet. Rivers have cut the resulting plateau up into a mass of flattish-topped hills separated by steepsided valleys, but ridges and summits of more resistant rock often rise above the general plateau level. To the south, between the Angara tributary of the Yenisey and Lake Baykal, the relief becomes bolder and more mountainous. To the east, the middle and lower courses of the Lena, together with that of its left-bank tributary, the Vilyuy, occupy a large lowland.

In the plateau area, the rivers often run at depths of nearly a thousand feet below the general level of the upland, and the steep sides of the valleys are notched by numerous terraces, marking successive stages in the uplift of the plateau. The current of the streams is much swifter than the sluggish waters of West Siberia, and rapids and falls are characteristic.

The effect of this greater relief is masked to some extent by the forest cover, which restricts visibility and lends a sameness to areas of vast extent but differing height and slope. The characteristic forest is made up of the Siberian and Dahurian larches, flat-rooted trees that can establish themselves above the permanently frozen subsoil. The depth available to root growth varies from about a foot to 6 feet, with an average of about 3 feet. The Dahurian larch grows on rich and poor soils alike, and on well- and ill-drained land. It is slow-growing and long-lived, and is able to fight the upward encroachment of moss and peat by putting out fresh roots above the base of the trunk. In favourable conditions on the better loamy soils it grows 60 feet tall or more, and has an undergrowth of willow, juniper, dog-rose and whortleberry.

There is much less swamp than in West Siberia because summers are warmer, and there is less precipitation and more relief. But where the ground is boggy, the Dahurian larch is much shorter – 25 feet or less, because the permafrost is nearer the surface. On the other hand, on sandy ground, where in summer the permafrost is farther down, the pine flourishes and there is little or no moss cover.

In the more mountainous terrain a vertical zoning of vegetation is apparent. Spruce and cedar skirt the lower slopes to about a thousand feet above sea-level, where a light larch forest takes its place. This thins out with increasing altitude and at 2,000 feet has become a brushwood of alder bushes. Above this height the rocky summits have mountain tundra.

The seasonal contrast is heightened by the deciduous nature of the ubiquitous larch. Winter is stark and gaunt, compounded of white snow and black branches. The cold is extreme, with mean temperatures ranging from −20° C (−4° F) in the west to −45° C (−49° F) in the east, while absolute minima of −60° C (−76° F) and lower occur in valleys where the cold air collects undisturbed during the long winter nights. The short frosty days are often blessed with sunshine. Sounds travel amazingly through the still dry air, and the ground and the trees crackle and snap with the frost. The cover of fine powdery snow is shallow and often blown away by the strong wind, exposing the ground to the relentless cold until it is frozen to great depths. The rivers freeze so deep that water is expelled at the sides, giving rise to long ridges of frozen mud.

With so little snow to melt, spring – the season of thaw – is brief. Yet mornings in this freeze-thaw interlude produce the striking effect of trees sheathed in ice, glistening with hoar frost, and festooned with icicles. The sun plays upon this sparkling scene until it has dripped away, and by the afternoon the magic has gone. The larch regains its leaves and a warm sunny summer ensues. In the low, sheltered Lena valley, summers are warmer than anywhere else at the same latitude, and Yakutsk at 62° N has a July mean of 19° C (66° F). The heat is accompanied by a plague of mosquitoes and flies. Temperatures fall rapidly with the onset of night and a maximum afternoon temperature of 35° C (95° F) can drop to 5° C (41° F) by the following dawn.

The total precipitation is so low in places (5 to 10 inches), that with the warmth of summer much of the region would be too dry for tree growth, were it not that the thawing surface of the permafrost provides the roots with a constant supply of water throughout the growing season.

The mixed forest zone

This zone has a north–south width of over 600 miles in the west, but narrows eastwards until, at Gorky on the Volga, it has become a narrow strip about fifty miles wide, separating the tayga from the wooded steppe. This narrow strip continues eastwards to the Urals. The total area of about 430,000 square miles is twice the size of France. In its natural state, the zone was almost wholly covered by a forest in which the coniferous evergreen spruce and the broadleaved deciduous oak were the dominant species, hence the appellation 'mixed'. Many other trees were common, however, especially the pine, linden, maple, ash, elm, alder, birch, and in the west only, beech, hornbeam and holly.

In the main, this is a lowland composed of moraine-covered hills, undulating or level plains, and ill-drained depressions. The morainic hills are littered with haphazard mixtures of boulders, gravels, sands and clays which were carried forward by the ice sheets of the glacial period and abandoned on their retreat. Many picturesque lakes nestle among their knolls. There are over 1,400 named lakes in the Valday Hills, and the Baltic Heights are sometimes called the Lithuanian Switzerland. The surfaces of these morainic hills are often flattish and marshy. The Volga, the West Dvina and Dnieper, all rise in the same flattish, swampy part of the Valday Hills at a height of about 700 feet, and the streams flow in broad marshy valleys which they often fill during the period of the spring flood.

Although the relief is generally flat or undulating, there are some steep drops: the Valday Hills, with a highest point of about 1,000 feet above sea-level, have a steep fall of 300 feet to the Lake Ilmen depression on their west, and the Smolensk–Moscow ridge drops sharply nearly 200 feet to the Volga plain on the north. Where drainage is satisfactory and deep loamy soils have developed, these moraine-capped hills carry the spruce–oak association typical of the region as a whole. The light-loving oak, in ideal conditions, grows to 60 to 70 feet, with spruce, maple, linden and aspen forming a second canopy beneath it. There is undergrowth of hazel, spindle and raspberry, etc., and a rich moss cover on the ground. But where the soils are podsolic, the oak drops out, leaving the spruce dominant, and where sands predominate, the pine takes their place. The birch is present almost everywhere.

Most of the morainic uplands owe their elevation in part to some uplift of the basic rocks, normally limestones. When these are exposed on the surface, as they occasionally are, karstic features resulting from the solution of the rock lend a new aspect to the scenery – swallow holes, underground streams, caverns, etc. Such karstic features are also found in the Baltic region where gaps in the morainic cover have exposed the Silurian limestones beneath.

Ill-drained flats and depressions are found in the Baltic region, in the upper Volga valley, in the Polesye area (which occupies the southern part of the White Russian republic and extends southwards into the Ukraine) and in the Meshchera, southeast of Moscow. The Polesye and Meshchera are shallow tectonic depressions which were occupied by postglacial lakes. The Polesye includes the Pripyat marshes: there are numerous streams, lakes and swamps, and the watersheds between the streams are low and flat, but there is also much forest. The postglacial lake left behind broad sandy stretches, since colonized by pine and birch. Sixty per cent of the Polesye forest is pine, 15 per cent birch and 13 per cent the swamp-tolerating black alder. There is often a thick undergrowth of bilberry, cranberry, rosemary and bog whortleberry, and there are thick beds of peat. The smaller Meshchera is very similar in character: almost a third of its area is bog, with peat 25 feet and more in depth.

There are many other sandy areas, besides those in the Polesye and Meshchera. They often have dunes and have been colonized by pine forest. Two of the largest are along the north bank of the Volga, from Gorky to Kazan, and along the east bank of the Dnieper below Gomel.

In the Baltic provinces the morainic heights are surrounded by boulder clay flats which extend southwards into White Russia and southeastwards into Russia proper. The lack of relief derives from the horizontal bedrock beneath. There are numerous bogs. Elsewhere, the soils are podsols and of indifferent fertility. Spruce forest dominates large expanses of these northwestern areas which are not easily distinguishable from the tayga.

Besides the morainic and tectonic uplands (mostly above 600 feet) and the

23. *The winter landscape at Arkhangelskoye, a village on the Moskva river*

swampy lowlands (mostly below 300 feet), there is much gently undulating or level land, surfaced with boulder clay or sandy loams, which is better drained. Having carried the typical oak–spruce forest for thousands of years, it has developed superior brown forest soils. There are also a few areas, notably the Opolye, a large, flat, treeless area in Vladimir *oblast*, which have very fertile, dark-earth soils reminiscent of the steppes. But these better lands have been cleared for cultivation, and it is the spruce and birch forests of the podsols, the pinewoods of the sandy areas, and the undrained marshes that survive to represent the natural landscape of the region. They give a misleading impression of the original natural environment as a whole.

Climatically, the landscape here has four seasons, and although these are of unequal length, they are more marked than in tayga regions, where the contrast between summer and winter is all-important. Winter has a snow cover lasting from four to five months, but partial thaws prevent a deep accumulation; mean January temperatures decline slowly eastwards from $-3°$ C ($27°$ F) to $-12°$ C ($10°$ F), but on the Valday Hills winter is colder and snow cover longer than on the surrounding lowlands (Fig. 23).

Spring is the brief season of melting snow, slush and water on the land, of flood-filled valleys, and of breaking ice on rivers and lakes; but the deciduous trees are not fully out in leaf. In summer, shades of green possess the landscape, and vegetation grows rapidly as sudden warmth follows the soil-drenching snow-melt. July mean temperatures range from 17° C (63° F) in the Baltic northwest to 20° C (68° F) east of Kazan. Thunderstorms darken the sky of many a sultry afternoon and provide additional moisture throughout the hottest months.

Cultural landscapes

The natural resources of the tayga zone are many and varied: forest materials such as bark, timber and pitch; fur-bearing animals and mammoth tusks; peat; soils that respond to manuring; long warm summer days; fish in the rivers and natural meadows in the valleys; water power; a wide range of minerals, including both fossil fuels and metals; and natural navigable waterways. Against these must be set formidable natural difficulties: the coldest winters on earth, with the subsoil often permanently frozen; podsol soils infertile in their natural state; vast expanses of swamp with plagues of mosquitoes in summer; drought-stricken areas and broken relief in the east; boulders spread by former ice sheets in the west; great distances combined with physical conditions hostile to the building of roads and railways.

The difficulties have prevailed over the opportunities to such an extent that even today the zone is, taken as a whole, one of the more sparsely peopled parts of the earth's surface. Except where their activities led to the burning of the forest, the primitive peoples – few in numbers – left scarcely any mark upon the natural environment. Their hunting and fishing were not extensive enough to deplete the wild life, and a few rude log huts, birch-bark tents and dug-out canoes, with wisps of smoke rising above the forest, made up their contribution to this vast wilderness before the Russians came.

It was the wild life of the forest that drew the Russians into the tayga zone, and the fur traders of Novgorod, situated on its southern margin, were the first to exploit this resource. Between the tenth and twelfth centuries, they subdued the various tribes of the North Russian spruce tayga and even crossed the Urals. Ivan IV's conquest of Kazan in 1552, and Yermak's defeat of the Tartars of western Siberia (1581), made possible the entry of fur traders, Cossacks and Russian officials into Siberia. So quickly did they move along the waterways and so effectively did they pacify the forest-dwelling tribes that they had reached the Sea of Okhotsk and the Pacific by 1649. The seventeenth century was the heyday of the fur trade, and furs remained, well into the eighteenth century, the country's chief source of wealth and the main means of payment for foreign imports. The Russians were active almost everywhere, using boats and canoes on the rivers, and carts and sledges on land. They not only collected furs from the natives but trapped themselves. So thorough was the hunt that supplies were rapidly depleted and the fur trade declined steeply during the eighteenth century. Russian settlement and activity in the tayga declined with it.

During the nineteenth century and early twentieth, a second tide of Russians flowed into the zone. But on this occasion they were not fur traders, but exiles and prisoners convicted of political and criminal offences. Banishment to Siberia went back to the seventeenth century, but it was not until the nineteenth that numbers were large. At times, the convoys of the banished, dragging their chains, stretched almost unbroken along the highway from Moscow. As a rule, the prisons, camps and settlements were made at or near the old fur-trading posts. There was also a certain amount of agricultural colonization by peasants near the chief posts and along the main routes, wherever conditions made this possible. The Church also made its contribution by the foundation of monasteries.

At the end of the nineteenth century, the population of the tayga was about 12 million, and of these $10\frac{1}{2}$ million were Russians. Almost all of these lived in the North Russian region. The West Siberian and Central Siberian regions were very sparsely populated indeed and counted about 800,000 inhabitants in all, the vast majority of whom were settled along the southern margins. Of these, perhaps 500,000 were Russians. It is obvious, therefore, that the effect of the Russians upon the landscape was much greater in the west, where they were counted in millions, than in the centre and east.

Wherever the Russians were settled, the trees, growing vertically in the forest, were cut down and arranged horizontally to make forts, stores, log izbas, windmills, etc. Logs were often laid on streets and roads to make them passable in the muddy season. There was often a church. The churches, however, were usually walled with sawn timber and ornately crowned with gilded bulbous cupolas, each surmounted with a cross (Fig. 24). In 1901 Stadling described Siberian villages, which had originated either as fur-trading posts or convict settlements, thus:

Surrounded by the forest as by a dense wall, the villages ... extend sometimes to a length of three or four miles. In the middle or at one end, the gloomy and weather-beaten station prison towers above the rest of the houses, with its courtyard surrounded by a high wooden fence.

On either hand stretches the long row of one-storeyed houses or huts, grey and black from exposure to the hard climate or from smoke. The further away from the centre, the smaller and more poor-looking do these houses and huts become, till they reach the forest as mere earth-covered yurtas. The inhabitants of these izbas and huts are the foster-children of the prison, which they have more or less recently left, and year after year this row of huts increases.[1]

The forest was not only attacked for building purposes. Wood was cut for the fuel needed to keep alive during the harsh winter, to make charcoal near ironworks, and for clearing farm and meadow land. The trees were burned

24. *A village church in the Karelian tayga*

and the newly won ground often gave good yields in the first year; but these soon fell off, and the farmers moved on to new clearings. The abandoned land was soon colonized by birches. By such methods it was found possible to cultivate varieties of rye, oats and barley, potatoes, turnips and cabbage, almost anywhere in the zone, although untimely frosts were liable to ruin a crop. Naturally such agriculture was more common in the southern margins, and most widespread on the southern border of the North Russian tayga, where flax was an important industrial crop round Kostroma, Vologda and Vyatka. In Siberia such clearings were almost wholly confined to the neighbourhood of the rivers.

Communications played a big part in humanizing the landscape. Enormous rafts of timber floated down the rivers, and from the late nineteenth century, steamers – squat, flat-bottomed, paddle-wheeled craft – operated on the great Siberian rivers. They burned wood, even though, on the Yenisey and Lena, they sailed past huge coalfields. There were also crude native boats, often mere floating boxes, and dugout canoes. Barges loaded with barrels of fish, flour and salt, were towed along by man-power. Sometimes the cargo also was human: 'not only common criminals, but also some followers of Leo Tolstoy, and others of the best and noblest sons and daughters of Russia, on their way to Yakutsk, to Verkhoyansk, and – hundreds of miles beyond – to Kolymsk, to be buried alive in the most dreary land on the surface of our globe.'[2]

Besides the waterways, there were the rutted tracks, often portages leading from stream to stream, and sometimes corduroyed with logs. By 1914 many of them had been lined with telegraph poles and wires – the Siberian telegraph went as far north as Yakutsk. Everywhere sledges, horsedrawn in the south and pulled by dogs in the north, formed part of the winter scene.

During the twentieth century, the population of the tayga zone has risen from approximately 12 million to about 18 million. Much of this growth has been urban and the larger towns of the southern margins of the North Russian tayga have been the chief beneficiaries. Most of this urban increase has been housed in the large new blocks of flats which are characteristic of all Soviet cities, but some of the new and greatly expanded towns have individual townscapes linked with their special functions.

In spite of Soviet development and activity, the area of man-modified landscape, away from the southern agricultural borders, remains small compared to the vast expanse of the tayga. Yet its indirect effect upon the landscape of the country as a whole has always been great, since tayga products have always been foremost in foreign trade, enabling goods to be imported which have changed the face of much of Russia. Furs and timber in the prerevolutionary period, timber and gold since, have made possible the import of materials, machinery and skills upon which successive Russian cultures have largely depended. Now natural gas and petroleum can be added to the exportable treasures of the tayga zone.

The North Russian spruce tayga region
This region was originally peopled by Finns, Chuds, Votyaks, Komi, Udmurts and Karelians, and the latter three remain numerous enough to form autonomous republics within the Russian republic; but 90 per cent of the population

is now Russian. The total of 13 million represents a density of 22 per square mile, far greater than that of the Siberian regions.

The sixteenth and seventeenth centuries were the most splendid in the region's prerevolutionary history. In 1553 English traders arrived on the shores of the White Sea and made their way through the forests to Moscow. As Moscow had no free Baltic outlet, its main link with Europe became the route across the tayga via Yaroslavl, Vologda, the Sukhona river, Ustyug and the Dvina river to Kholmogory and Archangel. This much-frequented way attracted considerable Russian settlement, and when, towards the end of the sixteenth century, Giles Fletcher listed the sixteen chief cities of Muscovy, four of them – Vologda, Ustyug, Kholmogory and Kargopol – lay on the Moscow–White Sea trade routes. Archangel, founded about that time (1584), soon joined the ranks of leading Russian towns. It was thus described in 1701:

> The citadel, in which the Governor himself resides, abounds with shops, where the Russians, who come there at such times as their fairs are kept, expose their various merchandises to public sale. There is a wooden wall which extends to the very river, and surrounds it. All the houses in this city are built with wood. . . . The streets are covered with broken pieces of timber.[3]

At the same time, Vologda contained sixty-four churches, twenty-one of which were built of brick or stone. Its position was such that Ivan the Terrible (1533–84) considered making it his capital. But Peter the Great's foundation of a new port on the Baltic at Petersburg (1703), meant that Russia's overseas commerce no longer had to cross 800 miles of tayga to reach Archangel, and the settlements along the White Sea route declined.

Railways brought renewed life to the North Russian tayga at the end of the nineteenth century. In 1898 the railway from Moscow, which already reached Vologda, was continued to Archangel. The trans-Ural line from Tyumen via Yekaterinburg and Perm was brought westward to the Dvina river system at Vologda and Kotlas. Early in the present century, Petersburg was linked with Vyatka via Vologda. And in 1916, on the eve of the Revolution, the difficult route across Karelia from Petrograd to Murmansk was opened (Fig. 25).

Mining ventures were of long standing in the North Russian spruce tayga. Iron had been mined round Lake Onega since early times, and Peter I had set up a charcoal-using ironworks on the west side of the lake at Petrozavodsk. Karelian mica was already being exploited in the sixteenth century, when Giles Fletcher wrote:

> In the province of Corelia, and about the river Duyna towards the north sea, there groweth a soft rock which they call slude. This they cut into thin flakes, which naturally it is apt for, and so use it for glass-lanthorns and such like.

It ... is better than either glass or horn: for that it neither breaketh like glass, nor yet will burn like the lanthorn.[4]

Salt was associated with the upper Kama valley. Here, in Peter I's reign, between fifty and eighty brine pits were worked by the Stroganov family; the brine was evaporated in large pans.

The prerevolutionary towns differed little from the villages, except in size, being merely large congregations of wooden houses. But their churches were usually more splendid than the rural ones, and often built of stone or brick. The chief industries were linen manufacture, rope-making, pitch preparation, leather-tanning, tallow-melting and sawmilling. Rybinsk, because of its situation at the junction of the Volga with the canalized waterway to Petersburg, was distinguished by the size and number of its flour mills.

The Soviet development of the difficult tayga environment has depended largely upon the expansion of means of communication and sources of energy. The Baltic–White Sea Canal was one of the achievements of the first five-year plan and completed in 1933. It involved deepening the channels in the rivers

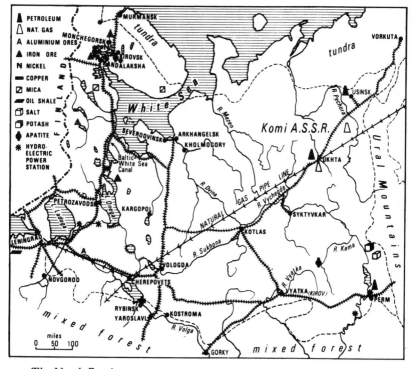

25. *The North Russian spruce tayga*

26. Preparing the route of a new railway (Archangel–Leshukensk) through the tayga

and lakes of the Karelian isthmus, and linking them with canals and locks. The main freight is timber and ore from the mines around Kirovsk. In 1964 the deepening of the old waterway linking the Volga at Cherepovets with Leningrad was completed for the use of modern river craft such as are used on the Volga itself. The new 225-mile-long waterway has only seven locks and carries a heavy tonnage of timber, wood-pulp, grain, coal, oil, salt and fertilizer.

Notable additions have been made to the railway system. An important line crosses the tayga from Kotlas to Vorkuta in the tundra belt. Kotlas has been connected with the Vologda–Archangel line, which has itself been linked to the Murmansk line by a branch south of the White Sea. Another transport feature of the landscape is the system of oil and gas pipelines which follow the Vorkuta railway across the region from northeast to southwest. The oil pipeline begins in the oil- and gasfields of the Komi republic; the 'Northern Lights' gas system, originating at Urengoy in the tundra belt, passes through them. The Komi fields produce some 3 per cent of Soviet oil and natural gas, and the chief centre is Ukhta (89,000). Oilfield gas fuels a large (1,260 MW) thermal power station at Pechora (57,000). Titanium has been discovered at Yarega, near Ukhta. Water has been extensively harnessed for electric power. There are numerous small dams in Karelia, and the Volga above Rybinsk and the Kama above Perm have been widened into reservoir lakes by hydroelectric barrages.

With the help of these newly-developed communications and energy sources, man's exploitation of the forest is now more vigorous. Lumbering is the chief occupation, and is concentrated along waterways and railways and close to power stations. The North Russian tayga, although possessing only 14 per cent of the country's total timber resources, produces 40 per cent of the sawn wood. From the air, the exploited forest appears striped: cutting proceeds in parallel bands separated by similar strips of standing timber. Diesel tractors bring in about 500 logs each, carried on a train of sleds. The logs are assembled in vast timber yards occupying old clearings in the forest. Thence they make their way to river, canal or railway for transport to the sawmills. Villages of lumberjacks' wooden cottages have been built near the central timber yards. Besides the sawmills, other woodworking factories, making matches, veneers, furniture and prefabricated houses have been added along with a whole new industry, that of wood chemistry. This manufactures pulp and paper from timber not fit for lumber, and produces wood alcohol, glucose, etc. from the waste arising from other woodworking industries.

The Kola peninsula, within the Arctic circle, has become an important mining and industrial area. Aluminium, nickel, copper and iron ores are mined. Iron ore is shipped to Cherepovets from the fully-automated Lake Onega port of Medvezhyegorsk. On Kola also are large deposits of apatite, used as a fertilizer: the mines are located on the steep mountain sides.

Agriculture has been extended and improved, although it is confined in the main to the southern margins and the river valleys. Fresh clearings have been made, especially near new and expanded settlements, and lime, fertilizers and machinery have made their appearance. Tayga agriculture cannot, however, be mechanized to the same degree as elsewhere, because the fields tend to be small and scattered. Livestock rearing and dairy farming have shown the most improvement, but cereal and vegetable cultivation has been increased also. Winter rye is the leading grain. Perhaps the most striking change in the Soviet period has been the establishment on tayga collective farms of large acreages of greenhouses. Reindeer herding has been encouraged in the northern regions.

The chief towns are listed in Table 5. Perm and Izhevsk were both the sites of charcoal-mining ironworks in the eighteenth century. Perm, although to the west of the Ural range, is usually classed as a Ural town. Situated near the confluence of the Kama and the Chusovaya, it is a great machine-building, petrochemical and woodworking centre: its industrial establishments line both banks of the Kama for 15 miles. Above the city is the hydroelectric station from which it obtains its power. The dam holds back a 600-mile-square reservoir. Izhevsk still has metallurgical works and produces steel for its machine-building and motor industries.

At the opposite corner of the region, Archangel receives masses of timber floated down the Dvina; this is stacked in rectangular piles covering a vast acreage. Alongside the wharves, the variegated colours of foreign flags and the painted funnels of foreign ships, as well as the presence of foreign seamen ashore, indicate the importance of the export trade. Archangel also has pulp and paper mills. The modern city centre is composed of multi-storey stone, brick and concrete buildings interspersed with parks and gardens, and there is a long waterfront with the towers and cupolas of numerous churches silhouetted against the skyline. Nearby Severodvinsk is a shipbuilding and machine-building centre and an important submarine base.

TABLE 5. *Population and rank of principal towns of the North Russian spruce tayga region* (thousands)

	1926	1959	1981
Perm	120 (25th)	629 (17th)	1,018 (19th)
Izhevsk	63 (64th)	285 (48th)	574 (35th)
Kirov (Vyatka)	62 (67th)	252 (57th)	396 (67th)
Archangel	77 (46th)	256 (55th)	391 (69th)
Cherepovets		92 (166th)	279 (100th)
Vologda	58 (74th)	139 (109th)	247 (115th)
Rybinsk	56 (80th)	182 (77th)	245 (117th)
Petrozavodsk	27	136 (110th)	241 (121st)
Severodvinsk		79 (195th)	208 (140th)
Syktyvkar		64 (231st)	180 (158th)

Across the White Sea is the Kola group of mining and smelting towns, which includes Monchegorsk (53, 000), Kirovsk (39,000) and Kandalaksha (37,000), all founded in the 1930s. Syktyvkar, near the mouth of a Vychegda tributary, is capital of the Komi republic, and reindeer mingle with motor cars in the streets. The town is built up both sides of a natural amphitheatre, and crowned by the modern building of the Komi Soviet. The inhabitants work in sawmills, in factories making prefabricated houses and furniture or processing furs, and in yards building river barges. Cherepovets has grown rapidly with the continued expansion of its large modern fully-integrated and highly automated steelworks. Here Kola ore, Vorkuta coking coal and Urengoy natural gas are brought together to make sheet steel for the motor industry and large-diameter tube for pipelines. Its power station, which provides hot water as well as electricity, works on peat extracted from the boggy land around the town.

The West Siberian swamp tayga region
Before the Revolution, the swamp tayga was almost completely uninhabited except for the Samoyeds in the extreme north, the Tartar peoples on the southern borders, and the Ostyaks along the Ob and Yenisey rivers. There were

27. Odes, a new settlement in the tayga on the Ukhta oil and gas field

only about 20,000 of them and perhaps 80,000 Russians. The population now is nearly 2 million, most of whom are Russians, but the density is only three per square mile. There were a few small towns. Most of them had begun as fur-trading posts or *ostrogi* – log huts and stores garrisoned by Cossacks and surrounded by wooden stockades.

Tobolsk, founded in 1587, soon became the largest town in Siberia. But its population of 15,000 in 1772 grew to only 18,500 a century later. It was built on a hill commanding the confluence of the Tobol with the Irtysh. In 1852 a Polish exile described how its 'streets were laid with planks and large trunks of trees'.[5] Most of its houses also were of wood. Yeniseysk, near the junction of the Angara and the Yenisey, was second in size among Siberian swamp-tayga towns, having a population of 12,000 in 1914. Here, 'the mud and the ruts were just as deep as in the villages, only there was not so much cow dung'.[6] Berezovo and Surgut, both on the Ob, had each about a thousand inhabitants.

This desolate expanse of forest and bog has been transformed by the finding, early in the 1960s, of oil in the Middle Ob region. Despite the incredibly difficult conditions of permafrost, winter blizzards and summer quagmire, the oilfield has rapidly become the world's largest, with an annual production of over 300 million tons. Resulting human activity has affected the landscape in many ways with drilling wells, pipelines, oil-gas compressor stations, roads and settlements. The rivers are busy with barge traffic in the navigable season and the air is bright with flared gas and noisy with helicopters. A new railway runs northwards from

Tyumen across the region to the gas centre of Urengoy in the tundra belt. It passes through the old fur-trading towns of Tobolsk (65,000), its calm now shattered by the erection of the country's largest petrochemical complex, and Surgut (137,000), with a branch to the new oilfield centre of Nizhnevartovsk (134,000). Another new railway leaves the Urals at Ivdel for the Ob to serve the Berezovo gasfield. The building of railways across swamp underlain by permafrost is extraordinarily difficult, but their completion has opened up new areas to lumbering as well as to oil and gas development. The wasteful flaring of gas is being lessened by the construction of gas-processing plants, enabling the amount burned off to fall from 83 per cent in 1976 to 35 per cent in 1980. Oil-gas fires the 2,400 MW Surgut power station, which also provides the town with hot water. The gas travels in rail cars to the huge chemical complex at Tobolsk, and by pipeline to the industries of the Kuzbass in southern Siberia. There has been widespread pollution of ground, water and air, and destruction of wild life: hunting is the main recreation of drilling teams and other workers in this harsh region.

The Central Siberian larch tayga region

The valleys of the Central Siberian plateau were inhabited before the Revolution by about 10,000 Tungus who lived by hunting and fishing. Far more numerous were the Yakuts of the Lena lowland, a semi-nomadic, pastoral people who had come originally from the south. They added pastureland of their own to the Lena meadows by burning down the forest. An open parkland landscape resulted, with birch woods and meadows. But in the harsh climate of the eastern tayga they often had to subsist on roots, grass and bark, as well as on meat and fish. The Yakuts caught their fish from dug-out canoes with small nets made of horsehair. They were described by a writer in Peter I's reign:

> They shift their abode as do the Tobolsk Tartars. Their winter huts are square and made of logs; the roof is covered with turf, and a hole is left in the middle to let out the smoke. Their summer dwellings are round and shaped like a sugar loaf. The outside shell of these huts is made of birch bark, carefully sewn together and embroidered with horse-hair, and dyed in different colours.[7]

They were forced to scour the forest for furs to pay the tribute (*yasak*) levied by the Russians, and suffered extreme extortion and cruelty. Nevertheless, there were 221,500 of them in 1897.

Salt was the only mineral mined before the Revolution. It was used for the river fishing industry and was prepared in works at Ust-Kut, a seventeenth-century trading post, and at Vilyuysk, both in the Lena basin. Gold was mined in the mountain belt on the eastern edge of the region, and Vitim and Olekminsk on the Lena were the towns that served the mines. The conditions in which the workers – most of whom were convicts and exiles – lived and toiled, were appalling: 'The miners have to work wading knee-deep in ice-cold water; and after the long day's work they spend the night in overcrowded barracks, begrimed with dirt and teeming with vermin. Disease, especially scurvy and diarrhoea, is rife, and the mortality enormous.'[8] They worked throughout the summer without wages, and were then turned loose with a single payment, which soon vanished in the saloons and brothels of Vitim or Olekminsk. Close to the latter town, and contrasting with its filth and debauchery, was the dissenting sect of Skoptsy's village of Spaskoye, distinguished by its cleanliness and surrounded – despite the climate – by carefully tilled fields.

Irkutsk and Yakutsk were the only prerevolutionary towns of note. Irkutsk, founded in 1652 on the Angara river near its outflow from Lake Baykal, grew rapidly as the capital of eastern and central Siberia, and in 1897, with more than 50,000 inhabitants was the second-largest Siberian town, after Tomsk. By 1914 it had many substantial buildings in brick and stone, including a Roman Catholic church in Gothic style, built for the large number of exiled Poles. It had also become an industrial centre, with tanneries, tallow works, fur-dressing establishments and sawmills. Yakutsk, older but smaller, was founded in 1632 in the centre of the Lena lowland at a latitude of 62° N; it was a miscellaneous collection of dilapidated Russian log houses and Yakut huts surrounding the prison. The streets in summer were liquid mud into which all refuse was thrown, fouling the air intolerably. Its population had risen from about 2,000 in 1775 to 8,000 in 1914.

The Soviet period, especially the past three decades, has witnessed a large-scale development of the region's power resources and of mining, so that in many areas the monotony of the tayga is now interrupted by the superstructure of

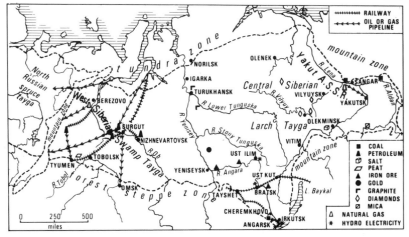

28. *The West Siberian swamp tayga and the Central Siberian larch tayga*

mines, the derricks of gas wells, and the dams, installations and pylons of hydroelectric projects. Enormous coal and lignite fields have been found on the Central Siberian plateau, but permafrost complicates mining, and they are only worked for local needs at one or two places in the Lena basin. On the other hand, in the southeast, where the Trans-Siberian railway runs through the Irkutsk coalfield, there has been active development, especially around Cheremkhovo.

There has been notable hydroelectric development on the Angara, where natural conditions are very propitious: the river is fed by Lake Baykal and its level is therefore remarkably constant; it does not freeze; its valley has firm, steep, high banks. Consequently costs are extremely low (0.03 kopeks a kWh compared with an average of 0.15 to 0.2 elsewhere in the Union). Two very-large-capacity stations are already operating at Bratsk (4,500 MW) and Ust Ilimsk (3,600 MW), while a third, lower down the river at Boguchansk, is under construction. No fewer than twenty pylon transmission lines radiate from Bratsk, taking power to the Kuzbass, Novosibirsk, Tomsk, Barnaul, etc. The abundant cheap power is also fed to a growing industrial complex with aluminium-smelting, saw-milling and wood-chemical industries. It also drives the machinery of iron-ore mines in the mountains bordering the Angara.

A large diamond industry has been established in the Vilhuy basin, where the kimberlite pipes are a legacy of Palaeozoic and Mesozoic vulcanism. Mining began in 1949 and now satisfies domestic needs and a valuable export trade. The Vilhuy hydroelectric station, which provides the power, has given rise to a 250-mile long reservoir lake known as the Vilhuy Sea. The largest deposits of graphite in the Union are mined on the Lower Tunguska river. Billions of tons of common salt have been discovered near Olekminsk and are now worked.

Furs are still an important product of the tayga, but now come mostly from large state fur-farms, where the animals are housed in cages arranged in parallel rows hundreds of yards long, and covering several acres. The fur-farmers live in neat new wooden cottages. The whole farm is hemmed in by the forest, through which a road links up with a town or with rail or water communication. The Central Siberian larch tayga accounts for a third of Soviet furs. The fur-farms produce black or silver fox, mink and blue fox, while sable, squirrel, muskrat, white fox and ermine are still obtained wild.

Agriculture has not been neglected, and particular progress has been made in the Lena lowland, where quick-growing varieties have made possible a considerable expansion in the acreage of summer wheat, rye, barley and oats.

Improved transport facilities serve these new activities. On the Lena large river ships loaded with trucks, tractors and bulldozers descend the great river to supply the mining sites of Yakutia. The new Baykal–Amur railway (BAM) begins at Tayshet on the Trans-Siberian and proceeds eastwards through difficult terrain via Bratsk and Ust-Kut. Road transport is usually only of local importance, but many old tsarist portage tracks have been made into modern highways, and the Aldan Highway has been built from the Trans-Siberian railway to Yakutsk. New roads branch off from the railways and waterways to serve lumber camps and mining centres. Air transport has obvious advantages over surface movement in a forested swampy territory, and all the major centres have airfields. Giant helicopters move heavy machinery from rail and water to construction sites, and dirigible airships are also used.

Irkutsk (568,000) remains the region's largest city. It is at the point of convergence of two fast-growing industrial zones. One of these lies along the Trans-Siberian railway from Tayshet eastwards and is based on the Cheremkhovo coal basin, while the other is in the Angara valley and powered by hydroelectricity. Angarsk (245,000), Bratsk (222,000) and Ust Ilimsk (82,000) are fast-growing new towns.

Modern Yakutsk, capital of the Yakut republic, represents a triumph over permafrost. To the old wooden town have been added a seven-storey hotel, modern apartment blocks, and institutional buildings such as those of the Yakut University. They have been erected on piles driven, with the aid of steam jets, 25 feet into the permafrost, here 600 feet or more deep; they are insulated from the ground, so that their heat will not thaw it, causing them to sink lopsidedly into the mud. They are supplied with natural gas from a nearby field. The 1981 population was 159,000.

Igarka, founded in 1929 on the lower Yenisey, is a sawmilling town within the Arctic Circle. It also has fish-processing and canning plants. The town is all wood – wooden houses, wood-paved streets, wooden wharves, etc. The fields and glasshouses of state farms, where potatoes, carrots, radishes, onions and tomatoes are grown, surround the settlement. Among the newer towns of Central Siberia, diamond-working Mirny, founded in 1958, is noteworthy: the concentration mills have frostproof walls of insulated aluminium. A new town centre of large concrete buildings, raised on piles driven into the permafrost, rises amidst an expanse of wooden houses.

The mixed forest zone

This zone holds about 65 million people, three times as many as in all the tayga regions, in about one-sixth of their total area. This much greater average density of population, amounting to about 150 per square mile, has resulted in much modification of the landscape. Nearly two-thirds of the forest has been cleared to make way for farms. Large cities have grown up, and a relatively dense network of communications has been developed to serve them.

Of the natural resources which have favoured this development, by far the greatest has been its watershed position. Here, within easy reach of each other, like the headwaters of rivers which lead to the five seas: Baltic, White, Black, Azov and Caspian, and thence to the lands beyond. As a result, prosperous

29. *The pipeline from the Taas Tumus gasfield to Yakutsk. Because of the permafrost and the extremes of temperature, the pipe zigzags on trestles through the tayga forest*

trading cities developed at strategic points early in the Middle Ages. Some of these towns have preserved ornate churches and citadels (kremlins) dating from this early mercantile prosperity.

Other natural resources were the forest, peat, bog iron, and more recently, oil shale and low-grade lignite coal. But the zone as a whole is deficient in sources of energy and in metals, although it does have valuable reserves of mineral salts. The soils are mostly leached podsols, often strewn with boulders in the northwest. Boggy ground is widespread, notably in the Polesye and Meshchera, and there are many sandy or gravelly pine-clad morainic hillocks. Thus agricultural possibilities were limited.

The mixed forest zone may be subdivided into four regions, according to geographical position and historical development:

1. The Baltic lands and northwestern Russia.
2. White Russia (Belorussia), western Russia, and northern Ukraine.
3. The Industrial Centre.
4. The Trans-Volga strip.

The Baltic lands and northwestern Russia

The Baltic lands are not Russian historically, and this is apparent in the

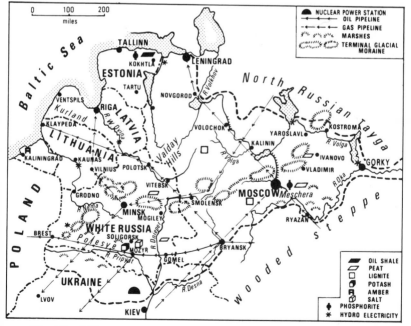

30. *The Mixed Forest zone*

architecture of the towns and villages, as well as from the languages spoken. But, as they stood between Muscovy and the Baltic, and as they were often in hands hostile to Russia, they were inevitably of interest to tsar and Soviet alike. They were repeatedly devastated in wars between the Muscovites on the one hand and Lithuanians, Poles, Swedes and Germans on the other. Their inhabitants – Lithuanians, Latvians and Estonians – were successively under German, Polish and Swedish rule before entering the Russian Empire. Peter I acquired them in 1721, and after a brief period of separate existence between the wars, they became Soviet republics in 1940. After the Germans had been driven out in 1944, the German Baltic city of Königsberg was also annexed, and renamed Kaliningrad.

Although forests, mainly coniferous, cover much of the ground in the Baltic region, and poor soils are widepsread, there are areas of profitable agricultural specialization. Latvia and Lithuania have a large grain-growing area in the former province of Kurland. Along the Estonian coastland there is intensive production of meat, milk and vegetables to supply Leningrad. Flax is a noteworthy crop around Pskov, and can be seen at harvest time spread out over the ground for rain and sun to separate the fibres, and hung on long pine hurdles to dry.

The largest towns of the Baltic region are shown in Table 6.

TABLE 6. *Population and rank of principal towns of the Baltic region (thousands)*

	1926	1959	1981
Leningrad	1,690 (2nd)	3,367 (2nd)	4,676 (2nd)
Riga	(385 in 1935)*	580 (21st)	850 (26th)
Vilnyus	(208 in 1931)*	236 (61st)	503 (47th)
Tallin	(146 in 1938)*	282 (50th)	442 (58th)
Kaunas	(108 in 1931)*	219 (64th)	383 (71st)
Kaliningrad	(316 in 1933)*	204 (71st)	366 (74th)

*Not in the USSR

Peter the Great built Petersburg (Leningrad) at the nearest point on the sea to Moscow, and by creating it his capital, made it the symbol of a Russia dependent on overseas trade. The Soviet return of the capital to Moscow was equally symbolic of a determination to base the country's economy on its own resources. But although Leningrad's commercial function is now less vital than in late tsarist days, its industrial role is greater than ever before. The concentration here, as at Riga, of highly skilled labour has made the city a leading centre for high-quality engineering. The generators for the great Siberian hydro stations and the equipment for most Soviet nuclear power stations are made here. The city suffered severely during the wartime siege. Its northerly position on the 60th parallel gives it short, dark, cold and damp winter days, but almost continuous daylight in summer. The timber rafts floating down the river remind one that it is on the edge of the tayga. To protect Leningrad from the flooding it periodically suffers, a 16-mile dyke is being constructed across the Gulf of Finland some 20 miles to the west of the port.

The location of Peter's town on the northwestern borders of Russia necessitated linking it with other parts of the country, and especially with Moscow and the Volga. In the eighteenth century the Vishny Volochok canal, which joined tributaries of the Volga (Tvertsa) and Volkhov (Msta), was kept extraordinarily busy carrying timber, metals and foodstuffs to Petersburg. The waterway left the Volga at Tver (Kalinin), which in consequence became a busy commercial centre. It also brought a little more life for a time to Novgorod, which remained, however, but a shadow of its medieval self. The Petersburg–Moscow railway (1851) bypassed it, and in 1959 its population was still only 61,000. It was more numerous in the twelfth century when Novgorod was a member of the Hanseatic League and capital of a vast fur-yielding empire extending to the shores of the White Sea and Urals. But the establishment of a gas-chemical industry has led to a revival, and by 1981 the population had risen to 198,000. The imposing kremlin, enclosing a beautiful eleventh-century cathedral and other handsome buildings, looks over the Volkhov river to the low-lying marshy country beyond. Much of the Soviet Union's export trade (chiefly oil, gas and petrochemicals) now makes its way across the Baltic region by rail, road and pipe to the large new chemical export terminal at Ventspils.

Of the five largest Baltic towns, other than Leningrad, three are capitals of Republics: Riga (Latvia), Tallin (Estonia) and Vilnyus (Lithuania). This status has given them administrative, educational and cultural buildings, as well as new blocks of flats and factories devoted to light industry and machine-building. But they also preserve medieval quarters with old walls, gates and towers, narrow crooked streets and ancient Germanic buildings, as does Estonia's second city, the historic university town of Tartu (107,000). Kaunas was the former Lithuanian capital, while Kaliningrad has been built on the site of the East Prussian city of Königsberg, almost totally destroyed in the war. Amber is quarried nearby. These Baltic manufacturing centres, which before the Revolution worked on imported coal, need power: hence the energetic exploitation of the Estonian oil shales at Kokhtla Yarve (74,000). This has led to the opening of vast quarries, to the building of a large tall-chimneyed processing plant, and to the erection of thermal power stations, while at Maardu, east of Tallin, a large shale-chemical works belches smoke. The large Leningrad nuclear power station (4,000 MW) has been built on the Baltic coast at Sosnovy Bor, 50 miles west of the city. Small hydroelectric stations have also been

31. Leningrad: the river Neva and the baroque Winter Palace (1754–62)

established on the Volkhov, Dvina and Neman rivers, and natural gas is piped into the region.

White Russia (Belorussia), western Russia and northern Ukraine

White Russia, long under Lithuanian and Polish rule, was not brought into the Empire until the partitions of Poland in the late eighteenth century. Its western areas again formed part of Poland from 1920 to 1939. Consequently, it did not benefit from the industrialization of the early Soviet five-year plans, and when recovered by the USSR in 1944 had been mercilessly ravaged by war, as had most of Russia west of Moscow. Its better-drained lands are farmed. Rye is the traditional grain, but potatoes and dairy farming are also important. Flax has always been a special crop in the north, hemp in the south. On the poorer ground, villages and farms have long had a poverty-stricken and backward appearance, but where the old izbas remain, they have usually been reroofed, often with asbestos. Farm buildings are almost all modern, and new administrative, social and educational buildings have been erected by collective farms. Some attempt was made to improve the bogs of the Polesye in the 1870s, but since 1966 over 3 million acres have been drained, and twenty-one new state farms, with silage towers, long barns and urban-type settlements established on the reclaimed marsh. Fodder crops are increasingly grown.

The population of the larger western towns is shown in Table 7. All suffered

TABLE 7. *Population and rank of principal towns of Belorussia and western Russia (thousands)*

	1939	1959	1981
Minsk	237 (32nd)	509 (24th)	1,333 (8th)
Bryansk	174 (45th)	207 (68th)	407 (64th)
Gomel	139 (58th)	168 (86th)	405 (65th)
Smolensk	157 (53rd)	147 (102nd)	311 (87th)
Vitebsk	167 (48th)	148 (100th)	310 (88th)
Mogilev	99 (89th)	122 (123rd)	308 (90th)

heavy damage during the 1941–45 war and, as a result, most dropped in rank between the 1939 and 1959 censuses. It may be noted, however, that recently all have improved their relative position. Having recovered from wartime destruction, their advantageous situation on routes between the Industrial Centre and the socialist countries of eastern Europe is being fully exploited with the help of oil and natural gas brought in by pipe, and large local deposits of mineral salts.

In no Republic has the urban population increased so fast as in Belorussia. In 1959 it formed only 30 per cent of the total, but in 1981 it was 57 per cent. Minsk has grown much faster since 1959 than any other large town in the USSR, both as administrative capital of developing Belorussia and as a leading engineering centre, making lorries, motorcycles, cranes, machine tools and refrigerators. The city has broad boulevards of handsome white-balconied blocks of flats. Gomel manufactures farm machinery, wood–chemicals, wallpaper, and fertilizer from nearby phosphorite mines, while Mogilev makes dump trucks and synthetic fibres. Grodno (212,000) produces textiles and nitrogenous fertilizers. Other large industrial centres are Bobruysk (203,000), Baranovichi (138,000) and Borisov (117,000). These are old cities with a chequered history, and have spent long periods under Polish rule, but Novopolotsk (72,000) and Soligorsk (72,000) are new Soviet towns specializing respectively in petrochemicals and potash fertilizer. Mozyr (79,000), on the *Druzhba* ('Friendship') oil pipeline which crosses southern Belorussia to eastern Europe, also has petrochemicals. A new steelworks, using scrap in electric furnaces (capacity 500,000 tons), is being built at Zhlobin, forty miles northwest of Gomel. Hitherto the region has had to import all its steel. In the marshy country of northern Ukraine is the Chernobyl nuclear power station (2,000 MW).

The Industrial Centre
To the area lying between the upper Volga and the Oka geographical position offered not only commercial opportunity but military security. Into this

naturally moated refuge there migrated, during the hazardous Middle Ages, thousands of fugitives from Tartars in the east, from Poles and Lithuanians in the west, and from Germans and Swedes in the northwest. Here alone an independent Russia survived, and this was the base from which its growing power thrust along the rivers in all directions towards the distant seas. Here too, ancient towns have preserved their beautiful medieval kremlins and churches: Vladimir, Rostov, Suzdal, Yaroslavl and, of course, Moscow.

Position enabled the population to import the raw materials of early industry: flax, hemp, hides, wool, wood, bog iron. The skills acquired in working these encouraged the growth of factory industry in the late nineteenth and early twentieth centuries, and have helped the Soviets in the introduction of modern technology. Large new manufacturing distincts have been added to the ancient centres and, occasionally, entirely new towns established. The *oblasts* of Moscow, Vladimir, Gorky, Ivanovo and Yaroslavl, with parts of contiguous oblasts, form the most important single industrial area in the USSR: factories, houses and blocks of flats often dominate the landscape, and there is an unusually dense network of busy roads and railways, and a growing number of pipelines, most of them converging on Moscow. The Moscow Canal (completed in 1937) climbs and descends the morainic ridge which separates the capital from the Volga. The landscape, however, is by no means wholly urbanized or industrialized: forests, woods, fields, meadows, marshes, and, near the towns, market gardens and dairy farms predominate, even in the most densely populated part. Thirty-eight per cent of Moscow oblast is still forested, 40 per cent of Kalinin, Ivanovo, and Gorky oblasts and 42 per cent of Vladimir. [9]

Although swamps are frequent and woods never far distant, much land is farmed. Rye was the chief crop until the 1870s. But when the railways made it possible to import cheaper grain, there was a shift to industrial crops (flax and potatoes) and to fodder crops, dairying and market gradening. This change in the rural landscape has continued during the Soviet period. Orchards, with apples, cherries, pears and plums, absent from the tayga, are usual in the villages. War damage notwithstanding, many old log izbas remain, misshapen through age and intermingled with newer cottages. Television aerials perch on tall sticks, not always straight, while the results of electrification – pylons, poles and wires – add to the general air of untidiness. The smaller towns are but intensified manifestations of this rural pattern – higgledy-piggledy collections of wooden houses in gardens and amidst trees.

A radical landscape change is being effected through drainage of the Meshchera marsh, which has long supplied Shatura power station with peat fuel. Reclamation began in 1964, and the new farms produce mainly milk, meat and vegetables.

The larger towns of the Industrial Centre as here defined, excluding suburbs and satellites of Moscow, are listed in Table 8. Industrial expansion and

32. A seventeenth-century church at Yaroslavl

population growth were greater here during the first five-year plans than anywhere else, and most of the towns more than doubled their population during the brief thirteen years between the 1926 and 1939 censuses. Since then growth,

TABLE 8. *Population and rank of principal towns of the Industrial Centre, excluding suburbs and satellites of Moscow (thousands)*

	1939	1959	1981
Moscow	4,542 (1st)	6,053 (1st)	8,203 (1st)
Gorky	644 (6th)	941 (5th)	1,367 (6th)
Yaroslavl	309 (20th)	407 (32nd)	608 (32nd)
Ivanovo	285 (22nd)	335 (39th)	470 (54th)
Ryazan	95 (88th)	214 (66th)	470 (54th)
Kalinin	216 (35th)	261 (54th)	422 (61st)
Vladimir	67 (139th)	154 (94th)	307 (91st)
Kaluga	89 (99th)	134 (111th)	276 (103rd)
Dzerzhinsk	103 (79th)	164 (86th)	263 (108th)
Kostroma	121 (70th)	172 (81st)	259 (109th)
Rybinsk	144 (62nd)	182 (77th)	245 (117th)

though substantial, has slackened off, and many of the towns have declined relatively. The capital and its environs form a special case. Migration into Moscow has been impossible to stop, and new building is seen everywhere. Its continued growth is due to its possession of the largest pool of skilled labour, the best educational and research facilities, the richest market, and also to the pull of the metropolis – the desire of men and women to live and work in or near the big city.

Much of Soviet textile production is located in the Industrial Centre. The cotton industry is most important, and found mainly in towns along the Klyazma valley and at Ivanovo. Woollens are manufactured in and around Moscow, and the ancient linen industry survives at Kostroma. Machine-building has developed rapidly under Soviet rule, although there is no primary iron and steel production, apart from steel-rolling mills at Moscow and Gorky. Moscow manufactures cars, lorries, machine tools and electrical equipment, and Gorky, motor vehicles and machines tools. Yaroslavl (diesel engines), Kostroma (diesel locomotives, railway rolling stock), Kineshma (car parts), Vladimir (tractors, car instruments) and Ivanovo (textile machinery), as well as many smaller towns, are also important. More recently, there has been a growth of the chemical industry, with production of synthetic fibres at Kalinin, Serpukhov, Vladimir and at Dzerzhinsk, which also manufactures fertilizer. Voskresensk produces fertilizer from phosphate mined at nearby Fosforitny. Oil brought by pipeline from the east is refined where it crosses the Volga near Gorky and at Yaroslavl, where synthetic rubber is made into tyres. Pulp and paper are manufactured on the borders of the tayga zone at Pravdinsk (for *Pravda*), near Gorky, and at Rybinsk.

The heavy concentration of industry in a region almost totally devoid of sources of energy has led to the exploitation of low-grade lignite and peat which are converted into electricity in power stations, and to large imports of coal, oil, gas and electricity. These imports find landscape expression in freight trains, pipelines and pylon-carried cables. Although Russia's first nuclear power station was built in the postwar decade at Obninsk, southwest of Moscow, its output was very small, and there is no major modern nuclear power station in this relatively densely-peopled area; instead the capacity of the thermal stations continues to expand; that below Kostroma, for instance, to 3,600 MW by the installation of a 1,200 MW gas-fired unit.

Until the middle of the nineteenth century, Moscow was, in the main, a vast and motley sprawl of mansions, gardens, wooden shacks and hovels, without the benefit of regular streets. This agglomeration surrounded a more compact and solid centre, consisting of – besides the Kremlin – churches, a few institutional buildings and the brick houses and shops of the merchants. The late nineteenth and early twentieth centuries saw the addition of industrial districts with large dingy brick dormitory-factories and wooden workshops.

The Soviet period has witnessed the transformation of the city outside of the

Kremlin, which alone remains much as it was in former times. Ramshackle wooden houses have been swept away. Administrative buildings, shops and hotels have been concentrated in the central area, while large blocks of flats make up the residential quarters. The new streets are broad and tree-lined. Many of the larger buildings, including the university, are built on the principle of a symmetrical arrangement of towers, with the tallest in the centre. The television tower in the Ostankino suburb is, at 1,756 feet, a widely visible landmark. The twelve main motor roads that converge upon the city end at the dual-carriageway ring road, the outermost of the concentric circular boulevards that are the distinctive feature of Moscow's plan. It is the city boundary and encloses an area of 340 square miles, beyond which the built-up area is not allowed to spread. Moscow's continued increase in population has been accommodated within this restricted area by the replacement of low-density districts of wooden houses by tall blocks of flats.

Red Square owes its fame, not only to the architecture of the Kremlin wall and towers and to the ornate domes of St Basil's cathedral, but also to its having been the scene of parades, processions, uprisings and state executions for many centuries. Its large rectangular shape cleaves the ancient walled town into two

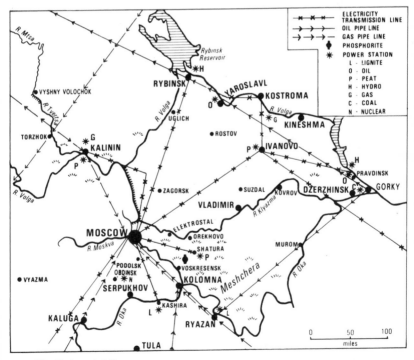

33. The Industrial Centre

34. Moscow: this western district, within a loop of the Moskva river, is crossed by Kutuzov Avenue, the main road to the west. It has been rebuilt during the Soviet period

halves: the Kremlin, the prince's stronghold, enclosing churches, palaces and gardens, and the Kitaygorod, or merchants' town. Here, where the great markets of earlier times were held, the GUM or State Universal Stores now stands, in which whole arcades of shops arranged in three storeys are included in one immense building. Its façade faces the Kremlin wall and the Lenin mausoleum, which forms the chief Soviet contribution to the square. In winter, the dark 'crocodile' of pilgrims to the tomb traces its black line across the snowy expanse of the square. In summer, the sun illumines the many colours of St Basil's and the star on the Kremlin tower (Fig. 35).

Gorky (Nizhny Novgorod), at the confluence of the Volga and the Oka, occupies a central position in the waterway system of Russia, and during the nineteenth century was renowned for its great fair. It is now a major industrial centre and the site of great engineering industries. Many works were transferred here from more exposed territory during both twentieth-century wars with Germany, and its has benefited much from the traditional metal-working skills of the surrounding villages. It has a lower town, or port area, crowded along the river's edge, and an upper town.

The Trans-Volga strip
From Gorky eastwards, the Mixed Forest zone continues to the Urals in a belt 50

35. *Central Moscow: in the right foreground, the Kremlin and the Lenin
Mausoleum; in the middle ground, St Basil's and the GUM department store,
with modern buildings in the background*

to 100 miles wide, the Volga and Kama rivers forming the southern boundary for
much of the way. There is much cultivation, but also much forest surviving,
especially pinewoods on the sands bordering the Volga. Apart from the farms,
the chief man-made aspects of the landscape are the city of Kazan, the main-line
railway from Kazan to Sverdlovsk in the Urals, and wells of the northern outliers
of the Volga–Ural oilfield.

This country was opened to the Russians after the conquest of the Tartar
khanate of Kazan in 1552. Once the cutting of the Vishny Volochok canal in 1720
had given a through waterway to Petersburg, grain and timber both moved in
large quantities from this area to the capital. Eighteenth-century Russian navies
were built largely of Kazan oak. Adjoining the Tartar city, which was a collection
of hovels built on marshy flats adjoining the river and adjacent to the fortress,
the Russians built a new town of wooden izbas. Because of its position near the
junction of the Volga and the Kama, it soon became a great commercial centre
and industrial town. Leather and livestock products were its chief prerevolutionary industries, to which it has since added engineering, food-processing and
petrochemicals. As capital of the Tartar autonomous republic, the city has,
besides new blocks of flats, various Tartar administrative, educational and
cultural buildings. Until burnt to the ground in 1815, this gateway to the east was
the largest town in Russia after Petersburg and Moscow. It has since declined in
order of population to twentieth, but none the less had over a million inhabitants

in 1982.

Cheboksary (340,000), between Gorky and Kazan, has grown rapidly with the building there of the last hydroelectric station of the Volga 'cascade' (capacity 1,400 MW). Its population grew between the 1959 and 1979 censuses from 94,000 to 303,000; as well as being the administrative centre of the Chuvash ASSR it has a variety of manufactures, including a large pulp and paper combine which, working on deciduous timber, is likely to have a serious impact on the local forests.

6
The steppe belt

Natural landscapes

The steppe landscape belt is usually divided into two zones, the wooded steppe (*lesostep*) in the north and the grass steppe to the south. Sometimes a third zone of broadleaved forest is interposed on the north between the mixed forest and the wooded steppe. But although a narrow strip along the northern margins was possibly once completely covered by deciduous forest, 'the presence within it of islands of meadow steppe points to its inclusion with the wooded steppe'.[1] Thus, the presence of natural steppe grassland, rather than the absence of forest, is the criterion used to define the steppe belt, which is about 2,500 miles long and stretches from the Carpathian to the Altay Mountains. Beyond them it reappears in relatively small areas. The total extent is about $1\frac{1}{4}$ million square miles. Although this chapter is mostly written in the present tense, the natural landscape has been so greatly modified by man, that much of the following description relates to the past.

Climate varies the landscape of the steppe belt from season to season and from year to year. The whole belt experiences a winter frost during which the ground is snow-covered. But whereas these conditions last two months or less in western Ukraine, they endure for three or four months in central and eastern Russia, and for five months and over in Siberia and northern Kazakhstan. However, although the Siberian-Kazakh winter is longer, it has less snow: winds are able to blow it off the ground, exposing the bare steppe to deep freezing. Despite the low total amount of snowfall in the treeless zone, furious blizzards frequently fill the air with snow and pile up enormous drifts.

Because there is so little snow to melt, spring is soon over, but not before it has wet the soil, filled the stream beds and depressions, and replenished the flow of the rivers. Summer is the season of desiccation, during which soil, vegetation and pools dry up, and rivers become shallow. Although most precipitation falls in summer, much of it is lost in evaporation by hot dry winds. The steppe regions are therefore highly dependent on the much smaller amount of winter precipitation, accumulated in the form of snow, and for this to be blown away can be more serious for the vegetation than a summer drought. Annual precipitation decreases both southwards and eastwards, but increases with altitude.

The natural landscape, therefore, changes latitudinally, longitudinally and altitudinally. Southwards, as the climate becomes drier and the summers hotter, forests shrink and eventually disappear, except in the valleys. Eastwards also, the climate becomes drier, and winter more severe. Trees common in the west – beech, hornbeam, ash and oak – drop out, and the birch dominates the woodlands. With increased elevation, and therefore usually with greater precipitation, woodland reappears. The Donets Heights form an outlier of wooded steppe within the grass steppe.

Mean July temperatures range from 19° C (66° F) along the northern margins to 24° C (75° F) along the southern borderland. Combined with a decrease in the total annual precipitation from over 20 inches to well under 15, this represents a sharp negative change in the moisture balance – sufficient to bring about the transition from luxuriant and complete forest cover in the north to near-desert vegetation in the south. Mean temperatures do not tell the whole story. The entire belt, but especially the grass steppe zone, experiences dry, scorching winds – *sukhoveys* – which raise shade temperatures to 35° C (95° F) and even to 40° C (104° F), while lowering the relative humidity to 15 or 12 per cent (the mean is between 60 and 40 per cent). At certain seasons, the winds are so laden with pollen, especially from the ubiquitous fescue grass, that the phenomenon known as 'white mist' occurs. The great heat also produces shimmering and mirage effects.

Summer precipitation varies enormously from year to year. At Rostov-on-Don, where the average annual amount received is just under 20 inches, 30 inches fell in 1956 but only three in 1959! Violent thunderstorms are characteristic. One storm alone can bring two or three inches of rain, briefly converting low-lying surfaces into sheets of water, or painting the ground white with hail. If these storms do not occur, but instead the *sukhovey* blows, severe drought results: droughts occur on an average once in every three or four years. Autumn,

36. *The steppe zones and regions*

unlike spring, is a protracted season during which night frosts return. These are especially keenly felt in the gullies, ravines, deep valleys and depressions sheltered from the wind.

The wooded steppe zone
The wooded steppe zone may be defined as that in which woodland appears along with steppe grassland outside of the valleys. Its area is about 550,000 square miles. Large stretches of almost continuous forest in the north dwindle southwards to mere copses. In the far west, large beech forests clothe the Kodra Heights in Moldavia, but most of the forest west of the Dnieper is of the oak–hornbeam type. Lofty oaks form the upper canopy, with hornbeam beneath, and because of the shade they cast there is little bush undergrowth. Not much hornbeam is found east of the Dnieper. From that river to the Urals, the oak is associated with maple, linden, ash, aspen and elm, but the ash drops out at the Volga. Beneath such typical oak forests there is a vigorous undergrowth of hazel, hawthorn, blackthorn, dog-rose, spindle and Tartar maple. Woodland has a tendency to keep to the higher, moister land.

Most of the zone west of the Urals is covered by thicknesses of the straw-yellow fine-grained coherent deposit known as loess. Deep gullies with near-vertical sides have been cut in this, but the surface remains level and unbroken to their very brink, so that they are quite invisible from certain directions and often, therefore, not a noticeable feature. But seen from a river into which they debouch, the deeply gashed bank which they form is stark and striking. The gullies (*ovragi*) work back rapidly, branching in all directions, and when newly formed, are too steep to hold much vegetation. With time they develop into deeper, rather wider ravines (*balki*), whose somewhat less steep sides are wooded.

Much of the land between the principal river valleys is fairly level, but climbs gradually eastwards to give a high right bank to the southward-flowing rivers. Such high right banks (*yary*), which are usually broken by gullies and deep wooded ravines, dominate the Dniester, Dnieper and Don in turn. The plateaux which terminate in the Don *yar* lie between 650 and 1,000 feet above sea-level and are known as the Central Russian Heights. A dense and ever-growing system of ravines has been cut in the sedimentary rocks which compose them. Towards the Volga the land rises even higher, and in the bend at Kuybyshev, the ravine-pierced, forested Zhiguli Mountains rise a thousand feet above the river.

These interfluvial plateau surfaces were covered with oak woods and grass steppes, but in the southern part of the zone, where the grassland is more extensive, numerous shallow depressions (*pody*) are characteristic. Spring melt-water collects in these and slowly dries away in summer. Aspen woods, with willows on the margins, usually fill the *pody* east of the Don. In some areas,

37. Typical western lesostep *landscape: arable fields with modern harvesting machinery, intermingled with patches of forest*

aspen woods in depressions are so numerous that 'seen from afar, they look like a great forest. Only on closer approach is it realized that they are individual islands scattered over the whole plain' (Berg).[2] A hundred distinct aspen woods were counted in an area of about 5,500 acres, few of them more than 30 acres in size.

The grasslands of the *lesostep* also change their character southwards. Among the extensive oak forests of the north, they are meadow steppes or prairies, with a luxuriant growth of tall grasses intermingled with a rich variety of flowering plants. In the drier, hotter, southern regions, the grasses are not quite so high and the flowering plants not quite so many. Areas of scrub become more common in the southern wooded steppe, particularly on broken ground.

Apart from the *ovragi* and *balki*, relief is seldom strong. An exception is the Volynian-Podolian upland, situated in western Ukraine between the low-lying swampy Polesye of the forest belt, and the Dniester river. Granite summits rising to heights of 1,500 feet, limestone masses trenched by deep gorges, and a loess covering riddled by gullies give rise to striking scenery. The slopes are often too sheer to support vegetation.

Beyond the broad flats that extend eastwards from the low left-hand bank of the Volga, the land rises, at first gradually, and then more steeply, towards the

Urals. Across the Volga are strongly dissected plateaux: between the deep valleys only narrow, flattish-topped ridges are left, their grassy slopes contrasting with the trees and bushes which cling to the rocky slopes of the ravine sides. In places limestone outcrops give rise to a karstic scenery of caverns, etc.

Here and there, in regions of otherwise uniform relief, some geological accident has thrown up an outstanding feature. Sometimes a mass of rock has escaped erosion. Occasionally a severe dislocation of the rocks gives a surprising eminence, as with Mt Pivikha near Kremenchug. Other irregularities are caused by the presence, beneath the surface rocks, of buoyant low-density salt deposits which have pushed up the overlying formations.

The overall impression is, nevertheless, of wide extents of flattish land. The most uniform of these featureless stretches is the region lying between the Oka and the Don at a height of between 500 and 600 feet above sea-level. The streams flow in broad swampy floodplains, with numerous abandoned channels and oxbows. Only the forested, dissected, high right banks of the main rivers provide relief. Pines grow on sandy terraces above the flood line. The grassy steppe interfluves are remarkably flat and lack ravines. As elsewhere, shallow depressions in the flat steppe support bushes of aspen.

The narrow zone of wooden steppe in West Siberia has certain characteristics which distinguish it from the broader zone west of the Urals. Some of these result from its more northerly position, others from its more continental climate, and yet others from its more uniform relief and the higher salt content of the underlying rocks. Drainage is poor, the ground water – often saline – is near and sometimes at the surface. Sphagnum peat bog is therefore common, especially on the low flat watersheds between the Irtysh and the Ob, including the area known as the Baraba steppe; stunted pines and birches grow in these swamps. Saline soils – *solonchaks* and *solonets* – are also widespread, and consequently salt-tolerating species have a larger share in the vegetation than west of the Urals.

The forested areas are much poorer in species, and the birch, not the oak, now preponderates. Along the northern margins there is an almost continuous birch forest, the white trunks of the trees forming a main constituent of the landscape at all seasons. The aspen is the only other common species. Southwards, the areas of birch forest contract to become small islands (*kolki*) amidst meadow grass steppe or peat bog. Birchwoods of poor, low, but dense growth are also found on the higher ground of depressions otherwise occupied by bog. They often have an undergrowth of willow and aspen.

Grivy – long, low ridges, running sometimes straight and sometimes winding across the country, are another characteristic feature of the central section of the West Siberian *lesostep*. They vary in height from 10 to 50 feet; they are usually about a mile wide, and of any length up to a hundred miles. Their flattish tops carry grass steppe or pine forest according to their composition, and they are often pitted with hollows which contain lakes and marshes. They generally run from southwest to northeast and result from the washing away by the floodwaters of the immediate postglacial period of the intervening land, which is composed of loose and easily eroded material.

Between the *grivy* are low-lying and ill-drained flats covered with reedy marshes, black poplar swamps, shallow lakes interspersed with birch *kolki*, and wet meadows. In the western or Ishim steppe there are over 2,000 lakes, most of them only a few hundred yards across and a fathom or so deep; in the central or Baraba steppe there are about 2,500 lakes, some fresh, some salt. They fluctuate greatly in depth, size and shape from season to season and from year to year.

The valleys of the large rivers have a landscape of their own. Their sides give the only strong relief, being occasionally steep and etched with ravines. The floodplains offer a mixture of water meadows, pinewoods on sandy terraces, and low, flat stretches colonized by reeds, rushes, sedges and Siberian willows.

Two sections of the West Siberian *lesostep* escape many of the generalizations about relief and drainage given above. The first is in the extreme west where, from the Urals to the Tobol river, a sloping well-drained country was occupied formerly by a mixture of pine and birch forest and grass steppe. The second is made up of the plateaux which border the upper Ob. Here the gently undulating loess-covered surface was the domain of steppe meadows and birch copses. The wooded tributary valleys are deeply entrenched, often 300 feet and more below the plateau surface. Extensive pine forests clothe the sandy terraces that border the Ob itself.

The pine is the only needle-leaved tree to form forests and woods within the zone. As in the mixed forest zone, sandy terraces and ridges are its main home, but it is also found successfully holding on to slopes of weathered chalk, limestone and granite, or struggling to exist in peat bogs. On less sterile sandy soils – as along the Dnieper right bank – it may be found mixed with the oak, ash, birch and hornbeam.

The grass steppe zone

This may be defined as the zone in which woodland is confined to the valleys, while the interfluves support grassland. It is widest where it borders the shores of the Black and Azov Seas and the northern foothills of the Caucasus. From this broad front, it narrows northeastwards to a mere sixty miles at the Volga. In Kazakhstan it expands again to an average width of 250 miles.

The zone is, with few exceptions, remarkably level, a factor which combines with the grassland vegetation to give unbounded horizons. The absence of major relief owes much to the widespread cover of fine-grained, wind-blown, yellow loess which has smoothed over inequalities in the surface beneath. Upon this, the rich black-earth (*chernozem*) soil has developed. The grassland consists of an association of steppe fescue (*Festuca sulcata*) with various feather grasses (*Stipae*) and flowering plants. Increasing aridity leads to changes southwards. In the north, broadleaved grasses like *Stipa joannis* and a multitude of flowering plants join with the other steppe grasses. Southwards, bulbous plants and flat-rooted, narrow-leaved grasses which can better survive the summer drought predominate. They fail to cover the surface completely, leaving room for mosses.

Virgin steppe can still be seen at the Ascania Nova reserve, thirty miles southeast of Kakhovka on the lower Dnieper. When, in early spring, the snow melts away, the ground becomes bright green with moss. In March, clumps of new grass soon overshadow the moss, and the first flowers – the small white blossoms of whitlow (*Draba verna*) and the yellow and lilac-coloured *Gagea* appear, followed in April by the flowering of sedges and tulips. The large blue, yellow and violet flowers of the *Iris pumila* and the purple of the hyacinth-like *Bellevalia sarmatica* add to the varied beauty and bright gaiety of spring in the steppe. Soon, however, the grasses hide them from view. Most of the grasses flower in May. Their growth depends very much on the weather: after a wet spring nothing can be seen by the beginning of June but a silver-grey mass of *Stipa lessingiana* billowing in the wind. But if the season has been dry or the snow-melt inadequate, the grass will be less luxuriant, and thistles will soon thrust their crimson heads above it.

From the middle of June, the awns of the Lessing feathergrass begin to fall, the steppe fescue ripens and dries out, and the dominant shade passes from grey to yellow. Flowering plants continue to bloom in the shade of the grass, and much of the surface is carpeted with blue sage. In July, when other grasses and plants wither and scorch beneath the unrelenting sun, another feather-grass, *Stipa capillata*, dominates the scene, its 6-foot-long stems drooping to knee-height. In a very dry year, however, it is unable to make this growth, its bloom is lost, and the steppe takes on a brownish hue. In autumn, *Stipa capillata* in turn loses its bearded awns and dies away, leaving its stalks to protrude above the thin covering of winter snow.

Where conditions are too dry, either because of climate, soil or aspect, for the typical steppe grassland, a more xerophytic association is found. There is a sharp diminution in the number and variety of flowering plants. The drought-resistant feathergrass *Stipa sareptana* replaces *Stipa capillata*; the *Kochia prostrata* sends out roots up to 6 feet long in search of moisture; the ox-eye daisy and the bitter wormwood spread over large areas, especially on saline soils.

In the typical steppes of the Ukraine and south Russia, the only pronounced relief is found in the high right-hand banks of the rivers (*yary*) where gullies in the loess, ravines in chalk, and steep ghylls in limestones and sandstones, present a sharp contrast. Where slopes are not too abrupt and moisture is adequate, broadleaved woods of oak, ash, elm and maple have established themselves. Sometimes a typical low steppe scrub is found, the principal constituents of which may be white-flowering blackthorn, meadowsweet, dwarf cherry, dwarf almond with its rose-tinted blossom, laburnum, guelder rose and, commonest of all, the little Siberian pea-tree. Thickets of these shrubs may also occur in the drier southern regions of open steppe. As everywhere, pinewoods occupy the sandy terraces along the river sides, while in the floodplains wet meadows alternate with woods of willow, poplar and black alder; birch, hawthorn, hazel and aspen take up the drier spots.

As in the wooded steppe, there are shallow depressions (*pody*) which fill with water after the spring snow-melt, and remain swampy until the heat of summer dries them out. In the Black Sea coastlands, temporary streams flow into long, narrow, salt-water lagoons (*limany*). These fail to find an outlet to the sea, though often ending only a mile or two from the coast.

From the river Prut to beyond the Volga, a distance of over a thousand miles, the level steppes extend at a height of about 350 feet above sea-level, rising much beyond this only when approaching the right banks of the main rivers, and dropping much below it only in the valleys and towards the sea. There is but one main exception to this great sweep of steppe – the Donets

38. Ploughing in the Kustanay district of the North Kazakhstan steppe

Heights, in which folded Palaeozoic and Mesozoic strata have been uplifted to form a plateau block with a gently undulating loess-covered surface, broken here and there by the rugged outcrop of the bedrocks. The flanks of the massif have been incised by ravines and valleys to depths of up to 500 feet; their precipitous sides give an almost mountainous effect, but the maximum elevation of the Heights is only just above 1,000 feet. This is enough to attract the extra precipitation needed to support wooded steppe within the steppe zone.

Extending southwestward from the Donets Heights and stretching crescentwise towards the Dnieper are the low, worn, granite Azov Heights, with an average elevation above sea-level of 500 feet, and summits rising to over 900 feet. The granites are concealed beneath more recent deposits, including loess, which supports steppe grassland. Although these hard granite ridges are subdued to the general level by the time they reach the Dnieper, they gave rise there to a series of noisy, swirling rapids. Across the Dnieper, they continue as the low Dnieper Heights.

The chalk and limestone hills to the west of Kerch in the Crimean steppe have mud volcanoes built up by escaping natural gas. The largest of these was described by Seymour in 1855:

The mud is grey and thick, and gives out a strong smell of sulphur and bitumen. Here and there on the thick mud are liquid spots, whence bubbles of hydrogen gas rise, of a foot in diameter, and sometimes they burst into fire, and the volcano is in a blaze. When this violent commotion happens, the mud flows on all sides over the borders; but in ordinary times it escapes in a little stream.[3]

Across the Volga towards the southern Urals, the normally horizontal beds of limestone and sandstone that compose so much of the Russian lowland have been arched up into a dome. The resulting upland, which has an average elevation of about 700 feet, and rises at one point to 1,100 feet, is known as the Obshchiy Syrt. It has been cut up by rivers into a series of flattish-topped ridges (*syrty*) and deep valleys. The *syrt* tops carry grass steppe with islands of oak–birch forest in the west; steppe scrub clings to the steep valley sides.

Some 300 miles southeast of the Obshchiy Syrt, the 200-mile-long Mugodzhary range interrupts the level steppes of western Kazakhstan with heights of up to 2,000 feet. Nevertheless, it remains covered with the monotonous steppe grassland: only the dry ravines and gorges, their often bare slopes blotched with steppe bush, give variety.

Most of the Kazakh steppe forms part of the relief province known as the Kazakh Folded Upland, which has a general level of about a thousand feet above sea-level. Its surface is varied by sharply sculptured ridges and rounded hills of hard igneous rock which rise some 200 to 500 feet above the surface. These are particularly numerous around Karaganda, giving the locality the name of 'land of little round hills'. But there are also larger mountains, with granite peaks soaring to 2,500 feet and more. A poor growth of stunted pines, juniper, birch and aspen is found on the mountainous granitic outcrops, and there are many rocky stretches colonized by diminutive bushes of Siberian pea-tree and meadowsweet. The steppe-covered plains around the eminences are pocked with hollows which fill with water after the spring thaw. Many hold permanent lakes, of which Tengiz is the largest.

The streams of the Kazakh upland dry up in the summer and only a few reach the main Siberian rivers, Ishim and Irtysh. Most of them disappear into depressions inhabited by salt-loving meadow-steppe plants. The most successful river is the Nura which eventually makes its tortuous way to Lake Tengiz. The dependence of these streams on spring snow-melt from the higher land is shown by the Nura's seasonal changes of volume. Eighty-eight per cent of its water comes in spring, compared with only 3 per cent in summer, 2 per cent in autumn and 7 per cent in winter. There is a great deal of irregularity of flow from year to year.

The Kulunda steppe, in the northeast, lies lower and has an extremely hot and dry summer climate. Its dry steppe surface, which is dotted with salt lakes and supports feathergrass and wormwood, is crossed by ridge-like southwest–northeast-trending *grivy*, on which pine woods grow.

Some minor landforms on the steppe owe their origin to animal activity, such as the yellow mounds of loess thrown up by the steppe marmot, and the corresponding burrows which disfigure any sloping ground and speed its erosion. Numerous small rodents – gophers, hamsters, ground squirrels, hares, jerboas, voles and mice – populated the steppe, the most numerous being the gopher (*suslik*). A more obvious part of the living steppe landscape, now departed, were the larger animals – bison, antelope, wild horse and ostrich. Enormous flocks of birds might be seen rising, disturbed, from grass or lake, including geese, ducks, snipe, coot, bustard, lark and bunting.

Cultural landscapes

The wooded steppe zone

The two divisions of the *lesostep* zone, the Ukraino–Russian and the Siberian, are so distinct as to require separate treatment.

THE UKRAINO–RUSSIAN WOODED STEPPE REGION. This extends from the Carpathians to the Urals, and its black-earth soils exposed to view by ploughing and – all too often – by erosion, are its chief natural resource. They mark it off from the forest regions to the north, with their podsolic soils. In fact, the boundary between the two soil types is the most important dividing line in Russian economic and social history, and tsarist and Soviet writers alike speak of the 'black-earth' and 'non-black-earth' provinces. The black earths are much more fertile, and do not suffer from surplus moisture. Bogs no longer contribute significantly to the landscape. Soils and climate combine, therefore, to make this region the richest agriculturally in the country. Here alone is there sufficient, but not excessive, moisture and warmth for a wide variety of crops and fruit. The region is also rich in minerals. The rivers have hydroelectric potential. The islands of broadleaved forest offered reserves of timber not to be found in the steppe zone to the south. On the negative side, a limited water supply, aggravated in many areas by a porous chalk or limestone subsoil, and the proneness of the soil to erosion, are handicaps.

The natural advantages of this region attracted a relatively dense agricultural population in early times, and the river routes fostered populous commercial centres. But nomadic incursions from the steppes, culminating in the Tartar onslaught of the thirteenth century, depopulated the region. Not until the sixteenth century were the Muscovites able to enter its central and eastern parts, and many of the present towns began their existence as frontier posts. Orel was founded in 1564, Voronezh, Ufa and Samara (Kuybyshev) in 1586, Belgorod in 1593. The western parts were occupied by the Polish–Lithuanian state. Once secure, the population of the region grew rapidly to become the densest in the country, and its surpluses of grain enabled Muscovy to concentrate its attention on industry and commerce.

The last quarter of the nineteenth century brought calamity. The dissolution of serfdom in 1861 left the peasants with smaller holdings than before, and cut them off from the domainal woodland and meadow. As railways reached southwards, cheaper grain from the steppes undercut their produce in the markets. Population continued to grow rapidly, but there were few industries to absorb the surplus. Mass migrations in search of work, seasonal and permanent, disrupted families and villages. Poverty, hunger and disease characterized the region well into the Soviet period and were reflected in rag-covered peasants and the shacks they lived in. Overcropped and eroded soils declined rapidly in fertility. Pasture and fallow were sacrificed to extract more foodstuffs, so that horses and cattle dropped in number. Only east of the Volga, where serfdom had not been established and where population was less dense, was the situation better.

Densely-peopled occupation of the region for several centuries has transformed the natural landscape. The forest islands have shrunk and the steppe grasslands have been ploughed. Table 9 shows the contrast in land use between two oblasts in the mixed forest zone and two nearby in the wooded steppe.[4]. But the drier, eastern part of the region, less densely populated and with large stretches of sandy soil, retains more forest. The clearing of woodland and the ploughing-up of the grassland have encouraged the formation of gullies and the erosion of soil. Hilly Kursk oblast, one of the worst affected, loses from 10 to 20 tons of soil per acre each spring.

TABLE 9. *Land use in the Mixed Forest and Wooded Steppe zones*

| | PERCENTAGE OF AREA UNDER | | | |
	ARABLE	HAY & PASTURE	FOREST	BOG
MIXED FOREST				
Moscow oblast	28·5	4·6	38·3	5·6
Vladimir oblast	24·7	6·9	42·0	6·6
WOODED STEPPE (northern)				
Tula oblast	67·7	2·3	12·7	0·0
Orel oblast	74·7	3·7	4·9	0·1

The first half of the twentieth century has witnessed some drastic rural landscape changes. The revolutions of 1905 and 1917 led to widespread burning of landowners' mansions. The collectivization and mechanization of agriculture in the early 1930s transformed the appearance of the countryside. The 1941–45 war produced wholesale destruction of villages in the west. But the density of rural population remains relatively high.

The nature of the crop grown dominates the summer landscape. Grains do not predominate as much as formerly, except in the east. Whole districts specialize in hemp, maize, sugar beet or sunflowers. Sugar-beet refineries, upon which countless trucks converge in autumn, characterize the sugar-beet areas, but in the far west, the same season sees trucks laden with fruit make for the jam factories, canning plants and wine presses of the Moldavian Republic.

As a result of wartime destruction and the reorganization of agriculture, old rural buildings have often given way to new-style cottages, barns, etc. But the traditional Ukrainian house, with thatched roof and whitewashed clay-plastered walls, set amid a group of shade trees, still survives, and many of the newer houses have been built in this style.

Except for the great Ukrainian administrative and manufacturing centres of Kiev and Kharkov, this region remained predominantly agricultural well into the Soviet period. Deposits of iron ore had led early to a profusion of rural forges in the districts around Tula, Yelets and Lipetsk, and to the foundation of ironworks in those towns themselves, but for the most part there was little

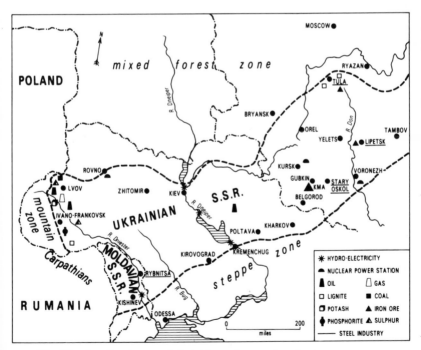

39. *The Ukraino–Russian wooded-steppe region: western part*

40. Iron-ore mining at Krivoy Rog

industry other than the working up of farm produce. From the 1960s on, however, large-scale industry has made a growing impact upon the landscape. In the far west, around Lvov, an industrial district has arisen on the basis of West Ukrainian oil, gas, coal, lignite, potash and phosphate. West Ukraine produces half the Soviety output of sulphur. Industry has also advanced here because of the advantages offered by the crossing of the territory by railways, roads, pipelines and transmission lines linking the Soviet Union with its partners in Eastern Europe, e.g. at Zhitomir (pop. 1959, 114,000; 1981, 254,000). In the central area, integrated steelworks at Tula and Lipetsk, large nuclear power stations at Kursk and Voronezh, and the exploitation of the iron ores of the Kursk magnetic anomaly, have led to widespread industrialization. And beyond the Volga, in the far east of the region, the Volga–Ural oilfield has given rise to a large petrochemical district, with particularly intensive development in the Lower Kama valley.

The Kursk magnetic anomaly (KMA) is the largest iron-ore deposit in the world, with reserves of 40 billion tons of rich hematite and magnetite (56–69 per cent metal content) and 200 billion tons of low-grade quartzites (31–9 per cent metal content). Despite its name, the KMA lies mostly in Belgorod oblast. Although worked sporadically in the 1930s and again in the 1960s, large-scale development did not begin until 1971, since when the KMA has become 'one gigantic construction area'.[5] There is some deep underground mining of the rich ores, but most of the annual output of 50 million tons comes from opencast mining of the quartzites. Large concentrating mills and associated activities have given rise to the new towns of Zheleznogorsk (67,000) and Gubkin (65,000). The concentrates are sent to Eastern Europe and to the expanding steel centres of Cherepovets and Lipetsk, enabling the latter to become, with an annual output of 10 million tons, the Soviety Union's third-largest producer.

Iron concentrates are now fed also to steelworks on the KMA itself. Twelve miles southwest of Stary Oskol, a frontier town founded in 1593, the world's first large-scale direct-reduction steelworks, dispensing with blast furnaces and coke ovens, is taking shape with West German technical assistance. The ore is crushed, concentrated to about 70 per cent metal content, and pelletized at Gubkin, whence the pellets flow through a 20-mile pipeline to the Oskol works. Here the impurities – carbon, phosphorus, silicon, etc. – are burnt out with natural gas, and the resulting iron 'sponge' is then converted into steel in electric-arc furnaces. Electricity for the complex comes from the large nuclear stations at Kursk and Voronezh; gas is brought in by pipeline, and water by the new Don–Oskol canal. The first-phase capacity is about 3.5 million tons of steel and 2.7 million tons of rolled products. The steel is both cheaper and of higher quality than that produced from blast-furnace pig-iron. Iron 'sponge' from the plant also goes to West Germany for direct-reduction plants there.

It is planned also to erect a giant conventional steelworks at Stary Oskol, to supply the needs not only of the Soviet Union but of Eastern Europe as well. A variety of metal-working and machine-building industries are being built to use the steel locally. The population of Stary Oskol, which was only 27,000 in 1959, had grown to 130,000 by 1981, and is planned to rise eventually to 800,000. Administrative and industrial activity has been greatly stimulated in the oblast capital of Belgorod (pop. 1959, 72,000; 1981 255,000).

The overburden from the opencast workings – sand, chalk, shale and clay – is used to make building materials: bricks, glass, cement, etc. The chalk and clay are raw materials for a large cement works at Stary Oskol. The landscape over large expanses has been transformed by extensive open mines, spoil heaps, tailing dumps, sludge pools, new roads, railways, transmission lines, growing industrial works and widespread urbanization. Although the steel works itself is enclosed and emission-free, smoke and fumes arise from many other plants. Blasting with explosives and the wind lift huge quantities of dust into the air.

The Volga–Ural oilfield, developed in the 1950s and 1960s, became the major Soviet supplier until overtaken by West Siberia. Several new oil-refining and petrochemical centres were built, notably Salavat (142,000), Almetyevsk (113,000), Novokuybyshevsk (110,000) and Oktyabrsky (94,000), while the small town of Sterlitamak has expanded to a city of 228,000. The heavy sulphurous oil lends itself well to chemical transformation. Tolyatti, sited near the Kuybyshev hydroelectric station (2,300 MW), is the site of the world's largest ammonia-producing plant, much of its output proceeding by pipeline to a new export terminal near Odessa; it is better known as the home of the Volga motor works, producing 700,000 Zhiguli cars (Ladas) and Nivas a year. The landscape of the oilfield is distinguished by oil derricks, the lurid glow of burning gases, and the complex equipment of refineries and chemical works.

The Lower Kama valley is 'a constellation of heavy industrial giants'.[6] Heavy industry is gathering along the Kama to benefit from closeness to the great Volga–Kama waterway which, with its extensions, links the Urals with the Baltic and Black Seas, and which, by means of a new fleet of river–sea vessels, gives contact also with the ports of the Mediterranean, the North Sea and English Channel. Nizhnekamsk (143,000), founded in the 1960s, has several petrochemical and gas-chemical plants, and from its own synthetic rubber makes tyres for the Soviet motor industry. Nearby at Naberezhnye Chelny (pop. 1959, 16,000; 1981, 346,000) is the mammoth KamAZ truck-building complex, the largest heavy-truck and diesel-engine producer in the world, approaching its full capacity of 150,000 vehicles and 250,000 engines a year. Much of the German equipment installed at KamAZ came direct from Hamburg, without transshipment, by river–sea freighters. Dump-trucks are made at Neftekamsk (77,000), another new town and petrochemical centre. The Lower Kama industries consume vast quantities of energy, and will need even more as their number grows. The large oil-burning station at Zainsk (2,400 MW) and the hydro plant at Chelny (1,248 MW), along with smaller stations, provide 6,000 MW, and a nuclear plant is planned. There is the usual reservoir-lake above the hydro station, and a new railway uses its dam to cross the river.

The region is crossed by the Dniester, Dnieper, Don and Volga rivers. The latter three are navigable, except in winter, and carry much freight; and all except the Don have hydroelectric power stations, dams and reservoirs within the region. The largest is the Kuybyshev reservoir, which forms a lake extending up both the Volga and Kama valleys. Overhead transmission cables, pipelines, railways and roads make from all directions across the zone for the Industrial Centre, as well as for major towns within the region, notably Kiev.

Kiev was the metropolis of the Russian state which, based on Dnieper commerce and wooded-steppe agriculture, flourished in the tenth and eleventh centuries, before the rise of Muscovy. Beginning as a stockaded hill on the high right bank of the Dnieper, it became, after its prince's conversion to Christianity in 989, a city of churches in the Byzantine style. The ancient but, according to contemporary travellers, beautiful city, had increasing difficulty in defending its wealth against the steppe nomads, and in 1239 it was destroyed by the Tartars. It subsequently fell into the hands of the Lithuanians and Poles, and not until 1654 was it reunited with Muscovy. Its vulnerable frontier position prevented it from being much more than a garrisoned outpost until the late eighteenth century. With renewed security, the natural advantages of its site reasserted themselves, and it grew into a large industrial and commercial city. Many fine buildings in the Ukrainian baroque style were added, some of them reconstructions of earlier edifices.

In September 1941 it was taken by the Germans. When liberated in November 1943 whole quarters had been utterly destroyed. It has since been rebuilt on spacious lines, with fine new buildings in neo-classical and Soviet styles. Broad avenues planted with chestnuts are lined with new blocks faced with white tile. In 1934 it had become capital of the Ukrainian republic, and it has many administrative, cultural and educational structures, and extensive new residential and industrial areas have been added. In its factories, machine tools, motor-cycles, agricultural and electrical machinery and textiles are manufactured. Its area, 67 square miles in 1917, has increased to nearly 300. On the opposite low bank, beaches, playgrounds and sports areas have been laid out. From these one may look across the Dnieper, gay in summer with pleasure and sports craft of all kinds, to the hills on which the city is built, with white walls, green domes and gilded cupolas emerging from the trees. And from one hill, the 66-foot-high monument to Prince Vladimir (980–1015), who ruled Kievan Russia at its prime, looks down to the river.

The great industrial city of Kharkov is noteworthy for its great tractor plant, built early in the first five-year plan, to make possible the mechanization of agriculture. The city was also the site of some of the first 'ensembles' of concrete buildings in the severe gaunt early Stalinist style, notably the House of State Industry. Kharkov was founded in 1654 as a frontier outpost, and with the settlement of the surrounding area, it became a market town. Its growth at the

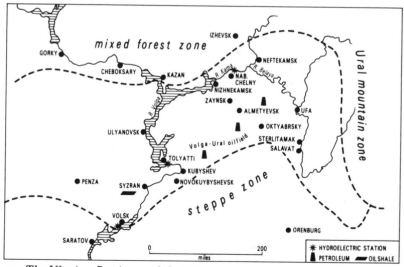

41. The Ukraino–Russian wooded-steppe: eastern part

TABLE 10. *Population and rank of the principal towns in the Ukraino-Russian wooded-steppe region (thousands)*

	1939	1959	1981
Kiev	846 (3rd)	1,110 (3rd)	2,248 (3rd)
Kharkov	833 (4th)	953 (4th)	1,485 (5th)
Kuybyshev	390 (17th)	806 (8th)	1,238 (10th)
Ufa	246 (29th)	547 (23rd)	1,009 (21st)
Voronezh	327 (19th)	447 (28th)	809 (29th)
Lvov	340*	411 (30th)	688 (30th)
Kishinev	216*	212 (67th)	539 (42nd)
Tolyatti		61	533 (43rd)
Tula	272 (26th)	351 (37th)	518 (44th)

*Not in the USSR in 1939

end of the nineteenth century resulted from its excellent rail links, and its position in the heart of the most densely populated part of the country. Besides agricultural machinery, it makes machine tools, turbines and ball bearings. It was the administrative capital of the Ukraine until 1934.

Voronezh is an old-established industrial town. Peter I began the manufacture of river boats here, and later the livestock-products industry (tallow, candles, soap, etc.) developed. Like Kharkov it acquired a large tractor works before the war and became a very important engineering, food-processing and chemical centre (textile and milling machinery, diesel engines, synthetic rubber, sunflower oil, canned fruit). Twenty-five miles to the south, on the left bank of the Don, is a large nuclear power station (2,500 MW).

The expansion of Kuybyshev and Ufa has been due to two facts: first, they escaped devastation by the Germans during the war, becoming instead recipients of refugee industry; and second, they are on the Volga–Ural oilfield, and have become its two leading refining, processing and transporting centres. Kuybyshev benefits also from the power generated at the great hydro station above the city. Founded in 1586 as Samara, it grew rapidly with the settlement of the trans-Volga steppes, shipping produce across and along the Volga, a function which was intensified by the railway. It also developed a large livestock-products industry, principally tallow and leather. On the hilly right bank of the Volga below Kuybyshev, townscapes are affected by industrial plant at Ulyanovsk (485,000) – a motor works and a worsted mill, at Syzran (169,000) – an oil refinery and thermal power stations using locally-mined oil shale, and at Volsk (65,000), where dusty cement works line the heights overlooking the river.

Kishinev, capital of the Moldavian Republic, has benefited from the growth of administrative and social occupations common to all such capitals, as well as from industrial development. It is an expanding machine-building centre, and a new steelworks, using scrap in electric furnaces (annual capacity 500,000 tons), is being built at Rybnitsa, 50 miles to the north, to supply its growing needs.

THE SIBERIAN WOODED-STEPPE REGION. Black earth soil, a climate suited to arable agriculture, hydroelectric potential, and minerals are among the natural resources that have encouraged man to modify the landscape here. Rich veins of silver, lead and copper lay in the foothills of the Altay Mountains. Large and easily-worked deposits of coal occur in the Kuznetsk basin (Kuzbass) and in the Kansk-Achinsk lignite field. Immediately to the north lies the West Siberian oilfield. Pine forests, found locally on sandy ridges, contain high-quality timber. Natural disadvantages are few, the chief being the saline or marshy character of many soils and the severity of the winter.

Not being a source of the coveted furs, the *lesostep* remained a frontier zone between the Russian-held tayga and the nomadic Tartars and Kazakhs of the steppe until the nineteenth century. This frontier was defended by wooden fortified posts garrisoned by Cossacks (Tyumen 1586, Tomsk 1604, Kuznetsk 1618, Krasnoyarsk 1628). It did, however, gradually encroach southwards: Ishim 1670, Biysk 1709, Omsk 1716, Barnaul 1738, Troitsk 1745, Petropavlovsk 1752. Meanwhile the older forts grew into small towns, with a little agriculture round about to feed them. Apart from these posts, the main impact of the Russians on the landscape was in the mining and quarrying activity that began in the basin of the upper Ob in 1728, and as the number of mines increased, thousands of workers were brought into the district. They were mostly peasants who grew food for the population, worked in the mines, and brought the ore to the smelters of Barnaul in their carts. There were also convicts and exiles. Cottrell in 1841 noted that

the environs of Barnaul are highly cultivated, the quantity of corn necessary to

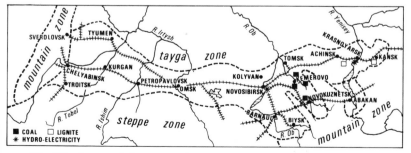

42. *The Siberian wooded-steppe region*

supply it and the other *fabriques* in the vicinity being very great. Within a few versts of the town, we passed through some immense forests, which are, however, becoming every day rarer from the immense quantities of wood required for the furnaces . . .[7]

By the 1860s some of the towns had become quite populous: Tomsk 25,000, Omsk 20,000, Tyumen 14,000, Barnaul 12,000, Krasnoyarsk 9,000. And enough peasants had settled around them to provide raw materials for industries working up agricultural produce, mainly distilling and leather-working. But it was not until the 1880s that Russian peasants settled the *lesostep* in large numbers. Their invasion became a flood in the 1890s. The completion of the Trans-Siberian Railway as far as Irkutsk in 1898 was a prime factor in bringing 3 million migrants into Siberia between 1901 and 1914. The wooded steppe's narrow belt of good soil, sandwiched between the short-summered swampy tayga to the north and the arid steppe to the south, was in itself sufficient to concentrate by far the greater number of these settlers within its bounds. The railway, which ran entirely within the zone, intensified this concentration.

Despite massive immigration, the rural population density never reached the degree of saturation found in the Russian and Ukrainian sectors. Land was more

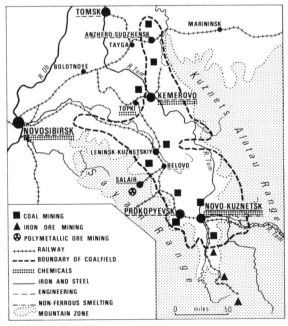

43. Kuznetsk coalfield (Kuzbass)

plentiful, agriculture more extensive and expansive. The steppe areas were not wholly ploughed up, and the birch woods and pine forests escaped the fate of the oakwoods of the Russo–Ukrainian *lesostep*. Typical Russian izbas and wooden churches appeared in the numerous villages that sprang up. The railway made commercial farming possible on a large scale, with exportable surpluses of wheat, butter and eggs.

The Trans-Siberian led to the swift expansion of towns where rail and water transport met. To government buildings and churches in brick and stone, and the surrounding mass of wooden houses – some beautifully adorned with wooden carvings, others thrown crudely together – was added the railway station. The local scene now included not only bands of dejected exiles, waiting at the landing stage for craft to take them north along the rivers, but crowds of immigrants at railway stations. The most remarkable urban development was at the Ob crossing, where no town had stood in 1897. By 1914 Novo–Nikolayevsk (Novosibirsk), with 85,000 people, had become the largest city in the region.

The Kuzbass coalfield, exploited only for local purposes before 1928, underwent rapid development under the first five-year plans and during the war. Small towns, villages and greenfield sites mushroomed into cities (Table 11). But

TABLE 11. *Population of the principal Kuzbass towns (thousands)*

	1926	1959	1981
Novokuznetsk	4	380 (35th)	551 (39th)
Kemerovo	22	289 (47th)	486 (50th)
Prokopyevsk	11	282 (50th)	267 (107th)
Leninsk-Kuznetsky	20	132 (112th)	133 (209th)
Kiselevsk	0	128 (117th)	123 (217th)

although coal production has continued to grow, and is now about 150 million tons a year, those urban centres which have not attracted new industry have stagnated or declined in population since the 1960s when mechanization began to displace labour. Novokuznetsk became the site of the first Siberian steelworks and is now the fourth-largest plant in the USSR, making about 8 million tons a year. Kemerovo has heavy machine-building. Mines, coke ovens, blast furnaces, slag heaps and thermal power stations have transformed the local landscape. The Kuzbass field produces good coking coal, but the Kansk–Achinsk field, to the west and east of Krasnoyarsk, has only low-grade and untransportable lignite, although it can be easily and cheaply mined. It is to form the basis of a power complex in the 1980s: four vast open mines yielding up to fifty million tons of lignite a year will fuel four 6,400 MW mine-side power stations.

Hydroelectric power has been developed on the Ob and Yenisey, and gas and oil brought into the region by pipe. The single-track Trans-Siberian has widened into a complex transport artery which includes the electrified double-track railway, a main road, an oil pipeline and electric transmission lines. The rail network in the Kuzbass and upper Ob valley has been developed. Metallurgical, engineering, chemical and woodworking industries have been established in the towns, and agriculture has expanded in the countryside. The great river–rail towns continue to make strong growth, with new residential blocks and modern industrial quarters (Table 12).

TABLE 12. *Population and rank of Siberian river–rail towns (thousands)*

	1926	1959	1981
Novosibirsk	120 (24th)	885 (7th)	1,343 (7th)
Omsk	162 (17th)	581 (20th)	1,044 (17th)
Krasnoyarsk	72 (55th)	412 (29th)	820 (27th)
Barnaul	74 (52nd)	303 (45th)	549 (40th)
Tomsk	92 (32nd)	249 (60th)	439 (60th)
Tyumen	50 (87th)	150 (97th)	378 (73rd)
Kurgan	28	146 (101st)	322 (82nd)

Novosibirsk at the junction of the TSR and the Ob is now the largest city in Siberia with, at a few miles distant, its *akademgorodok* or scientific suburb devoted entirely to research. It is a great commercial centre, with the Turk–Sib railway from Central Asia and lines from the various Kuzbass towns converging upon it. Omsk occupies a strategic position where the railways from Sverdlovsk (via Tyumen) and Chelyabinsk unite to cross the Irtysh. It has expanding textile, oil-refining and petrochemical industries. Tomsk, situated on oil and gas pipelines making their way south to the Kuzbass, is the site of the Soviet Union's largest plant processing materials for the plastics industry – polymers, polypropylene, methanol, etc. Kurgan has grown up where the main lines from Sverdlovsk and Chelyabinsk unite to cross the Tobol, while Tyumen is the capital of a vast west Siberian province which extends northwards to the Arctic shores and is now the scene of large-scale oil and gas development.

Barnaul is situated where two important Soviet-built main lines intersect and cross the Ob: the Turk–Sib from Novosibirsk to Tashkent and the Kuzbass–Magnitogorsk line. The old gold- and silver-smelting town now has textile mills, food-processing factories and a new oil refinery. Krasnoyarsk's remarkable expansion has been more recent, and has resulted largely from the building of a giant hydro station on the Yenisey above the town where, behind a

420-foot-high dam there is a 2,000-square-mile reservoir-lake. It now has modern electric steel mills, aluminium smelters, river-shipbuilding yards, wood-working and wood-chemical industries, and a growing light industry producing – among other goods – televison sets.

The steppe zone

The natural resources available here included an abundant store of fish in the waters, grassland for pasture, rich soils for the plough, prolonged summer warmth and generous endowment of minerals: abundant coal and iron ore, manganese, lignite, natural gas and many other deposits (Figs 45 and 48). The Donets basin (Donbass), with an annual production of over 200 million tons, and the Karaganda basin, producing 50 million tons a year, are first and third respectively amongst the hard-coal fields of the USSR. The Ukraine (Krivoy Rog) produces more iron ore than any other ironfield in the world, and the newer Kustanay deposits are worked on a large scale. Against these assets must be set drying and dust-raising winds, periodic drought, severe winters, proneness to soil erosion and, historically, a lack of natural defence against enemy attack.

Until the nineteenth century the steppes remained the domain of a succession of mainly nomadic pastoral peoples: Cimmerians, Scythians, Sarmatians, Khazars, Pechenegs, Cumans, Tartars and Turks, but the natural prairie landscape was little affected by their presence. Clarke could write as late as 1800 that 'all the south of Russia, from the Dnieper to the Volga, and even to the territories of the Kirgissian and Thibetan Tartars, with all the north of the Crimea, is one flat uncultivated desolate waste'.[8]

THE WESTERN STEPPE REGION. At the end of the eighteenth century the western steppe became Russian and was opened up to colonization by many peoples: Germans, Bulgarians, Serbs, Greeks, etc. as well as Ukrainians, Russians and Cossacks. Wheat-growing at once expanded rapidly in the river valleys, along coasts, and wherever the opportunity existed for getting grain to the world market, but Tartar and Kalmyk tribes, and large flocks of sheep, continued to roam undisturbed over wide expanses of open steppe. In the last quarter of the nineteenth century the railway came to the western steppe, and the growing of wheat became almost universal. The steppe was ploughed up, leaving the black soil exposed to frost, snow, wind and rain until early summer, when it was covered by the growing crop. Clouds of black dust were raised by the strong winds, adding to the loss of soil from water run-off. Only the extensive fallow, with its regrown grass and weeds, offered some poor semblance of the vanished steppe. Whether the fields would lie drought-stricken or swell with golden grain depended on the vagaries of an unreliable climate.

The coastal ports, particularly Odessa, Nikolayev and Rostov-on-Don, throve upon the export of grain. The railway also made possible the industrialization of the Donbass coalfield and the Krivoy Rog ironfield. Nowhere was the landscape

44. Maryanovka, a newly built collective farm village in the Donetsk region

more thoroughly transformed than in the Russo–Ukrainian steppe between 1880 and 1910. But the spread of cultivation over the steppe did not lead to a similar extension of human settlement. Population crowded more than ever before into the valleys. In the west, the Ukrainian *khata* was the typical peasant dwelling, but many of these traditional homes were destroyed in the 1941–45 war.

The Soviet period has witnessed further transformations. In the early 1930s the intermingled strips of the individual peasants were merged into collectives. These have been subsequently formed into larger units and increasingly mechanized until, today, the commonest harvest sight is the combine pouring grain into a lorry alongside. Fertilizer spread over the fields, and helicopters spraying insecticide are seen increasingly. In western areas ravaged by the Germans, the old Ukrainian thatched cottages have often given way to modern wooden houses roofed with asbestos, iron or slate. Typical now are rows of long livestock sheds, silage towers, pits and troughs, new communal buildings, pylon-like windmills for generating electricity, and small hydroelectric stations on local streams, built and operated by the collective. Large areas of the Russian steppe, especially in the lower Don region, have been altered by the plantation of tree shelter belts. Here the steppe is no longer 'limitless', but the view over the fields extends only as far as the forest strip.

Irrigation, associated with hydroelectric power stations, makes an important contribution to landscape modification. The lake-like reservoirs accumulated behind the dams supply water to increasing areas of dry steppe. Further diversification of crop is thus made possible, and maize, cotton, rice, sugar beet, fruit and vegetables are grown on the irrigated land. A series of hydroelectric dams on the Dnieper have converted the river into a string of reservoir lakes. From the Kakhovka reservoir an irrigation canal brings Dnieper water into the Crimea. Above Volgodonsk is the Don reservoir known as the Tsimlyansk Sea. The Volga in this zone has been raised and widened by the Volgograd dam, so that now only the tops of the high chalk and limestone bluffs on the right bank are visible.

Eastwards from the Sea of Azov the Kuban, a traditional grain area, produces a million tons of irrigated rice a year, besides 8 million tons of wheat. The open landscape is now interrupted by natural gas installations. Large towns are found only on its southern borders where the Caucasus foothills begin: Krasnodar (581,000), Armavir (163,000) and Stravropol (265,000).

As elsewhere in the country the Soviet period has brought additional railways, roads and bridges, and introduced pipelines as well as electric pylons and cables. It has linked the Volga and Don rivers by the Volga–Don canal (1953).

The Ukrainian part of this region – with the adjoining Russian Rostov oblast – is one of the most highly industrialized and densely populated in the country. The Donets coalfield (Donbass), already a leading industrial area before the Revolution, saw its towns grow rapidly as coal production increased and coal-

45. *The western steppe*

using industries concentrated here (Table 13). But since the 1960s growth rates have slowed markedly. As in the Kuzbass, increased mechanization has lessened the demand for labour, and the output of coal peaked in 1976 at 224 million tons; it was 204 million in 1980. Oil has intruded into this coal-dominated land with an oil refinery on the North Donets river at Lisichansk, which is connected by pipeline with the new petrochemical town of Severodonetsk (115,000) on the opposite bank. Ammonia is made at Gorlovka. And although most electricity used in the Donbass comes from coal-fired plants, there is now a nuclear station (2,000 MW) at Konstantinovka. An aqueduct brings Dnieper water to the Donbass, an area critically short of water. Slack heaps disfigure the countryside and billows of smoke rise from the chimneys to darken the sky, but some of the well-planned new towns are exceptions to this dirty industrial landscape.

TABLE 13. *Population and rank of principal towns of the Donets coal basin (Donbass) (thousands)*

	1926	1939	1959	1981
Donetsk	174 (15th)	462 (12th)	708 (10th)	1,040 (18th)
Voroshilovgrad*	72 (57th)	213 (36th)	275 (52nd)	474 (53rd)
Makeyevka	79 (43rd)	240 (31st)	407 (32nd)	442 (58th)
Gorlovka	23	109 (85th)	308 (43rd)	338 (77th)
Shakhty	41	155 (54th)	196 (73rd)	214 (134th)
Kramatorsk	12	93 (93rd)	115 (130th)	183 (156th)
Kommunarsk	16	55 (162nd)	98 (149th)	121 (220th)
Lisichansk	7	26	104 (143rd)	120 (223rd)
Severodonetsk			33	117 (229th)
Konstantinovka	25	95 (90th)	89 (175th)	114 (236th)
Stakhanov†	17	46	91 (167th)	108 (248th)

*Formerly Lugansk   † Formerly Kadiyevka

The same tectonic uplift that cradles the Donbass forces the Dnieper to make a large eastward bend, within which lie the enormous iron-ore deposits of Krivoy Rog. The vast open mines produce over 100 million tons of ore a year. The river bend itself is lined with great cities (Table 14) whose main function is heavy industry – Kremenchug, Dneprodzerzhinsk, Denepropetrovsk, Zaporozhe and Nikopol, where most Soviet manganese, essential to the steel industry, is mined. The Dnieper towns all have iron and steel, metal-working and machine-building works. Chimneys, blast furnaces, coke ovens and steel mills

TABLE 14. *Population and rank of the towns of the Dnieper bend (thousands)*

	1926	1939	1959	1981
Dnepropetrovsk	237 (9th)	501 (11th	690 (12th)	1,100 (11th)
Zaporozhe	56 (78th)	289 (21st)	449 (27th)	812 (28th)
Krivoy Rog	38 (110th)	198 (41st)	408 (31st)	663 (31st)
Dneprodzerzhinsk	34	148 (56th)	194 (75th)	257 (110th)
Kremenchug		90 (98th)	93 (163rd)	215 (134th)
Nikopol	14	58 (158th)	83 (183rd)	150 (183rd)

are prominent features of the townscape, and the lurid red glow of molten metal lights up the sky at night.

Krivoy Rog ore, Donbass coal, Dnieper hydroelectricity, Nikopol manganese and Shebelinka natural gas are the basis of the Ukrainian steel industry. The main centres are Zhdanov on the Azov Sea, with two large integrated plants producing 15 million tons a year, and Krivoy Rog, with an output of 14 million tons. Iron ore is also mined east of Kremenchug, at Kerch in the Crimea, and at the new town of Dneprorudny (67,000) on the Kakhovka reservoir-lake.

Before the Revolution, when the Russian economy was heavily dependent on overseas trade, and the farm produce of the steppe gravitated to the coast, its ports ranked high. Odessa was the third city of the Russian Empire at its last census in 1897. The new Soviet state struggled for self-sufficiency; foreign trade declined, and so did seaports relative to inland industrial centres. Odessa, fifth in population in 1926, had fallen to nineteenth by 1968; Rostov-on-Don, seventh in 1926, was twentieth in 1968; Nikolayev, thirty-second in 1926 was sixty-fifth in 1968. Since then, with the return of the USSR to a more active role in international commerce, these ports have resumed rapid growth. Odessa (1,072,000), founded by Catherine II in 1794, still has the fine buildings in the local white limestone with which she endowed it, despite heavy war damage. At Yuzhny, east of the port, is the export terminal of the ammonia pipeline from Tolyatti and Gorlovka. Nikolayev (449,000), also founded by Catherine II as a naval base, and built of the same white limestone, is now a centre of heavy industry. South of the city, on the Bug estuary, the world's largest alumina plant processes bauxite from Guinea. Both the export terminal at Yuzhny and the import terminal at Nikolayev are indicative of the Soviet Union's growing involvement in world trade. Rostov (957,000), the leading Azov port, near the mouth of the Don, is a great flour milling and agricultural machinery centre. Lesser ports, whose trade has always been more local than international, include

Kherson (324,000), Taganrog (278,000) and Kerch (158,000).

On the Tsimlyansk Sea, a hydroelectric reservoir on the Don, where the Volga–Don canal begins, is Volgodonsk (126,000), a new town dominated by *Atommash*, a plant manufacturing nuclear-power-station machinery.

Table 15 shows the Volga towns in this zone (Fig. 48). Volgograd, on the high west bank, totally destroyed in the great battle of 1942–43, has been rebuilt, and is now one of the most beautiful modern cities in the world: broad avenues, their carriageways separated by gardens, are lined by attractive blocks of flats. Its complex of memorials to Russia's war dead, on a suburban hill, is a most impressive sight. Steelworks and other industrial plant lie along the river below the high bank. Across the Volga, near the great hydroelectric dam and power station, Volzhsky manufactures wide-diameter gas pipe. Saratov, a river-crossing town with machine-building works, is the centre of an important gasfield. Its hydroelectric power station (1,300 MW) and dam are by-passed by a 7-mile long navigation canal. A two-mile-long road bridge (1965) links the city with Engels, on the opposite bank of the Volga. Engels and Balakovo, higher up the river, make rayon, using natural gas and cellulose, while Kamyshin has a big cotton-textile combine.

TABLE 15. *Population and rank of the Volga towns (thousands)*

	1926	1939	1959	1981
Volgograd	151 (19th)	445 (13th)	591 (19th)	948 (24th)
Saratov	220 (11th)	376 (18th)	579 (22nd)	873 (25th)
Volzhsky			67	220 (130th)
Engels	34	69 (133rd)	91 (167th)	168 (167th)
Kamyshin		24	57	113 (239th)

THE EASTERN STEPPE REGION. Eastward across the Volga farming was less intensive before the Revolution. There were large wheat farms cultivated with machinery, but pastoral activities remained important, especially on the Kazakh steppe, where only the northern margins were cultivated. This situation changed little until the 1950s, when a landscape revolution occurred similar to that which had taken place in the west in the nineteenth century. The 'virgin and idle lands' were ploughed up and sown to wheat. State farms were organized to receive an army of 350,000 immigrants from Russia, the Ukraine and Belorussia. But whereas the western transformation had been accomplished by the ant-like efforts of thousands of peasants using primitive implements, the eastern steppe

46. Volgograd (Stalingrad) today: Prospekt Lenina

was attacked by modern machinery. The results have, as expected, varied greatly from year to year in these drought-menaced lands. In 1963 there was almost complete failure; in 1966 a bumper crop. This shift of grain-growing eastwards has permitted greater diversification on the richer and rather better-watered soils of the west where, besides wheat, increasing amounts of maize, barley, millet, sunflowers and hemp are grown, and more land is sown to fodder crops and sugar beet.

On the 'virgin lands' themselves there has also been more diversification. The initial policy of ploughing up vast areas and sowing to wheat, regardless of local soil and moisture conditions, quickly led to dust-bowl formation, especially in the Kulunda steppe. Soils are much more varied in Kazakhstan than in the west: the predominant dark-chestnut and chestnut-coloured soils often give way to saline soils unsuitable for arable farming. The *pody* depressions and temporary lake beds grow meadow grasses and are better suited to livestock. There has recently been more adaptation to the natural environment, with the cultivation of silage, maize and fodder crops to support an increased measure of livestock farming. The irrigated area is expanding in the drier east. Ob water is brought westward into the Kulunda steppe by the new Kulunda irrigation canal. The building of hydroelectric stations on the upper Irtysh at Bukhtarma (675 MW), Ust-Kamenogorsk (331 MW) and Semipalatinsk (1,350 MW) has not only made possible irrigation from their reservoirs for the surrounding countryside, but also a much-needed water supply by aqueduct for the Ekibastuz and

47. *Reaping machines in the steppes of North Kazakhstan*

48. The eastern steppe

Karaganda–Temirtau industrial areas. Rice is the usual crop on the newly irrigated land.

As a consequence of these dry-farming and irrigation schemes the colonization of northern and eastern Kazakhstan has proceeded apace. The population of Kazakhstan has grown from 6 million to 15 million since the war, faster than any other Republic. In landscape terms this means the creation of large villages of wooden houses with farm buildings, schools, clubs, hospitals, etc., numerous roads making for the rail stations, and rapidly expanding towns with grain elevators. Many of them have developed into industrial centres. Orenburg serves a large gasfield producing over ten per cent of the Soviet Union's enormous output: the city's plants extract over a million tons of sulphur, as well as other useful chemicals from the gas before sending it via the 'Soyuz' pipeline to Eastern Europe. Orsk, supplied with oil from the Volga–Ural field, and Pavlodar, similarly supplied from the West Siberian field, have oil refineries and

TABLE 16. *Population and rank of principal towns of the trans-Volga steppes (thousands)*

	1926	1939	1959	1981
Karaganda		166 (50th)	383 (34th)	583 (33rd)
Orenburg	123 (22nd)	173 (45th)	267 (53rd)	482 (52nd)
Semipalatinsk	57 (76th)	110 (83rd)	156 (93rd)	291 (93rd)
Pavlodar		29	90 (171st)	288 (94th)
Ust-Kamenogorsk	14	20	150 (97th)	286 (96th)
Orsk	14	66 (144th)	176 (79th)	254 (112th)
Tselinograd	13	32	99 (146th)	241 (121st)
Temirtau		5	77	217 (131st)

petrochemical works. Orsk also has a steelworks, while Pavlodar has a large tractor combine and an aluminium smelter.

Karaganda is a coal-mining, iron-and-steel and machine-building town created by the first five-year plans; there is also a steelworks at nearby Temirtau. Karaganda produces about 50 million tons of good coking coal a year. The other great Kazakh coal basin is that of Ekibastuz (81,000), where great level masses of lignite between 500 and 650 feet thick lie close to the surface, making for cheap and easy working. Already vast open mines are yielding 80 million tons a year, much of it going at present to thermal stations in Kazakhstan, West Siberia and the Urals. However, four great power stations, each of 4,000 MW capacity, are being constructed on the coalfield to absorb an expanding production. Surplus power will be sent to Russia by a long-distance transmission line.

7
The arid belt

Natural landscapes

The arid lands cover an area of $1\frac{1}{4}$ million square miles, 15 per cent of the total extent of the USSR (Fig. 49). Because of the lack of moisture and the great heat of a long summer, much of the ground is bare. Plants are mostly low in stature and widely spaced, although in some parts a denser cover of vegetation temporarily clothes the surface in the wetter season. There are two landscape zones: the semi-desert, covering somewhat under a quarter of the area, and the deserts.

The semi-desert zone

The semi-desert zone forms a relatively narrow strip, between 100 and 200 miles wide, separating the steppes from the deserts. Its aridity is determined by the great excess of potential evaporation (averaging 36 inches a year) over precipitation (averaging about 10 inches). If soil and ground moisture conditions are favourable this will support a dry steppe vegetation, but if they are

49. The Arid Lands: physical

adverse it can only be colonized by desert plants, and the zone is as much one of the interpenetration of these two types as of transition between them. Nevertheless, there is a typical semi-desert vegetation, even though its share of the total area is not large. In it steppe grasses, principally *Festuca sulcata*, are found along with varieties of wormwood (*Artemisia*). Generally, the grasses are fewer in species, lower in height and sparser in ground cover than those of the steppe zone.

In such a typical semi-desert area, the first little *Artemisia maritima* bushes appear in March. Temperatures rise very rapidly in April, and May is 25° to 35° C (45°–63° F) warmer than March. This rapid onset of heat, combined with the moisture available from the melted snow, enables black mosses and small ephemeral flowering plants to cover over the bare ground between the wormwood shrubs. The fescue and other grasses shoot up, giving a fresh green background to the yellow flowers and grey leaves of the wormwood.

During May the ephemerals die down, the grasses grow taller and flower. After the fescue come the feathergrasses, *Koeleria gracilis* and *Stipa capillata*. In June the grasses wither and die in the summer heat, and the wind lays low their yellowed stems. Only the dried-out stalks of *Poa bulbosa* and *Alyssum desertorum* remain upright, rising above the wormwoods. By July these too have lost their leaves, and the ground lies yellow, brown or grey beneath the scorching rays of the sun. Mean July temperatures range from 23° to 26° C (73°–79° F), and daily maxima may reach 40° C (104° F). There is little cloud and less rain. Scorching *sukhovey* winds are very frequent (on eighty-five days of summer at Novouzensk), and bring the relative humidity down to 15 per cent.

In September, when the weather has become cooler and moister, the wormwood revives for a while, until winter covers the ground with a thin layer of snow, above which a few stalks protrude. The snow is often blown off in snowstorms, allowing the frost to penetrate deep into the ground. January mean temperatures average −15° C (+5° F), but actual temperatures may drop to −50° C (−58° F). Yet brief winter thaws melt the snow, which freezes again in a glazed and icy form.

There are many depressions, large and small, that fill up with water in spring, and then dry off to make way for a cover of meadow grass, which in turn dries up and turns yellow. There are also areas of a light sandy mould which absorb enough moisture to sustain steppe grasses well into the summer, and even sufficient to support large bushes and trees, though these may appear stunted and deformed. Poplars, willow, wild olive and roses are the usual bushes, with some birch. On the other hand, there are even more extensive areas where, because salt-bearing rocks are widespread, soluble salts or saline water come near to the surface, leading to the formation of *solonchaks*, on which only salt-tolerating halophytes will grow. Here the black wormwood (*Artemisia pauciflora*) is often the only occupant of the ground, apart from black mosses, dark green algae and lichens. Its black stalks do little to relieve the barren appearance of the *solonchak*.

Throughout the zone as a whole there is little strong relief: ravines and gullies, so characteristic of much of the steppe belt, are few. In the west, however, between the Volga and Emba rivers and beyond, the flat surface is interrupted by numerous salt domes and dislocations of the overlying rocks, caused by the upward pressure of low-density salt deposits. For the most part, they rise less than 200 feet above the surroundings, but a few have a relative height of over 500 feet.

At its eastern end the semi-desert zone includes part of the 'land of little round hills', in which the fairly level surface of the Kazakh upland is broken by numerous rounded and conical hills caused by the upward thrust of granitic igneous rocks.

Some relief is also provided by the Yergeni Hills, which are a southerly continuation of the Volga Heights, and by the Mugodzhary Hills, which likewise are a southward extension of the Urals. The Yergenis rise gently from the west to heights of up to 700 feet, and drop in an abrupt, ravine-dissected slope to the east. The broader valleys in the west are covered by grass steppe, and trees and bushes fill the ravines. Between the Mugodzhary Hills and the Kazakh upland lies the Turgay tableland, a series of low plateaux formed from horizontal sedimentary rocks. Several hills rise a few hundred feet above the general level.

The northern part of the Caspian lowland and the Turgay tableland have numerous depressions, some of which hold permanent lakes. Those in the Caspian lowland, notably Lakes Elton and Baskunchak, are exceedingly salt, and each summer evaporation covers them with a pink or white salt crust. The two large permanent rivers that cross the zone, the Volga and the Ural, carry narrow strips of woodland southwards into the desert zone. Most other rivers dry up in summer or disappear into reed-filled depressions.

The desert zone
The extreme dryness of the climate, combined with several months of great heat, is the main factor affecting the landscape in the desert zone. Total annual precipitation is under 7 inches everywhere, except amongst the foothills of the southern mountain chain (Ashkhabad at 726 feet has 10 inches, and Tashkent at 1,570 feet, 14 inches), but many central areas have below 4 inches (Turtkul in the Amu valley, 3 inches). These are average figures, but there is great difference from year to year. In some years, one violent downpour alone may produce inches of rain.

The summers here are the longest and hottest in the Soviet Union. Shade temperatures of up to 50° C (122° F) are experienced, and the surface of the ground heats up to 80° C (176° F) and will burn the bare foot or hand. The scorching heat is aggravated by strong, drying *sukhovey* winds, which blow on over half the days of summer, often accompanied by dust storms. On windy days, a dust haze may obscure the cloudless sky, transforming the blazing sun into a dim red ball. 'Dry rain', which evaporates before reaching the ground, and dry thunderstorms, awesome and beautiful, but without a refreshing fall of heavy rain, are other peculiar features of the deserts.

Air currents rising from the heated surface cause mirages to appear:

> The waters of a shallow lake appear quite close, edged with reeds. Involuntarily, the driver increases speed. But the mirage is out of reach. Small vacillating outlines of its delusive banks recede into the distance, and then once more dance in front.
>
> One is perplexed by the phenomenon of inverted perspective. Telegraph poles along the side of the road appear taller in the distance than close up. The nearer ones stand upright and motionless, but those farther off seem to vibrate in the streams of ascending air. Sometimes they appear to 'take off' from the ground and hover in the air.[1]

In the late summer and autumn, the increasing temperature range between the days, which are still very hot, and nights that become longer and cooler, becomes so extreme that rocks exfoliate or 'peel', and the flaky debris is blown away by the wind.

Winters are short but sharp, and the weather can be very changeable. The whole region lies open to the north, and Arctic or Siberian air may bring snow and temperatures of $-30°$ C ($-22°$ F), followed in a few days by sunny summerlike weather, with shade temperatures up to $20°$ C ($68°$ F). Cyclonic activity may bring cloud and a little precipitation in the winter months. This may take the form of prolonged drizzle or snow. The amount of snow falls sharply from north to south, where only January and February are likely to have a wintry look. Duration of snow cover, over two months in the north, averages but two or three days between thaws in the south. The few inches of snow that fall and lie may be blown off by winds or melted by winter thaws. Spring comes suddenly (in April in the north, March in the south), and a fortnight is long enough to remove all traces of winter. Cyclonic activity increases and may be accompanied by brief but often torrential showers.

Only types of vegetation specially adapted to the long, dry, hot summers (xerophytes) can survive in this environment. Such adaptation takes several forms. There are small flowering plants which grow very fast, completing their life cycle in six to eight weeks. This enables them to thrive where there is a brief but fairly reliable moisture season, although their seeds are often capable of surviving for years, should such a season fail. These plants are known as ephemerals when they are annuals, and as ephemeroids if perennial. The latter often perpetuate themselves by bulbs, runners, tubers, etc., beneath the ground, rather than by seeds, which would be exposed to many hazards – burial by sand, drought, flood, wind, frost or insects. Thus *Ixiolirion tataricum* multiplies through lumps that form on the roots. Ephemeroids and many other desert plants and shrubs go seasonally into a state of rest (anabiosis), during which they may appear to be lifeless. The sand sedge (*Carex physodes*) and the meadow grass *Poa bulbosa* are such plants. After luxuriating in spring, they wither away in the hot rainless summer, but revive the following spring.

Within their stems, stalks and leaves, desert plants form many substances designed to store and conserve water, and to facilitate its intake from the soil: volatile and fatty oils, alkaloids, soluble salts. In consequence of this unusual biochemistry, many of them give off strong odours and aromas, as do many wormwoods and *Calligonum*. In order to hold moisture, stalks and leaves are sometimes thick and succulent. The leaves may also have thick, hairy, sticky or varnished skins to reduce transpiration (e.g. the desert spurge *Euphorbia*), or they may curl up or drop off during the summer drought. The *Smirnovia turkestana* has large leaves in spring which it discards in summer; but in autumn, when a little rain may be expected, it produces small leaves, which in turn die off in winter. Most of the larger bushes dispense with leaves altogether, using green shoots from their branches instead.

The necessity of adapting themselves to drought, to the great heat of summer, to the freezing cold of winter, to the lack of food and shelter, or to living in sand, gives the desert fauna distinctive features. Most of the creatures are small. Insects, especially beetles, arachnids, reptiles and small rodents are especially numerous. Spring, the moist season, when vegetation is briefly abundant, is also the time when the whole range of wild life is to be seen in action on the surface of the ground, busily storing up food and moisture, often by accumulating fat.

Because summer temperatures a few inches below the surface remain constant at about 30° C (86° F), compared with maxima of 80° C (176° F) on the surface, many small animals escape into holes in the ground. Several rodents, some lizards and the desert tortoise both aestivate and hibernate until the following spring. Others live in their holes by day but come out in the cool of the night, when the surface swarms with insects, and is alive with buzzing, chirping, whistling, rustling and other sounds.

The rodents have short forelegs armed with bristles to assist in digging and burrowing, and the desert gopher (*Citellus leptodactylus*) has long fingers for the same purpose: in places the surface is pitted with its holes at the rate of 5,000 to an acre. Long hind legs raise their bodies clear of the excavated material as it is thrown back, and enable them to leap over the scorching ground. The whistling mouse (*Dipus sagitta*) can jump twelve times its length. The jerboa (*Paradipus stenodactylus*) has springy pads on its paws, so that it will not sink into soft sand on landing. Long tails help with balancing.

Some of the reptiles are able to wriggle themselves into the sand, while others climb up into bushes away from the hot surface and into the breeze. The big-eared lizard *Phrynocephalus mystaceus* may be seen on the crests of dunes, its body held away from the sand by extended legs, and its tail up in the wind to cool. Most desert creatures are well camouflaged, and the largest Soviet lizard, the *Varanus griseus*, though up to 5 feet long, is difficult to recognize against the sand.

For those animals that live actively in summer, the succulent leaves and stems of the plants provide both food and water. Their needs are small, however, as they lose very little moisture in excretion. Ability to perspire, essential in such great heat, is facilitated by having light hairy coats rather than thick fur, and, in the camel, by having the fat concentrated in lumps instead of spread all over the body under the skin.

Apart from the two-humped Bactrian camel, the larger animals are either herbivores like the wild ass and antelope, which belong to the steppe, or beasts and birds of prey such as the wolf, fox, polecat and vulture. Owing to the sparse and low vegetation, shelter is difficult to find. Camouflage is resorted to and most desert creatures are yellowish or brownish in colour; most are able to get out of sight into the ground, and the larger herbivores can run very fast – the antelope up to fifty miles an hour and the wild ass to forty.

Differences in climate divide the desert into two subzones. In the northern, winter is longer and more severe, and summer is shorter and less hot than in the south (July means about 25° C: 77° F). The little precipitation is fairly evenly distributed throughout the year, with a tendency towards maxima in spring, early summer and autumn. In the southern subzone, summers are not only hotter and longer (July means about 30° C: 86° F), but almost completely rainless. Precipitation is concentrated in the December–May half of the year, with a maximum in March. This maximum corresponds with the snow melt, so that a large proportion of the total precipitation is made available in spring.

The important climatic distinction between the two subzones is reflected in the vegetation. Widely spaced xerophytic plants like wormwood characterize the northern area, whereas in the south, a green plant cover clothes the deserts for a brief period in spring.

THE NORTHERN (WORMWOOD) SUBZONE. The two principal deserts of the northern subzone are Ust-Urt and Bet-pak-Dala. The Ust-Urt plateau stretches southwestwards from the Aral Sea to the Caspian. It rises up towards its outer edges, which drop steeply on all sides: the precipitous eastern slope drops 600 feet to the Aral Sea. The name means 'level plain', and it is a tableland of horizontal Tertiary sedimentary rocks, mostly limestones, with a good deal of Quaternary clay on top. The clay bakes hard under the summer sun. The limestones form bold, broken, white cliff-like scarps with a scree of fallen rock beneath. Where they outcrop on the surface, the dazzling, barren surface is pocked with swallow holes. There are saline depressions in the clays, often with salt lakes, and the sandstones have disintegrated into masses of loose sand. Wormwoods and other diminutive xerophytic shrubs, little more than a foot high, sparsely dot the surface.

The Bet-pak-Dala extends westwards from Lake Balkhash to the Sarysu river. It is a plateau with an average height of a thousand feet, composed of horizontally-lying sedimentary rocks of Tertiary age. The surface is predominantly clayey. There are also sandy loams and gravels, and in the northeast, the rounded hills and ridges of the Kazakh 'land of little round hills'. There are numerous depressions and occasional ravines, especially along the western edge, which drops down steeply to the Sarysu. Although about a third of the scant 4 inches of annual rain falls in spring, it comes while the ground is still cold and is not therefore able to support much vegetation of the ephemeral type. Vast expanses of level plateau, which are frozen hard and dusted white with snow in winter, are dotted with little grey and black wormwood plants throughout the summer.

Besides the mainly clay-covered Tertiary plateaux, with their saline depressions, there are four large areas of sandy desert in the northern subzone: North Caspian, into which the Emba river drains (it seldom reaches the sea); Aralian, to the north and east of the Aral Sea; the Myun-Kum, between the Chu river and the Kara Tau range; and the Semirechye, the land 'of the seven rivers' which flow into Lake Balkhash. These are better supplied with water than the clayey deserts, since the porous sand is able to absorb all the moisture that falls upon it, and very little is lost, because in sand the upward capillary movement is weak. The water table is near the surface, and where the sands are fixed by vegetation, they are able to support grasses in early summer. After these have dried up, sand wormwood (*Artemisia arenaria*) predominates. In wet depressions, willow bushes and reeds give a remarkable impression of abundant moisture in regions receiving only 4 or 5 inches of rain a year. Moving sand in the form of live dunes is common in these northern deserts. It accounts for 20 to 30 per cent of the area of the Aralian sands and 45 per cent of that of the Caspian sands. Plants find these difficult to colonize, and shifting, crescent-shaped dunes form the landscape.

THE SOUTHERN [EPHEMERAL] SUBZONE. This subzone includes two large sandy deserts, the Kara-Kum, west of the Amu river, and the Kyzyl-Kum east of it. In the Kara Kum (despite the name, which means Black Sands), the sands are whitish-grey, but over most of the Kyzyl-Kum (Red Sands) they are rose-coloured.

According to the direction and constancy of the prevailing winds, the sand is arranged in long ridges, in crescent-shaped dunes (barchans), or in an irregular mass of sandhills. Sometimes it forms more or less level plains. In the ridged sand deserts, the dunes rise 50 or 60 feet above the depressions, which are about 200 feet apart. For the most part, the sand is fixed by a sparse vegetation of bushes and plants, although the barchans are usually mobile. But live dunes are less frequent than in the northern subzone and form only 5 or 6 per cent of the area. Even fixed dunes move slowly as winds constantly shift the dry surface layer. In daytime, when winds are strong, the barchans appear to smoke, as fine dust is blown off their tops, and in the evening they cast long shadows, which alternate with the warm colours imparted to the upper slopes by the setting sun.

Moisture conditions are surprisingly favourable in view of the low annual precipitation: almost all moisture is absorbed by the porous surface and stored. There is normally a permanent water table within reach of the long roots of the saxaul and other desert bushes, usually about 4 feet down. The white or sand saxaul (*Haloxylon persicum*) grows on ridged and hill sands to a height of 14 feet. The thick, bushy but leafless *Calligonum caput-medusae* is also found, growing up to 10 feet. In April its fragrant white or pink blossom first appears, and it defies the utmost heat and drought of summer.

In spring, besides the deeper water table that supplies the permanent bushes, a temporary layer of moisture is formed near the surface by snow-melt and showers. For a few weeks in March and April, the sand desert is transformed by a covering of green ephemeral and ephemeroid plants. These die off as summer advances and the moist layer descends beyond their reach. The ground between the saxaul bushes becomes bare, dry and sandy once again. The commonest ephemeroid is the sand sedge (*Carex physodes*) which withers away in mid-May. The desert lily (*Eremurus*), the lower part of its upright stem enclosed by green leaves, and the upper part bearing clusters of small white flowers, fastens itself even in the loose sands of mobile barchans.

In order to live in the sands and take advantage of the water they hold, plants have to be specially adapted to cope with the possibility of the sand being blown away from their roots, or of their being buried in it. They have to be quick-growing, so that if they are overwhelmed they can soon break through to the surface; they have to be able to send out fresh roots at the new level of the sand; they need to be able to hold enough sand round their roots (with a hairy covering) or otherwise protect them from drying out when exposed to the air; their seeds have to be made light and resilient to keep above the surface on a windy day, when the sands are moving. Plants so adapted are known as psammophytes.

The sands of the Kyzyl-Kum are interrupted by a range of isolated mountains (inselbergs), with summits rising above 2,000 feet, which are all that remains of an old range, now worn down to remnants. Their lower slopes are lost in thick screes of stony debris, which retains water and from the base of which springs issue forth.

50. An oilfield in the Kara-Kum desert

North of the southern mountain ranges – Kopet Dag in the west, Tyan Shan in the east – there is a piedmont subzone with a distinct individuality. There are large extents of loess and clay, as well as accumulations of sandy loams and loose material washed down from the mountains. The masses of yellow loess are often exposed on ravine sides, and overlook the deserts to the north with a low cliff. Precipitation here is often higher than to the north, and is usually between 6 and 14 inches a year. In many areas the supply of moisture is increased by streams flowing down from the mountains.

Spring comes early, and by the beginning of April the piedmont carries a thick cover of ephemerals and ephemeroids, mainly grasses and sedges, but also some flowering plants. In some areas, the red colour of masses of poppies contrasts with the neighbouring green vegetation. Umbellates, especially the giant fennel (*Ferula*), are characteristic.

With the onset of the long and very hot summer in May, the piedmont desert begins to turn yellow; the grasses and sedge dry off, and a sparse cover of the low cactus-like succulent *Euphorbia* takes their place. In June the ground dries out completely, and the surface bakes hard as a rock. Dust flies up in the wind, and in a particularly dry and windy year the sky is darkened by a dust pall. The brittle grass stalks are broken by the wind, only a few gaunt survivors remaining as reminders of the spring profusion. The melancholy of the torrid scene is deepened by the bleached bones of camels and asses tossed about on the cracked, grey surface by the wind. A few wormwoods and other xerophytes may see the summer through, and some areas may appear brownish-green from quite dense stands of the strong-smelling *Artemisia cina*. With rain again in autumn, the ephemeroids revive briefly before dying down for the winter.

A feature peculiar to the southern subzone is the *takyr*. Takyrs are flat clayey surfaces which are under water in spring, and then dry out to form a hard cracked surface. The cracks form a polygonal pattern: there are large polygons a yard or so across, formed by crevices, within which are smaller polygons of narrower cracks; a third series of fine breaks forms an inner polygonal net, with merely an inch or two between the cracks.

The typical takyr does not normally support plants. Throughout most of the vegetative season, it is as hard as rock; when moistened by rain, the ground expands and becomes so watertight that rain is scarcely able to penetrate an inch, but collects in pools. Immediately after the spring waters have dried off, there is a shortlived fuzz of lichens and blue-green algae, and this is renewed after any subsequent wettings by showers. There are also takyr-like areas where the ground is a little less heavy and less flat, so that moisture and roots can penetrate, though only to meet concentrated salts at a depth of a foot or so. Here, a vegetation of low salt plants, wormwoods, and often black saxaul bushes, establishes itself. The long saxaul roots are able to go far beyond the salt layer in search of moisture. Takyrs are found mainly in the southern subzone of the deserts, particularly in depressions along the Kopet Dag piedmont, in the old deltas of the principal rivers, and in the Kara-Kum sand desert. Here the finer clayey particles have been washed down into the interdunal depressions.

In some foothill areas a badland topography has developed, consisting of severely eroded saline clays and marls. There is no 'surface', but a maze of deep steepsided gullies and ravines, separating knife-edged ridges.

The river valleys

In contrast to the water-starved aspect of the whole arid belt are the valleys of the permanent rivers, fed not only by mountain snow-melt waters in early summer, but often by thawing glaciers throughout the hot season. Here there are black bogs, green reed thickets, white solonchaks and grey takyrs. There are meadow solonchaks consisting of the halophyte grass *Aeluropus*, its leaves white with salt granules, and woods of ungainly black saxaul in drier spots. Above all, there are *tugay*.

Tugay are impenetrable forests of trees, bushes, prickly halophytes and creepers, that grow profusely in the abundant, but somewhat saline, ground water of the river valleys. There are willows and specially adapted kinds of poplar, especially *Populus angustifolia*, whose hard, harsh, almost metallic leaves rattle rather than rustle in the wind. Fragrant, rose-coloured wild olive bushes scent the air, and mingle with the grey, salty, leafless tamarisk. The *tugay* forest and the tall reed thickets are ideal homes for wild life, which finds the neighbouring deserts so uninviting – Tugay deer, wild boar, Turkestan tigers, reed cats, hares, pheasants, nightingales and numerous other birds.

The Volga delta

The Volga delta is unique in the desert zone. When the level of the Caspian Sea was higher, deposits were laid down which have since been eroded, so that low, long, ridgelike hills, made of loamy sands and up to 60 feet high, rise above the lower islands. These hills have a semi-desert vegetation, in which a mixture of steppe grasses, notably *Stipa sareptana*, and wormwood (*Artemisia maritima*) are found; early ephemerals – tulips, fennel, etc. – bloom in spring. The delta is growing outwards at the rate of about 3 square miles a year, owing to the retreat of the Caspian, yet all but the higher land floods in spring. Once the water has receded it dries off very rapidly. The lower islands are covered with masses of reeds which give shelter to wild boar and ducks, geese, heron and other waterfowl. The various distributaries of the Volga are exceedingly rich in fish.

.   .   .   .

Certain types of landscape in the arid belt are not zonal in character, but occur in large or small areas in both subzones. *Solonchaks* are the commonest of these. They are found where the ground is highly salted with concentrations of sulphates and chlorides; that is, normally in low-lying areas which receive salts washed in from elsewhere, and where the water table is high, bringing the saline water up to the surface. They are sometimes the dried beds of salt lakes (*shory* or *playas*) or of impermanent streams; they often occur in river valleys, e.g. in that of the Chu, or in old abandoned river courses, such as that of the Unguz, whereby the Amu once flowed into the Caspian. They are found all over the arid belt, but especially along the shores of the retreating Caspian Sea.

The salt-crusted *shory*, which glisten white in the sun, are quite without vegetation, and often without life of any kind. It is dangerous for larger animals to tread upon them, as the crust might break and they would then be engulfed in the saline ooze beneath. When conditions are less extreme, solonchaks have a scanty covering of low, mean-looking halophytes. The typical *Anabasis salsa* is only 3 or 4 inches high. The individual plants may be spaced yards apart, leaving the whitish-grey surface bare between them.

Halophytes combat the salinity of their environment in various ways. Some have succulent fleshy organs which store up the water in spring – not because there will be none available later, but because only in spring is the saline ground water sufficiently diluted by rain and snow-melt to be usable. The drawback of this expedient is that their juicy stems or leaves are sought after by thirsty

51. Saxaul woods in the Kyzyl-Kum sand desert

animals, wherefore they arm themselves with prickles (e.g. *Salsola*). Others – like the tarmarisk – have means of expelling surplus salt, which is deposited on their stalks or leaves, giving them a greyish or whitish appearance. Others enter into a state of rest during the hot season, so as to avoid transpiration and the necessity for drawing in water from the ground. They all have to overcome the problem of osmotic pressure – the less saline liquid in the plant is attracted towards the more concentrated solution in the soil. As the plant needs to draw moisture from the soil, its cellular flow has to be specially controlled.

The botanical names of the plants tell their own story, bearing in mind that ἁλο is Greek and *sal* is Latin for salt: *Halocnenum, Halostachys, Salicornia, Salsola, Anabasis salsa*, etc. In less extreme conditions, a good covering of halophyte grasses may develop in spring to give a solonchak meadow.

The black saxaul wood is another landscape feature found in the desert, irrespective of subzone. The black or solonchak saxaul (*Haloxylon aphyllum*) establishes itself wherever sands have a tendency to be loamy or where there is a tendency towards solonchak formation. If soil conditions are favourable, it forms pure stands with up to 120 adult trees per acre. Individual specimens are 15 feet tall, and exceptionally they may reach 25 feet; their girth may expand to 4 feet. This is the only tree that can triumph over the true desert climate. It has a fantastic system of roots, which travel great distances, both horizontally and vertically: they have been known to go down 80 feet! A well-grown specimen branches into several trunks which run·along the surface for a foot or two before shooting upwards. Each trunk, at a height of 2 or 3 feet, again divides into several branches, which carry the small sharp leaves close to the stems. Often, however, an agonizing struggle with aridity is evident in the chaotic and gnarled growth of split and twisted branches. The hard, heavy wood is long-lived, and dead saxauls litter the ground for many years.

There are several types of stony desert: the outwash cones of boulders, gravels and sands deposited by mountain streams in the piedmont zone; the dry rocky surfaces of the Ust-Urt where limestone outcrops; the coarse, stony, gravelly surfaces of the Kara-Kum north of the Unguz depression; and the rocky screes that surround the rounded igneous hills of the eastern Bet-pak-Dala. In all, the vegetation is scanty and poor, consisting of a few xerophytic shrubs.

Cultural landscapes

The natural advantages of the belt are great and have led to a long history of exploitation by man. The length, heat and sunlight of summer favour a wide range of crops, and also modern military, aeronautical and space research. The Soviet space research centre of Baykonyr is located here. Many soils, especially the chestnut-coloured soils of the semi-desert zone and the desert grey earths, are potentially rich, and 'even the sandy soils of Central Asia are more fertile than the podsols' (Berg). The sands also retain valuable quantities of water. The rivers are priceless, especially those that rise in high mountains, as do the Syr and the Amu: the higher the mountains, the longer the snow-melt season, and where there are glaciers, these continue to melt throughout the summer. These rivers are, therefore, remarkably regular and reliable. The river valleys and deltas also have dense *tugay* woods which provide fuel and lumber, and act as natural shelter belts; their reeds and tall grasses provide thatch and are used for rope, fuel and sometimes fodder. The Caspian and Aral lakes have long been famous for their caviar-yielding fish. The natural vegetation offers a scanty but extensive pasture for sheep, goats and camels, and the saxaul tree is a source of fuel. The black fleece of the karakul sheep is especially highly prized.

Many desert plants, in adapting to the extreme aridity and salinity, produce various useful chemical substances: oils, alkaloids, resins, tannin, rubber, drugs such as salzolin (from the *Salsola*) and ephedrine (from the *Ephedra*), and pesticides like anabazin (from the *Anabasis aphylla*). Even the skins of the desert lizards can be used for fancy leather goods. The mineral wealth is great and varied. Natural gas, petroleum, gold, copper, molybdenum and salts are prominent, with coal, iron ore, lignite, chromite, sulphur and cement lime-stones also important.

The disadvantages, however, are formidable. Very low rainfall, excessive heat, strong dry winds, sandstorms, high evaporation, shifting dunes, saline soils and water, combine to make this a difficult environment for man. In addition there are poisonous snakes and insects, and, for browsing animals, poisonous plants like the charryk. Earthquakes occur in the south.

The arid lands have been used as sheep pasture for thousands of years, but the feed available varies greatly from year to year. In bad years, overgrazing is inevitable: the depleted vegetation then loses its hold on the sand, which begins to shift in live dunes. Pastures also vary regionally and seasonally. The northern semi-desert zone has summer pastures, but the thin and short-lasting snow cover in the south permits grazing in winter, when there is less salt in the plants and ground water. A large area of arid-land pasture is needed to feed a single animal – on an average 12 to 15 acres to a sheep. This, together with limited water supplies and the regional and seasonal variations in pasture availability, means that flocks have to be kept on the move. Hence, the pastoral peoples of Central Asia were traditionally nomadic. The Bactrian camel was particularly suitable for making long journeys across the desert.

Although water supply is everywhere a problem, it is less so in the sandy deserts, where the sands act as natural underground reservoirs, conserving snow-melt and rainwater within easy reach of the surface. There are ten thousand wells in the Kara-Kum, mostly old, their sides kept up with saxaul wood. During the Soviet period, many more wells have been dug, some of them

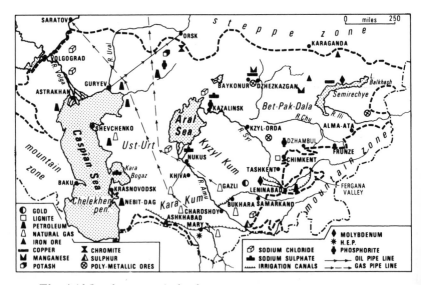

52. The Arid Lands: economic development

worked by wind, some tapping artesian sources; and small concrete reservoirs have been built to impound spring melt-water and run-off.

Besides improving water supply, the Soviets have changed the old nomadic way of life. Although the Kazakh and Kirghiz shepherds still spend the summer, with their flocks, in the Tyan Shan mountain pastures, living in tents, they now have permanent cottages in piedmont villages. The deserts to the north are used as winter pastures. In the Myun-Kum sand desert, for instance, bases have been built where stocks of hay brought from arable oases are held in case of need. At newly exploited water points in the deserts, oases growing fodder crops have been developed. These also offer various services to the shepherds: their meteorological offices use rockets to warn of an approaching *buran* which, in the desert, can be an unpleasant mixture of wind-driven sand and snow. The shepherds still work with horses and camels, but lorries ply between the new oasis villages and fodder bases.

Contrasting sharply with the desert and semi-desert landscape, modified only slightly by centuries of man's pastoral activity, are the irrigated oases, many of which have been the homes of sedentary man for three or four thousand years. Here the natural landscape has been utterly transformed. By bringing water on to the arid land, not only is the surface plant cover converted from sparse desert shrubs to arable fields, orchards and gardens, with farm and residential buildings, but the soil beneath and climate above both undergo considerable change. The climatic effects – higher humidity, lower temperatures and weaker winds – are felt well beyond the limits of the oases.

Large populations, advanced civilizations and splendid cities, all based on agriculture, were established in some of the irrigable areas. They were, however, vulnerable both to physical accident – the drying up, flooding or change of course of the river upon which they depended, and sand encroachment – and to enemy attack, especially by hostile nomads. The irrigation works so laboriously constructed over centuries could be quickly destroyed. Hence the history of the oasis districts is one of ups and downs, and large areas of abandoned water channels, ruined villages and derelict strongholds frequently occur.

Although the coming of the Russians in the second half of the nineteenth century had some important consequences, there was no fundamental change in the pattern. The irrigated area was greatly increased to make possible a larger supply of cotton, but the systems used continued to form a haphazard patchwork of old ditches, canals, dams and reservoirs. Turkmen, Uzbeks and other native peoples continued to provide the labour for the enlarged oases, and only in the Semirechye area, south of Lake Balkhash, was there much Russian settlement. The main prerevolutionary landscape contribution of the Russians lay in the railways and towns they built.

During the Soviet period, irrigation of the arid lands has benefited from

53. An irrigation canal in the Golodnaya-step desert

large-scale state planning, hydrological research, modern technology and heavy capital investment. Much primitive ditch irrigation has been superseded, old canals have been reconstructed and repaired, and sometimes lined with concrete, clay or plastic to reduce percolation. Seen from the air, the regular, rectangular pattern of the modern irrigation channels is easily distinguished from the confused network of the older works. Large reservoirs have been built on the rivers, often in connection with hydroelectric generation, and ambitious canals have been constructed to take water long distances from the rivers. The white concrete sluices, bare and strictly utilitarian in the early years, but now more ornamental and often watched over by a statue of Lenin, contrast sharply with earlier ramshackle methods of water control. Modern high-power earth-moving machinery has been an important factor in this technical revolution. Large sprinkler machines, some able to spray a strip nearly 400 feet wide, are also employed.

Large, landscape-transforming, Soviet irrigation works are too numerous to be described individually, but mention must be made of the Kara-Kum canal, which takes Amu water towards the Caspian. When completed, it will irrigate $3\frac{1}{2}$ million acres of arable land and supply water to 12 million acres of pasture. The Amu–Bukhara canal raises Amu water, by means of electric pumps, to the lower Zeravshan valley. Extensive state cotton farms are now replacing the desert in the Golodnaya-step – a result of bringing water through concrete conduits from the new Karkad reservoir, situated where the Syr river leaves the Fergana valley.

Irrigation is beset with problems, the worst being the process whereby irrigation water, when evaporated on the surface, leaves behind salts that it has brought up from the subsoil. Excess of salt in the soil seriously affects the yield of cotton. Difficult and expensive countermeasures have had to be introduced, involving draining off the irrigation water when it reaches a certain level in the ground. The water is pumped away to form pools which can be used for fish and for duck.[2]

In the semi-desert area, agriculture is practised locally without artificial irrigation, particularly in *limany* or large depressions which fill with water in spring from rain and snow-melt and then dry off, leaving a moist soil. And in some parts of the sandy deserts crops are grown – with fertilizer – in trenches excavated in the sand. The plants are thus enabled to reach the supply of fresh ground water stored up beneath the surface. Trench agriculture is found along the eastern shore of the Caspian.

Cotton is the main irrigated crop, and at harvest time its white lint dominates the oasis scene – in the fields, on the trucks and at the collecting stations. Its cultivation is highly mechanized. Fruits of all kinds (except citrus), nuts, tobacco, rice, mulberry trees for silkworms, fodder crops and sugar beet are also grown to meet local needs.

Dune-fixing and shelter-belt plantation to protect oases, railways, roads, etc., from sand encroachment, have been prosecuted vigorously. In Uzbekistan alone about 600,000 acres of mobile sands have been planted with shrubs. Such plantations are said to pay for themselves with the fuel they provide after five or six years.

The numerous mining activities, almost all introduced during the Soviet period, have obvious landscape importance, especially the installations associated with lignite, oil, gas and salt extraction. Massive deposits of lignite are worked at Angren, east of Tashkent, to fuel its 600 MW power station; a large 2,400 MW station is planned to make added use of this resource. The deserts of the Turkmen and Uzbek Republics yield about 125 billion cubic metres of natural and oilfield gas a year, and rank second only to the great tundra gasfield of West Siberia. Much of the gas has a high sulphur content which has to be removed before transmission. Pipelines serve the chief industrial areas of Central Asia and fuel local power stations, but most of the gas is piped off to the Urals and Central Russia. There are oil wells along the Caspian coast, especially in and around the Mangyshlak peninsula. Salt from Lake Baskunchak, east of the Volga, goes to Astrakhan for the fish industry there. This lake has a crust so thick in summer that it can be crossed by vehicles. Salt is also obtained by evaporation

54. Large areas of semi-desert near Lake Balkhash are being prepared for rice cultivation with irrigation

from the shores of the Aral Sea. The Kara-bogaz-gol gulf is a natural chemical factory, producing through evaporation, constantly renewed supplies of sodium sulphate. There are large copper smelters at Karsakpay (using Dzhezkazgan ore) and near Balkhash at Kounradsky. Since 1969 most Soviet gold production has come from the Kyzyl-Kum desert where it is mined opencast; there are three large concentrators operating. A large chemical combine producing phosphorite fertilizer has been built on the eastern edge of the Karatau range, where the largest phosphorite deposit in the USSR is situated. The Cheleken peninsula, besides its oil wealth, yields iodine, bromine and the rare ozocerite (mineral wax).

A great achievement of tsarist Russia was the building of railways from Krasnovodsk on the Caspian and from Orenburg on the Ural river across the waterless desert to Tashkent (1898–1906). In the Soviet period rail mileage has been greatly increased, and surfaced roads have been made in and around the oases. Trucks move over much of the desert without the benefit of made roads, and camel caravans still follow the ancient tracks.

The Republican capitals are among the largest towns (Table 17). They are now national administrative and cultural centres, but before the Revolution they were primarily Russian towns, representing the imperial authority. They are also considerable industrial centres (machine-building, textiles and food-processing).

TABLE 17. *Population and rank of Republican capitals in the Arid Belt (thousands)*

	1939	1959	1981
Tashkent (Uzbek SSR)	585 (8th)	927 (6th)	1,858 (4th)
Alma Ata (Kazakh SSR)	231 (33rd)	456 (26th)	975 (22nd)
Frunze (Kirgiz SSR)	93 (95th)	218 (65th)	552 (38th)
Ashkhabad (Turkmen SSR)	127 (68th)	170 (84th)	325 (81st)

Tashkent, on the Chirchik which flows into the Syr, was the only one of the four to have been already the site of a large native oasis town. It was taken by the Russians in 1865 and became the capital for conquered Central Asia. The Russian city was distinct from the Uzbek quarter, a large sprawling mass of low adobe houses, most of which were destroyed in the 1966 earthquake. Tashkent now has large modern districts with big residential blocks specially built to withstand earthquake shocks. Streets of new single dwelling-houses have been put up for the Uzbeks, who generally have such large families that they do not fit well into flats.

The other three capitals are Russian by origin. Alma-Ata was founded as the fort of Verny in 1854, in an oasis area connected with the Ili river. It lies amidst apple-tree-covered foothills. Frunze, in a foothill oasis area of the Chu valley, was founded as Pishpek in 1873, while Ashkhabad was established in 1881. Its slower growth is partly due to a severe earthquake in 1948. A great day in its history was 12 May 1962 when the Kara-Kum canal first brought Amu water to the town, for it has always had difficulty in finding an adequate supply. It is known for its film studios. Also in the Turkmen republic is the town of Mary (71,000 in 1981), established by the Russians late in the nineteenth century to the west of the ancient city of Merv. It is the centre of a large oasis irrigated from the Murgab river, and has textile and carpet industries, and a large hydroelectric power station. The reservoir holds back the erratic waters of the Murgab during the snow-melt season, and releases a controlled flow into the Kara-Kum canal, whose own supplies have – at this distance from the source – been diminished by evaporation, seepage and irrigation.

During the Soviet period the proportion of non-Russian inhabitants in these towns has risen sharply. The prosperity of the surrounding oases is reflected in the number of native farmers who come into town to shop; the thick round woollen caps of the men and the brightly-coloured cotton frocks of the women mingle with the European-style dress of the Russians.

Three ancient oasis towns in the Uzbek republic which have retained monuments from their magnificent past and have not been overshadowed by Russian settlement are Samarkand, Bukhara and Khiva. They are adorned with beautiful mosques, minarets, palaces and mausoleums, the walls of which are coated with intricately-patterned mosaics of coloured glazed tile. The native quarters – low flat-roofed adobe houses made from the yellow loess – are inhabited by Uzbeks, who wear cotton or silk black and white skull-caps, a reminder that theirs is a cotton-growing culture, just as the woollen caps of the other Central Asian peoples reflect the importance of sheep in their economies. Samarkand (489,000) has grown into a large modern city, processing cotton and silk, and making electronic and photographic goods. Bukhara (192,000) has also attracted industry since the coming of natural gas and the Amu-Bukhara canal, but Khiva remains a museum town.

All the towns mentioned above lie in the relatively well-watered loess-covered piedmont oasis zone, where streams issuing forth from the Central Asian mountains to the southeast debouch out onto the plain. In this zone there are also two large centres of the chemical industry: Chimkent (334,000), terminus of a new pipeline from West Siberia and site of a new oil refinery, and Dzhambul (277,000), which manufactures superphosphate from Karatau phosphorite. The piedmont oasis zone penetrates 170 miles into the mountains to form the rich and densely-peopled Fergana basin which supports several medium-sized towns: Namangan (241,000), Andizhan (238,000), Fergana (180,000), Kokand (156,000) and Leninabad (135,000). They are market and communications centres for the irrigated farms of their districts, and all of them process cotton and silk. Fergana also has an oil refinery working on local petroleum (Fig. 60).

Mention should be made of some special-purpose unifunctional towns created or greatly expanded during the postwar years. Shevchenko (122,000) is a fast-growing town created in the waterless desert to serve the Mangyshlak oilfield district, which is now also a source of gas, copper, cobalt, lignite and manganese. Its large nuclear-powered desalinization plant processes Caspian water for the needs of the region; the plant also generates electricity (110 MW). The town derives a distinctive look from the pink and yellow limestones with which its blocks of flats are faced, and its streets are lined with irrigated trees and shrubs. Growing industrial activity includes a new plastics factory, and population is planned to increase rapidly to 300,000. Nebit Dag (78,000) is an older oil town, dating from the 1930s. Bekabat (70,000) where Central Asia's first metallurgical plant was founded in 1944, has new electric furnaces and rolling mills. Chirchik (136,000), near Tashkent, has chemical industry. Navoi (86,000) was founded near Bukhara in 1958 to produce fertilizers, plastics, synthetic rubber and synthetic wool from the local natural gas.

Finally, there are the Caspian ports: Astrakhan (470,000), Guryev (135,000) and Krasnovodsk (54,000). All are termini of railways. Astrakhan, headquarters

55. The new gold discovery at Muruntau has already led to new settlements for prospectors and miners

of the Caspian fishery, where almost all Russia's caviar is prepared, has grown slowly. In 1811 it was sixth town in the Empire; at the 1926 census it was twelfth in order, but in 1981 fifty-fourth. Direct rail links between Russia and Central Asia have robbed it of much of its former importance, and it is adversely affected by the sinking level of the Caspian. Guryev and Krasnovodsk have oil refineries.

The level of the Caspian is falling because temperatures have become higher, and because less Volga water is reaching the lake: more of it is being used in industry and for irrigation, and more is evaporating from the broad expanses of new hydroelectric reservoirs. Much water has also been lost from evaporation in Kara-bogaz-gol, the gulf on the east shore; a dyke, completed in 1980, now prevents Caspian water from entering the gulf, but it will also arrest the formation of the valuable salts extracted there. The mining of oil and the building of 'oil towns' on stages offshore have not only introduced a new element to the geography of the Caspian, but injured the valuable sturgeon fishery through pollution. The Volga and Ural rivers carry much unwelcome industrial effluent into the Caspian. The Aral Sea is drying up fast, and its principal tributaries, the Amu and Syr, now yield most of their water to irrigation. The Syr no longer even reaches the Sea, which has retreated 35 miles from its eastern shore. Salt and dust blown from the dried-up lake bed and the deltas of former tributaries are furthering the 'desertification' of the region. Expanses of saxaul forest and meadow near the shores have died away through dessication, with the loss of hay, fuel and pasture. Most of the water still entering the Aral by the Amu is water drained off irrigated land and highly impregnated with sodium sulphate and sodium chloride. Both the valuable fishery and the large muskrat breeding grounds in the deltas are at risk. The third great lake of the region, Balkhash, has suffered by irrigation from the Ili and the building of a large reservoir in connection with a hydroelectric station on the river; the water of the lake has since declined both in quantity and quality.

The arid lands of Kazakhstan and Central Asia contain some of the fastest-growing populations in the USSR. That of Uzbekistan almost doubled between the censuses of 1959 and 1979. Population density grew faster in the Fergana valley in the 1970s than anywhere else in the country. Ideally the Soviets would like to see emigration to labour-shortage areas elsewhere, but the Uzbeks, Turkmenians and others are tenacious of their rural way of life. Many of them are reluctant to go and work in their own urban centres, although these have undergone much industrial development. To expand agriculture in the region sufficiently to employ the growing numbers would require further irrigation on a scale far beyond the capacity of local water resources. Such considerations have compelled the authorities to regard oft-repeated suggestions that water should be diverted from the West Siberian swamps to the deserts as not only attractive, but imperative, and the 25th Party Congress in 1976 directed that research be undertaken and definite proposals made. Under these it is planned to withdraw, in the first stage, 6 cubic miles of water a year from the Ob system from below the mouth of its tributary, the Irtysh. The water would be pumped back up the Irtysh valley to Tobolsk and thence by canal through the Turgay depression to the deserts.

8
The mountain belt

Natural landscapes

Soviet territory with mountainous relief covers about $2\frac{1}{2}$ million square miles, or 26 per cent of the whole area of the country. Most of this lies in the east, but it also forms an almost continuous belt of varying width along the southern borders (Fig. 56).

Because they mostly originated in thrusts against the Russian and Siberian structural platforms, causing the affected rocks to be ridged up in folds, Soviet mountains are usually grouped in parallel ranges which can be seen rising one behind the other. Often this parallelism is erosional as well as structural, rivers having worn down the softer rocks, leaving the more resistant standing up as high ranges. In the highest central ranges, the sedimentary rocks have usually been reinforced, and sometimes metamorphosed, by intrusions of molten magma from the heated interior. Such masses of granitic rock, elevated to great heights by mountain-building movements, resist erosion more effectively than rocks of sedimentary origin. They form most of the highest summits in the country. The ranges are often asymmetrical. Not only the Urals, but also the Sikhote Alin of the Far East, rise up gently from the west but fall steeply to the east.

Aspect is important in mountain landscape, especially the contrast between sheltered, sunlit, southern slopes and exposed, shaded, northern ones. Thus, in the Far East, the Mongolian oak (*Quercus mongolica*) and the maple grow 1,500 to 1,700 feet higher up on southern than on northern slopes; and in Transbaykalia, some southern slopes are clothed in grass while the northern carry larch and pine.

Temperature decreases, not only with increased latitude from the equator, but also with increased altitude from sea level. Average annual temperature drops about 0·6° C (1° F) for each degree of latitude northwards, or for each 300 feet of height. Consequently, a rather similar zoning of climate and vegetation is found as one ascends a mountain as when one travels north. There is a somewhat similar progression in precipitation as in temperature. In the USSR generally, precipitation increases from subtropical to middle latitudes, but falls off in high latitudes. So, as a mountain range is climbed, precipitation normally increases until a maximum is reached, and then falls off as summits rise above prevalent cloud levels. With both polar and high-mountain precipitation, the actual volume is much greater than the water-equivalent precipitation figures indicate, since it falls as snow.

Because the whole flank of a high mountain range can sometimes be seen rising up from the lowland, the vertical zoning of vegetation belts is often part of the visible landscape. In the western Alai Mountains, within a height range of 15,000 feet, a similar succession can be seen to that portrayed on a map of the latitudinal belts for 2,500 miles northwards: desert, semi-desert, steppe, forest, alpine meadows and tundra, eternal snow and ice. In the Urals, which are strung across 18° of latitude, the northernmost ranges (68° N) are wholly clad in tundra and permanent snow, whereas the southernmost hills (50° N) are wholly covered by wooded steppe. The greater part of most mountain ranges in the Soviet Union is covered by forest, usually a dense needle-leaved forest, which flourishes in the normal highland conditions of abundant moisture, long severe winters and heavy snowfall.

A fine fir-spruce forest covers much of the slopes of that part of the eastern Carpathians now included in the USSR. There are also extensive beech forests on the lower slopes and foothills. Coniferous forest clothes the lower slopes of the northern Urals (68°–61° N), the whole slope of the central Urals (61°–55°) to the treeline, and the upper slopes of the southern Urals (55°–52°). Broadleaved trees are absent from the eastern slopes, but a broadleaved deciduous forest or a mixed forest, including oaks, elms, lindens and maples, is found on the lower slopes in the west. In places, particularly in the north, steep and rugged rock masses break through the forest cover.

The dry limestone mountains of the Crimea are not heavily forested, but there are some pine woods high up on the southern slopes. The eastern Caucasus

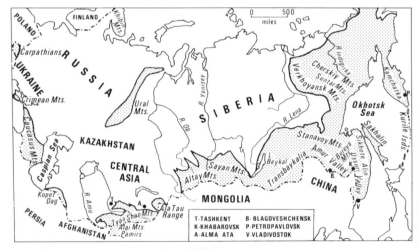

56. *The mountainous areas of the USSR*

ranges are also too dry for much forest, but the central and western ranges carry a progression from subtropical woodlands up through vast beech forests to a coniferous belt of spruce and fir, which ends with the treeline at about 5,000 feet. The subtropical or Kolkhid woods are mostly near the Black Sea, and consist of a mixture of alder, oak, hornbeam, maple and walnut, together with evergreens like the box and laurel. Lianes wind themselves around the trees.

The mountain slopes of Central Asia are among the least forested as they receive very little precipitation during the growing season. Oak and pine are absent and spruce and fir occur only in the wetter eastern regions of the Tyan Shan. Locally, in well-watered spots, there are woods composed largely of wild fruit trees and bushes – walnut, apple, pear, plum, apricot, almond, pistachio, olive, grape, etc., as well as hawthorn and maple. These make a fine show of blossom in early summer, and are especially noteworthy on the slopes enclosing the Fergana valley.

The only widespread needle-leaved tree is a juniper – *Juniperus semiglobosa*, which forms scattered dark patches on the otherwise barren-looking Turkestan and Alai ranges. It roots itself high up on steep slopes, between 5,000 and 10,000 feet, where it grows 20 to 30 feet tall. In certain areas of the Tyan Shan – the Fergana range, the eastern Kirghiz range, the slopes around Lake Issyk-Kul, the eastern part of the Transili Alatau – forests of the Tyan Shan spruce (*Picea schrenkiana*) flourish. This tree, which has a tall, tapering, extremely regular shape that looks as though it might have been trimmed by hand, can soar to 200 feet, but averages half this height. It shelters a lower growth of aspen, apple, bird cherry, blackcurrant, raspberry and juniper. It does best on shady and even stony slopes, particularly between 5,000 and 9,000 feet, forming an open woodland with plenty of light.

The Altay and Sayan Mountains of southern Siberia usually have a steppe grassland on their lower slopes, but with increased precipitation upwards, this soon gives way to coniferous forest which rises to a high treeline – 6,000 feet in the north and 9,000 feet in the east. This mountain forest is of two kinds. On the drier slopes of the east, it is a light, open woodland, consisting principally of larch, with an underwood of rose and currant bushes, and with rich meadows in gaps in the forest. But the wetter western and northern Altay carry a dense forest of cedar, fir and spruce, and little light reaches the dark moss-covered ground. Steppe grassland recurs, however, in the drier valleys and basins.

The Transbaykalian Mountains have a wooded steppe skirting their lower slopes. This soon gives way to unbroken coniferous forest of Dauric larch (*Larix dahurica*) up to 6,000 feet, but islands of grassland are found in the valleys and basins. The Transbaykalian forests are distinguished from the Siberian tayga by their dense undergrowth of rhododendrons and dwarf birches.

In the mountain ranges east of the Lena, increasing northerly latitude progressively forces down the treeline. In the Verkhoyansk Mountains, which run from 60° to 70° N, the Dauric larch forests that constitute the Siberian tayga rise to 3,500 feet in the south, but only to 600 feet in the north, and even then they are sparse and poorly grown.

The most noteworthy feature of the mountain forests of the Soviet Far East is the reappearance of broadleaved trees, although usually in specifically oriental species. Thus the lower slopes of the mountains bordering the Amur valley and the southern part of the Sikhote Alin have a mixed forest in which Manchurian and Korean species of broadleaved trees predominate: oak, maple, ash, linden, hornbeam, cork and walnut. Pines and firs constitute the needle-leaved element. There are also fruit trees and a dense undergrowth of hazel, syringa, spindle, honeysuckle, blackcurrant, guelder rose, etc. Numerous lianes wind around the trunks and branches of the trees, and epiphyte ferns are also found on tree trunks. These broadleaved forests change at about 3,000 feet to the Okhotsk mountain forest type, in which Ayab spruce forms the top layer, with a second canopy of Ermans birch and white-bark fir (*Abies nepholepsis*). This rises to the treeline in the south, but farther north it gives way to the typical east Siberian forest of Dauric larch, with an underwood of dwarf pine and shrub birch. The Okhotsk forest type is the prevalent vegetation cover over the mountains of Kamchatka.

A zone of dwarf trees and shrubs, often stunted and deformed, is normally found above the treeline. Besides the dwarf birch (*Betula nana*), the crooked birch (*B. tortuosa*) is common and grows up to 20 feet tall. The shrub alder (*Alnus fruticosa*) is also often present. At this high altitude, the spruce, pine, cedar and other trees often creep along the ground instead of growing away from it. They do this partly to avoid the wind and partly to keep close to the surface source of radiated warmth. Groups of such creeping, crooked trees, common in the Urals and east Siberia, are known as *staniki*. Bushes of bilberry, whortleberry, etc., often accompany the stunted trees of this zone, which can be compared to the wooded tundra.

The scenery above the treeline often owes most to the Quaternary ice ages, when more snow fell upon the summits of most of the higher mountains than could be disposed of by summer melting. Instead, from beneath the masses of snow thus accumulated, tongues of glacial ice crept downwards. In so doing, they created an entirely new mountain landscape. In the high places where the glaciers were born, rock was plucked away from the sides, leaving immense rounded, armchair-like amphitheatres (cirques), open at the front, with a hollow in the centre, and a steep back wall sheer up to the summit. With glaciers moving away on all sides, such steep walls were cut back towards each other, leaving sharp, knife-edged ridges and peaks. The valleys leading from the source region were carved into steep-sided troughs with rounded shoulders and bottoms, in which the tiny contemporary streams seem absurdly out of place. As the glaciers moved, they carried rock rubble of all kinds, which is now left behind on the valley sides and bottoms. Such former glaciation was particularly powerful in producing bold and sharp highland relief in the mountains of Central Asia, the Altay, northeast Siberia and Kamchatka.

The uppermost vegetation zone is that of alpine meadow or mountain tundra. Conditions at these high altitudes differ in some respects from those at high latitudes. The air is normally clearer and more heat is received from the sun in daytime on sunward slopes; because of the slope, there is better air and water drainage, so that permafrost and bog are far less common. But around the mountain summits there are more accumulations of rocks and boulders, the result of earlier glaciation and continuous frost-shattering. Consequently, on the one hand, there is more meadow, made up of grasses, sedges and flowering plants, but also more 'stony tundra' and more bare, steep rock faces.

The Arctic type of tundra, with mosses and lichens predominating, is found mostly on the more northerly mountains, such as the Khibins, the northern Urals and the Verkhoyansk Mountains. Alpine meadows are commonest on the Caucasus, the mountains of Central Asia, and the Altay ranges. They are often gay throughout the summer, with many colours of differing flowering plants, and although the plants may be small, the flowers may be large: e.g. *Anemone crinita*, *Aquilegia glandulosa*, *Gentiana ataica*, *Papaver nudicaule*, that bespatter the high-mountain meadows of the Altay between 6,000 and 8,000 feet. The mountain meadows are often accompanied by shrubs in steeper and rockier areas: rhododendron on the Caucasus, juniper and Tyan Shan spruce on the Tyan Shan.

Almost all the mountains of the USSR are covered with snow during the winter season, but almost everywhere it melts away in summer, revealing the vegetation or rock beneath. However, snow does not melt in crevices and in sunless places, so that the summer aspect of most mountain summits shows the rock surface streaked and blotched with white. The tops of the higher, wetter ranges carry a permanent snow cover under which, in some instances, small glaciers are formed; but their area is insignificant compared with that obtaining during the Quaternary ice ages.

The presence of permanent snow is not just a matter of extreme height, but of precipitation, especially winter precipitation. The greater this is, the lower the snowline descends. Thus in the wetter, western, high Caucasus Mountains it falls in places to 8,000 feet, whereas in the east it is up at 13,000 feet above sea-level. Aspect is important and permanent snow descends farther on northern than on southern slopes. Latitude, of course, is also a factor, and with similar precipitation conditions, the snowline falls northwards.

When the amount of snow falling in a year exceeds that lost through summer melting, the surplus is disposed of through the lower layers of the accumulated mass being squeezed out in the form of glacial ice. There are several areas in the USSR where this process takes place, and where clear azure-blue ice, illumined by sunlight, provides a rare sparkling addition to the mountain scenery: rare because, in the few places where glacial ice is still formed, it is soon covered by snow, dirt or debris.

The high mountains of the west-central Caucasus, above 13,000 feet, are the main centre of contemporary glaciation. There are here altogether some 1,400 glaciers covering an area of 8,000 square miles, several of them over 7 miles long. About three-quarters of them descend the northern slopes. Mt Elbruz (18,481 feet) alone sends out fifty glaciers from one snow cap. Whereas it is usually only on individual summits that eternal snow is found, the whole of the jagged crest of the west-central range of the Great Caucasus gleams white in the sun throughout the summer: only rock slopes too precipitous to hold the snow break through the dazzling mantle (Fig. 57).

Some of the higher ranges of the Pamir and eastern Tyan Shan also have crests continuously rising above the snowline for tens of miles, with some important areas of glacier formation. In the northwest Pamirs there is a knot of extremely high mountains, including such peaks as Mt Communism (24,559 feet) and Mt Revolution (22,880 feet), which give birth, among others, to Fedchenko, the longest glacier in the world. Like the glaciers of the Ice Age, this mighty ice river receives tributaries and moves majestically along its broad valley with serried and serrated peaks ranged along either side. In the eastern Tyan Shan, the knot of high mountains, which includes Pobeda (24,407 feet) and Khan Tengri (22,950 feet), is the chief centre of glaciation (Fig. 58).

In the Altay Mountains of southern Siberia, there are about 800 glaciers covering an area of 225 square miles, and some of them are over 5 miles long. The chief centre is Mt Belukha (14,773 feet) in the Katunsk range. In places they penetrate down into the forest zone at heights of only 6,500 feet above

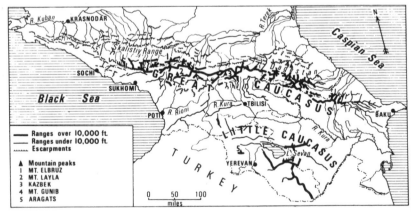

57. *The Caucasus mountain ranges and valleys*

sea-level. These Altay glaciers appear to be in rapid retreat: they are melting away at rates of 30 feet and more a year.

In some of the higher mountain masses of northeastern Siberia, particularly in the source region of the Indigirka river, glaciers are active. In the little-known Suntar range, the snow lies at 8,000 feet, but a score of summits rise above 9,000 feet, culminating in Suntar (10,171 feet), probably the highest point in northeast Siberia. It gives rise to five glaciers with a total area of 22 square miles. Near the source of the Indigirka, an icefield has been discovered from which over 2,000 glaciers descend, covering between them an area of 90 square miles. The Cherski Mountains also have glacier-forming centres.[1] In Kamchatka, the mighty volcanic Mt Klyuchevsky has a giant collar of snow and ice skirting its cone for a depth of 2,000 feet, from which dust- and ash-blackened ice tongues descend 7,000 feet and more. The northernmost volcano of the peninsula, Mt Shiveluch (10,943 feet), which erupted in 1948, has six glaciers.

The elevation of most mountains enables them to attract sufficient moisture to support forest up to a considerable height, but this is not always so. Steppe and even desert may take its place. Thus, in the eastern Caucasus, on the drier slopes and in the intermontane basins and valleys of the Altay, Sayan and Transbaykalian Mountains, a dry grass steppe-like vegetation prevails, usually accompanied by shrubs of *Caragana*, *Spiraea*, *Lonicera*, etc.

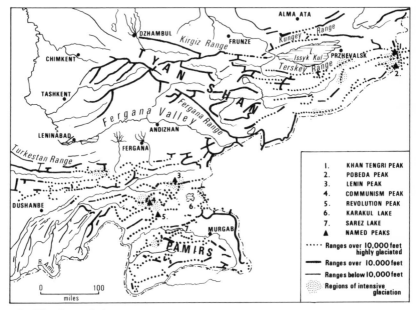

58. *The Central Asian mountains*

Much of the Central Asian mountain area is even more arid. The forward westernmost ranges, such as the Turkestan and Zeravshan ranges, and the lower ridges that run southwards to the Amu in western Tadzhikstan, are deeply eroded with narrow spines separating steepsided valleys, the slopes barren or dotted here and there with small desert plants and bushes. The valleys between the high Pamir ranges, with less than 10 inches of precipitation a year, have a sparse wormwood semi-desert vegetation. This thickens into a dry steppe (*Stipa-Artemisia-Festuca*) upwards of 10,000 feet, and at about 13,000 feet the Alpine meadows begin.

The eastern Pamir plateau, on the other hand, has less altitudinal range, and lying in the rain shadow of the high western mountains, is a cold desert. Murgab, at 12,000 feet above sea-level, receives an average of only 2 inches of rain a year. During one period of twelve months, no more than a tenth of an inch fell, and that on a single day. The July mean temperature is only 13·5° C (56·3° F), while that for January falls to −17·2° C (+1° F). Only two months of the year are frost free. Because the snow cover is so thin, the ground remains permanently frozen in places. The vegetation consists of a sparse cover of such diminutive plants as *Eurotia ceratoides* and the hairy *Artemisia skorniakova*, which grows only 2 or 3 inches high. There are also cushions of *Potentilla* and the pink-flowering *Sibbaldia*. A few shrubs of willow and barberry appear up to 13,000 feet. There are many takyrs, solonchaks and sandy stretches.

The western foothills and lower slopes of the Tyan Shan have an ephemeral desert vegetation, being almost barren for most of the year, but briefly covered with green sedge and numerous flowering plants in spring. Upwards, with more moisture, grasses – couch grass and *Poa bulbosa* – give a closer, but still incomplete, vegetal cover. Colour is imparted in spring by large tulips, red and yellow, by sword lilies, yellow and blue, by masses of red poppy and the violet *Malcolmia*. Not until mid-July do the grasses wither and die. At about 4,000 feet this ephemeral steppe gives way to mountain meadows and thickets of honeysuckle, rose and service, with woods of apple and hawthorn.

Soluble limestones are prominent in the composition of the Crimean and Caucasus Mountains, and because of the peculiar properties of that rock, especially its porosity and its solubility in rain water, large areas within these mountains have a distinctive limestone topography, and karstic features commonly occur. Limestone uplands are also impressive because of the whitish colour of the rock, its tendency to form massive blocks separated by deep gorges, and because of the often waterless appearance of its porous surface.

In the Crimean Mountains, the limestone masses whose steep slopes dominate the Black Sea have flattish tops between 3,000 and 4,000 feet, with the highest points reaching 5,000 feet (Mt Roman-Kosh, 5,069 feet). These upper surfaces or *yayly* (*yayla*=mountain pasture or alp) are mostly covered with grass and juniper bushes, but here and there the bare white rock breaks through abruptly. Rocks and stones are found scattered over the ground, which is pitted with sink holes, solution hollows and a whole range of karstic features. Occasionally, these hollows contain lakes, but more often the porous limestone surface is waterless, despite a total annual precipitation of from 50 inches in the west to 20 in the east. For about two months in winter, the whitish patches of limestone are superseded by whiter snow. In contrast to the plateau tops are the canyon-like valleys, filled with beautiful woods, including many wild fruit trees and fragrant flowering shrubs. Above tower the white, bare, sheer valley sides.

The *yayly* have a gentle, mostly forested, slope down to the north, but this gradual descent is broken by two successive lines of scarps, in each of which a buttressed wall of limestone, turreted with great rounded bastions of perpendicular rock, faces southeast. Both are broken by steep ravines and deep gorges.

Some 25 miles north of the main chains of the Great Caucasus Mountains is the Skalisty range, the first and highest of a series of southward-facing limestone escarpments. Its summits rise from about 3,000 feet at its western end to over 10,000 feet in the east. Its gentler northern slopes are full of karstic solution features. In the eastern Caucasus, in Dagestan, these forward limestone ranges form a confused mass of mountain blocks separated by deep canyons and broken up by ravines and gorges. Sometimes the rock masses are flattish-topped, while at others they appear as enormous up-tilted humps. Occasionally the highland feature is a mass of shale, deeply eroded, but protected by a cap of resistant limestones, e.g. Mt Gunib (7,611 feet). There are also massive limestone plateaux, ranges and ridges to the south of the main chains. Their surfaces are pitted with solution hollows and, owing to the extreme porosity of the rock, often quite waterless. Large subterranean caverns with stalactites and stalagmites abound. The highest of these southern ranges, the Svanetsky, rises to 13,171 feet in Mt Layla, which has small glaciers (Fig. 57).

In Kamchatka and the Kurile Islands, the Soviet Union possesses part of the circum-Pacific fault line through which the underlying heated interior of the earth makes contact with the surface through volcanic activity. Earthquakes are common and do much damage. Kamchatka has 150 volcanoes, twenty-eight of which are not yet extinct. They lie in groups on the two parallel ranges of mountains that form the backbone of the peninsula, but all the active ones are on the eastern range. These produce, periodically, great clouds of gas, and scatter dust and ashes over the snow, ice and tundra of the high mountain zone. Their eruptions may be so explosive as to alter their outline and change the landscape of the surrounding country with an outpouring of immense quantities of lava. Mt Bezymianny, which experienced a violent eruption in 1956, sent dust 27 miles up into the stratosphere, and ended with a completely different profile. The recently extinct volcanoes are distinguished by their conical form and the *calderas* and collar-like *sommas* that surround their craters. Those long extinct have often lost their symmetrical conical shape, but leave behind picturesque ruins – often volcanic 'necks' like the *puys* of Auvergne in France.

The greatest of all the volcanoes of Kamchatka is the symmetrical cone of Klyuchevsky, whose summit is 15,912 feet above sea-level, with a crater 300 yards wide and 160 feet deep. In its 1907 eruption it expelled over three billion cubic metres of ash, the sky became dark in daytime, and the snow in the surrounding country was so thickly covered that sledges could not be used in Petropavlovsk. In 1935, the volcano rained hot glowing stones. It erupted again in 1945 and in 1954.[2]

Hot springs are associated with this volcanic activity. South of the active volcano Kronoz (11,575 feet) lies the valley of the appropriately-named Geyser river – it has more than twenty geysers and is noisy with rumbling and hissing. This rocky valley is full of steam, and mineral deposits have painted the rocks red, pink, violet and brown. The largest of them, Velikan, shoots up a hundred-foot jet of almost boiling water ($95°$–$97°$ C) for four minutes every three hours. The steam cloud above it rises a thousand feet.

The highest summit of the Caucasus Mountains – Elbruz (18,481 feet) – is an extinct volcano, built upon the central nucleus of ancient rocks that forms the high central ranges. Not only does it stand out above the other peaks, but its gentle concave slopes, its twin summits and the saddle between them, are features quite distinct from the rest of the mountain landscape. Kazbek (16,559 feet) also is a prominent Caucasus volcanic peak, its snow cap in summer distinguishing it from the heights around.

A considerable area of the Soviet highlands does not possess a truly mountainous relief, but has a flattish, rounded or undulating appearance, broken here and there by higher summits, that may themselves be either rounded or given sharper relief by ice action. Most often, this absence of strong relief is a result of aeons of erosion. All but the hardest rocks have been worn down, and the largely levelled surface has been re-elevated in a subsequent upheaval. Relatively low, rounded relief is typical of large areas in the eastern Carpathians, the central Urals, the mountains of Transbaykalia and the Far East. When covered by coniferous forest, these rounded massifs resemble the mountains of Central Europe or the Appalachians. Locally, 'tors' of granite or gneiss give a more rugged picture. In the Pamirs and Sayan Mountains, extensive plateau surfaces are found at great heights. In the East Sayan they are plentiful at about 6,000 feet, and in the Pamirs at 10,000 and 12,000 feet. They often form platforms from which the highest crests rise to heights above sea-level of 20,000 feet or more. These lofty surfaces are often covered with broken rock and boulders.

Lakes, small and large, contribute to many mountain landscapes. Sometimes they are the round pools that occupy the hollows of glacial cirques near

59. *The northern slopes of the Great Caucasus mountains*

summits. Often they result from the deepening of a valley by glacial excavation, or its damming up by glacial moraine. In limestone areas, they can occur because a solution hollow in the rock has been blocked up by impermeable material. In the eastern Pamirs, Lake Karakul lies at about 13,000 feet above sea-level. Its still blue water, fringed with green, forms an oasis in a grey-yellow desert basin which is framed with mighty snow-capped peaks. In winter its surface freezes a yard thick. Another Pamir lake, Sarez, in the upper valley of the Murgab, has an unusual origin. In 1911 an earth tremor brought down a great mountain wall, 2,600 feet high and 3 miles long, into the valley. This dammed up the stream, and formed a lake 37 miles long and up to 1,600 feet deep. Another remarkable lake is Mertzbaher, 11,000 feet up amid snowy Tyan

Shan peaks. Every summer, as a result of the movement of glaciers, it disappears for a time, exposing some fantastically-shaped rock forms on its stony bed.

The Kungeya and Terskey ranges of the Tyan Shan, both with snow-capped peaks over 15,000 feet, enclose the large 112-mile-long Issyk-Kul (5,328 feet a.s.l.). A hot spring feeds it, whence its name which means 'hot lake'. It does not freeze in winter, and Przhevalsk, near its eastern end, is warmer in winter than Alma-Ata, 3,000 feet below. There is a strong contrast between the desert surroundings of the dry western end of the lake and the well-watered eastern end, from which forested slopes rise directly from the water's edge.

Lake Baykal – nearly 400 miles long, up to 50 miles wide, with an area of 13,400 square miles – occupies a deep chasm in the Baykalian Mountains. It is the deepest lake in the world – 5,315 feet. It is also the largest fresh-water lake in the USSR. Around its dark green waters rise the forested slopes of the mountains, but in winter its surface is white with ice and snow. On the volcanoes of Kamchatka and the Kuriles there are some crater lakes, notably the 400-feet-deep pool that occupies the crater of Kronoz.

Most of the Soviet mountains have undergone recent uplift, and the 're-juvenated' rivers are busily cutting down into the rocks, leaving their old valley bottoms above them as terraces. Where they come upon very resistant material they are less able to do this, but cross them in turbulent rapids, plunging down in falls as soon as less resistant rock is reached. Where the mountains are built of such hard rocks, the streams can carry little away with them and are always crystal clear; but where they have been able to attack softer schists and shales, their waters are muddy. The hardest rocks, however, are not proof against the shattering effect of frost, which constantly loosens and breaks up large masses of rock which fall into the valleys. These have usually also inherited morainic material – unassorted boulders, stones, gravels and sands – from the Ice Age. Consequently, mountain valleys often have a wild and chaotic appearance.

This chaos is strongest at high altitudes and high latitudes. Lower down and farther south, valleys tend to have gentler slopes, more soil and a more varied vegetation. Most of the valleys of the low central Urals are broad and open, though that of the Chusovaya is often bordered by perpendicular walls of bare rock instead of the usual forest. In the Crimea and Caucasus, despite the frequency of steep gorges cut into the limestones, many of the lower valleys are beautifully adorned with wild orchards and subtropical vegetation.

The climatic aspect of the landscape distinguishes the Amur valley and the Soviet Far East from the rest of the country. It has a strong monsoonal element, and almost all the annual rainfall is concentrated in summer, which is therefore a wet, cool and cloudy season. Because there is so little snow to melt, the floods in the valleys come, not in spring as elsewhere in the USSR, but in summer. Winters are cold and dry.

Valleys leading up to high mountains are subject to special climatic phenomena. The commonest of these is the föhn, a warm wind which, sweeping down the valley, raises temperatures sharply, and quickly melts the snow and dries up the vegetation. At Tashkent in Central Asia it is most frequent in February, when it soon dispels all trace of winter. In the Altay valleys its frequency – about a hundred days a year – is an important factor in the formation of a steppe grassland rather than a forest landscape.

Heavy rains on the mountains, coinciding with spring and early summer snow-melt, can funnel enormous quantities of water into the valleys, sometimes with catastrophic effect. There is much loose material available in the upper reaches and a really powerful torrent is able to bring it down the valley. Such an onrush of water and rubble descended the Transili Alatau as far as Alma-Ata early in July 1921. The weight of rock, sand, trees, etc., brought down was estimated at between 1 and 5 million tons and its volume at 10 million cubic metres. In April 1967 a similar combination of heavy rain with melting snow brought down destructive floods of water, rubble and mud on to many settlements at the foot of the Tyan Shan. Cotton fields were ruined, and in the towns of Samarkand, Andizhan, Zhalalabad and Fergana buildings were destroyed and lives lost.

As air cools on mountain tops and slopes, it becomes denser and heavier and drains downwards to the valley bottom. Hence, if there is no wind, valley bottoms may become intensely cold, colder even than the mountains above them. In Central Asia, almond trees and vines often suffer from frost at Tashkent (1,584 feet), but go unscathed in the nearby mountains at heights of up to 6,000 feet. When it is a regular feature of the local climate, this winter phenomenon of 'temperature inversion' produces a reversal of the normal vegetation zoning. Thus some valleys in the northern Urals have a tundra vegetation, while larch trees grow on the slopes above.

In the Soviet Far East, the frontier with China ceases to be mountainous, but follows the river Amur and its right-bank tributary, the Ussuri. Travelling north from Vladivostok to Khabarovsk, the Ussuri plain is flat and swampy, rising eastwards to the foothills of the Sikhote. Away from the river swamps, the forest cover here was a rich Manchurian broadleaved forest, made up of oriental species of oak, elm, ash, walnut, apple, plum, the cork tree, with wild vines and other creepers. Westwards from Khabarovsk for 200 miles the Amur valley is very flat and swampy, and floods widely. Birches, willows and oak (*Quercus mongolica*) grow here and there. This plain ends where forested spurs from the Bureya Mountains come south to the Amur. To the northwest extends another 200-mile-long plain as far as Blagoveshchensk and the Zeya. Here there were steppes along the Amur, with a forest, principally of Mongolian oak and black and white birch farther from the river. The level country is broken here and there by low mounds formed by volcanic basalt 'necks'. The river valleys are boggy, with poplars growing among the swamps. Beyond the Zeya, still farther to the northwest, the Amur lands become rolling plains, increasing in height and relief until the Transbaykalian Mountains are reached.

Cultural landscapes

The mountains of the USSR offer many resources: the forests that usually clothe their flanks; water reserves, held frozen in snow and ice and poured abundantly forth in mountain torrents; metals, raised from the depths by ancient upheavals and so made accessible to modern mining techniques; mineral springs, attractive scenery, clean fresh air, and sporting opportunities for health and recreation. Within them also are valleys and plateaux, sheltered and well watered, with possibilities for agriculture and communications. On the other hand, steep slopes and rugged topography, thin and stony soils, and severe climate have been obstacles to human settlement and exploitation.

The ranges most vigorously exploited by lumberjacks are the Soviet Carpathians, the Urals, and those regions of the Far East that adjoin the Amur valley and the Pacific Ocean. Accessibility determines which areas shall be worked. Hence it is those slopes of the Urals which are near the Kama system that produce most timber. The Kama is part of the great Russian waterway network, enabling Uralian timber to descend the Volga to the Volgograd sawmills or to reach the Industrial Centre via the Oka. The Carpathians possess valuable stands of hardwood which form the basis of the West Ukrainian furniture industry, notably at Ivano-Frankovsk (169,000). The new Baykal–Amur railway (BAM), which runs for 2,000 miles from Lake Baykal to the Pacific, at a distance of between 100 and 400 miles north of the Trans-Siberian, has opened up a vast new timber country in Eastern Siberia and the Far East which is remarkably rich in useful species, hardwoods as well as softwoods. Timber accounts for between a third and a quarter of the freight carried by the railway. All the lumbering areas have wood-processing plants, and it is planned to build several in the BAM zone.

The exploitation of minerals in the mountains dates from the Soviet period, with the exception of Uralian iron and copper and East Siberian gold. Peter I established iron- and copper-smelting works in the Urals, using local ore and charcoal and the skill of men who had been working small forges and foundries in the region. The first of these began to produce pig-iron in 1701. During the eighteenth century, the Ural industry spread and became, for a time, the leading producer of iron and copper in the world. The Urals have since proved to hold a wider range of mineral wealth than any other comparable part of the earth's surface.[3] Coal production is mostly lignite and used to generate electricity.

Many of the iron-ore bodies have now been depleted, but the large Kachkanar reserves near Nizhny Tagil continue to be worked. The world's largest deposits of the steel-strengthening alloy, vanadium, also at Kachkanar, are mined on a large scale. Huge deposits of asbestos are worked near Sverdlovsk, notably at Asbest (80,000), accounting for half the world output. Power is supplied from the coal-burning Reftinsky station (2,300 MW). Also in Sverdlovsk oblast is the Beloyarsk nuclear power station (900 MW) with its fast-breeder reactor. Three high-voltage transmission lines cross the Urals.

Until the late 1950s the Caucasus region (Azerbaydzhan SSR) was vital to Russia as her major producer of petroleum, and the forests of derricks around Baku, Grozny and other places, testifies to a history of oil-drilling going well back into the nineteenth century. The Baku area remains a leading refinery region, with complicated mazes of cylinders, spheres and pipes. The Caucasus is still an important producer of manganese, molybdenum and tungsten, all vital to the country's steel industry, and of copper and zinc, while good-quality coal is found in the west. Caucasus mines are often on difficult mountain slopes, necessitating conveying the ore to the processing plant by cable (Fig. 60).

The Tyan Shan Mountains of Central Asia also have rich and varied mineral wealth, and coal, lignite, salt, lead, zinc, iron ore, uranium, molybdenum, china clay, fluorspar, etc. are all mined. The Fergana valley, thrust into the Central Asian Mountains east of Tashkent, gives access to a rich diversity of minerals: coal, lignite, oil, gas, polymetallic ores, antimony, mercury and uranium. The Altay Mountains of West Siberia have long been known for their metallic wealth. This consists mainly of lead, zinc and copper, mined around Leninogorsk, but also of iron ore and gold. In the Transbaykalian Mountains, at Gusinoozersk, 50 miles southwest of Ulan Ude, a large lignite deposit is worked to fuel a new thermal power plant built to supply electricity to Mongolia. Also in the Buryat republic, about a hundred miles northwest of Chita, a large lead–zinc working with an associated new town is planned. Farther east, among the Sayan Mountains, are rich reserves of coal, iron ore, molybdenum, titanium and phosphorite.

The great complex of mountain ranges that extends eastwards from the Lena river and Lake Baykal to the Pacific coast has gold, coal and lignite mines scattered widely over its vast extent. Tin and molybdenum mining is also found at many widely separated places. In the far northeast of Siberia a small nuclear power station (Bilibino, 48 MW) supplies the expanding gold- and tin-mining activities in the mountain tundra region. Further power has been brought to the gold-miners with the completion of the Kolyma hydro station (900 MW) in Magadan oblast. The great new BAM railway has opened up a harsh rugged territory which abounds in minerals: coal, lignite, iron, lead–zinc, copper, tin, molybdenum, nickel, chromite, gold, mercury, asbestos, apatite, graphite, mica. A branch line leaves the BAM at Tynda and runs north to Berkatit and the

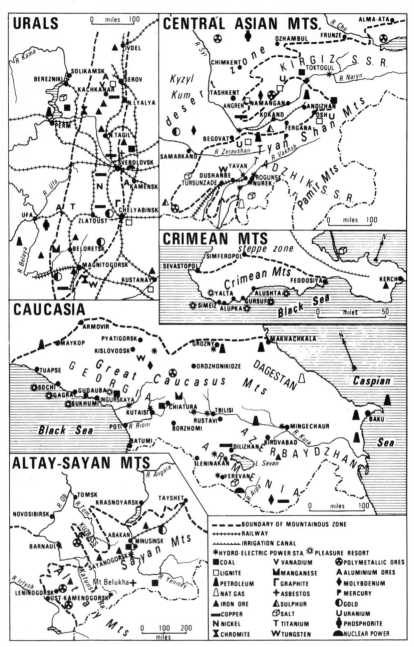

60. *The mountainous regions: economic development*

Neryungri coalfield, where an estimated 40 billion tons of coking coal lie in a great level mass. The open mining involves the removing and dumping of vast quantities of overburden to produce 13 million tons of coal a year: 9 million tons of coking coal travel to the Pacific coast for export to Japan; 4 million tons are fed into a large power station (ultimate capacity 2,400 MW). Offshore, on the island of Sakhalin, are valuable opencast coal-mines and oil wells, and a 380-mile-long oil pipeline runs from Okha in northern Sakhalin to the mainland to supply Komsomolsk and Khabarovsk.

During the Soviet period the water resources of the mountains have been increasingly used in the generation of electric power by damming up the valleys, thus creating large reservoirs and a fall of water to drive the turbines in the power stations. The construction of reservoirs also facilitates flood control and makes irrigation possible. The Caucasus region, with many small valleys and heavy precipitation in some areas, was ideal for the construction of the earlier power stations. The Minchegaur reservoir (1959) in Azerbaydzhan regulates the Kura river which used to flood disastrously in spring yet almost dry up in summer; it also provides irrigation water. The Inguri and Eristskali rivers, which flow into the Black Sea in western Georgia, have been dammed up to form a large reservoir. Power is generated at the Ingurskaya hydro station (1,300 MW) and at four small stations with a total capacity of 340 MW, all on the Eristskali. The Caucasus region also has a nuclear power station – the Armenian (810 MW).

In the Central Asian Mountains, the Vakhsh valley in southern Tadzhikstan has great hydroelectric potential. There is already the Nurek station (2,700 MW), while higher up the river at Rogunsk, an even more powerful installation (3,600 MW) is building. A large and varied industrial complex is being developed to use the power, including the Tursunzade aluminium smelter, and the Yavan electrochemical works which produces caustic soda and agricultural chemicals from local salt and limestone. The machine-building and textile industries of Dushanbe are being expanded. The Naryn valley in Kirgizia also has vast potential. It has developed a cascade of hydro stations, beginning with Shamaldy-Say (180 MW) in 1961, followed by Toktogul (1,200 MW), Kurpsay (800 MW) and Tashkumyr (450 MW). The Toktogul dam is 745 feet high: the power is used to work the varied mineral wealth of the Kirgiz Republic, while the reservoir, which took three years to fill, provides irrigation water.

The largest hydroelectric development in the world is the Sayano–Sushensk station (6,400 MW) under construction on the upper Yenisey in the Sayan Mountains of southern Siberia. The first of ten 640-MW units was brought into service early in 1979. Here are the three requisites for the building of a great new industrial complex in previously mountain wilderness: abundant cheap energy, a varied mineral resource, and accessibility, provided by a new railway – the electrified mountain line from Tayshet on the Trans-Siberian to Abakan, opened in 1965. Four industrial nodes are being formed, the new urban centres

61. *The valley of the Vakhsh river, the site of hydroelectric, irrigation and industrial projects now under construction*

of which will grow into large cities: Abakan (136,000) – non-ferrous metals, railcar-building, textiles, food-processing; Chernogorsk (74,000) – coal-mining, asbestos products, woollen textiles; Minusinsk (63,000) – electrical machinery, electrical goods; Sayanogorsk – ·aluminium smelting, prefabricated-building manufacture. Sayanogorsk, the youngest of the four, began life as the power-station construction base. The climatic conditions of the more sheltered parts of this southerly area enable the complex to have its own food base in intensive milk and meat production and the growing of spring wheat, vegetables and fruit. Wool is also produced locally for the Chernogorsk textile works.

Far Eastern power supplies have been boosted by the hydroelectric station on the Zeya (1,300 MW), where that tributary of the Amur is crossed by a highway linking the Trans-Siberian with BAM. Transmission lines run to various places along BAM and to Khabarovsk. A small geothermal station on Kamchatka uses hot geyser water to develop 11 MW, used in a nearby fish cannery.

In the Crimea and Caucasus, use for health and recreation has marked the landscape. The mountainous coasts are fringed by ever-lengthening resort development, and dotted with white villas, hotels, rest homes and sanatoria. Many of these were built by the aristocracy before the Revolution. Luxuriant plantations of subtropical vegetation – palms, cypresses, magnolias, etc. – are a distinctive feature of the resorts, most of which are growing rapidly as the holiday habit spreads in the USSR. Those on the east shore of the Black Sea are experiencing difficulty from the falling level of the land. This is taking place at the rate of an inch every twelve to fifteen years, and facilitates the erosion of the narrow coastal strips on which the resorts are built. To resist this, artificial beaches, groynes, shingle-traps and sea walls are being built, producing an increasingly artificial coastline. Sochi is the leading seaside resort in the USSR and its recent development finds expression in its resident population: 127,000 in 1959, 295,000 in 1981.

Away from the coast there are numerous spas in the Caucasus based on highly mineralized springs, e.g. Pyatigorsk and Kislovodsk in the north, Borzhomi and Dilizhan in the south. Also in the mountains are winter sports resorts, and lake resorts such as Lake Ritsa, whose waters carry many pleasure craft in summer. Even Lake Baykal, in distant eastern Siberia, is a resort area. Hydrofoils speed tourists across its waters in summer, just as lorries and cars use its frozen surface in winter. In the Caucasus there are also new permanent camp sites for young people, with cement paths and Nissen-type corrugated huts painted in many colours.

The mountainous regions of the USSR contain many valleys, basins and plateaux in which man has found it easier to settle, to make roads and railways, to pasture animals and sometimes to grow crops. In the lower valleys of the Caucasus and in Transcaucasia, wherever there is sufficient water, natural or artificial, subtropical crops are cultivated: tobacco, fruit, vines in the north, and tea, citrus, persimmon, avocados, olives, tung nuts, walnuts and winter vegetables in the hotter and better-sheltered areas of the south. Cotton, maize and mulberries are also grown, and in the extreme southeast, rice. Frosts are a menace, and near Sukhumi there are large greenhouses in which lemon plants are nurtured. Use of polythene sheeting now makes it possible to nurture young orange and lemon plants out of doors, and the long white plastic strips are

62. Harvesting tea by machinery in Georgia

increasingly seen in these subtropical fields. The most famous vineyards of the north are those of the Abrau-Dyurso state farm, where Soviet champagne is made. The Georgian tea fields are often vast, with straight rows of bushes stretching away to horizons made up of shelter-belt trees (Fig. 62).

The westernmost valleys and mountains of the Caucasus have a very heavy rainfall, and the ground is subject to periodic waterlogging. As a result, rural houses have steep roofs and are often built on piles. The broad valley of the Rioni, which opens on to the Black Sea, and is known as the Kolkhid lowland, was until recently malarial marshland. Much of this has been reclaimed during the Soviet period, and the land newly planted with trees from all over the world: cypresses, cedars, palms, magnolias, camellias, planes, tulip trees, cork oaks, bamboos, bananas, sugar cane, etc. The eucalyptus is especially valuable: it helps to drain the marshes and drives away mosquitoes with its odour.

In the Central Asian and Altay Mountains transhumance is common. The extensive steppes in the lower Altay valleys provide winter pastures, the snow cover often being negligible. In spring the shepherds move up to the forested zone where there are grassy glades, and in summer the high meadows are briefly usable. The valleys and basins are often too arid for agriculture, but irrigation water, associated with power-station construction, is increasingly available

Where water can be had, crops can be grown at surprisingly high altitudes – from 7,000 to 10,000 feet.

In the east the Amur and Ussuri valleys have become major agricultural regions, but the severity of winter and the wetness of summer are handicaps. Three-quarters of the farmland grows grain, and the laborious ridge and furrow method, whereby the seed is sown on the ridges, which are drained by the furrows, is often used on land that would otherwise be too wet. Flax, hemp and, locally, rice are also grown in the Ussuri valley. Sugar beet, soya beans and another oil-bearer, petilla, have increased their share of the sown area during the Soviet period. Despite its northerly location, the Kamchatka valley has some agriculture, mainly oats, barley and potatoes, and the geyser springs are used to heat hothouses. In the valleys of mountainous Yakutia, besides the mining settlements, there are a few villages of log huts inhabited by reindeer breeders and fur-trappers. Among such places are Verkhoyansk and Oymyakon, rivals for the distinction of having the lowest winter temperatures recorded, outside of Antarctica.

Railways hold the key to the development of the Soviet mountain belt. Not only are their engineering works landscape features in themselves, but they allow powerful economic forces access to new country and thus to do their own work of landscape transformation. The great BAM railway, built in the late 1970s and early 1980s through formidable territory, has tamed the most inhospitable terrain by means of numerous tunnels through ranges and ridges and innumerable bridges over rivers and streams: it has one tunnel nearly 10 miles long and one over 4 miles. Rail construction is followed by stations, access roads, settlements, tree felling, mines, quarries, factories and works. Rail-building is going on all the time somewhere in the belt – nothing as spectacular as BAM, but the closing of a gap here or an extension there. Thus in recent years a new line has crossed the Urals, which already have a well-developed network, making it possible for Magnitogorsk steel to go direct to Ufa; in the Caucasus the Krasnodar–Tuapse line has been completed across the western end of the range; and in Central Asia the Vakhsh valley railway from Termez has reached the new chemical town of Yavan.

Because of limited agricultural opportunities the farm population of the mountainous regions is relatively small. On the other hand, because of their mineral wealth and the concentration of communications upon a few strategically-placed points, the urban population is relatively large. The three largest cities of the Caucasus region are Tbilisi, Yerevan and Baku, the fast-growing capitals of the Georgian, Armenian and Azerbaydzhan Republics. Tbilisi (1,095,000) was a large town before the Revolution, and has some tsarist Russian buildings in classical style as well as old oriental quarters. And whereas many towns in the highland regions have situations not in themselves mountainous, Tbilisi is hemmed in by mountains. Much of it is built on difficult

63. *The Gusevogorsk mine of the Kachkanar ironfield in the Urals*

slopes ascended by cable cars, and the river Kura is here a steep-sided mountain torrent. Its industries are many and varied, principally machine-building, textiles and food-processing.

Yerevan was but a small and insignificant town before the Revolution. In 1926 its population was 65,000 and it stood sixty-second in rank among Soviet towns; in 1981 it had 1,055,000 inhabitants, ranking fourteenth. Its rapid growth is partly explained by the irrigation of the surrounding arid valleys and plateaux and by the building of hydroelectric power stations, but it cannot be explained wholly by geographical or economic factors. It owes much to the creative ability and commercial genius of the Armenian people for whom the Soviets have provided, after centuries of tribulation, a country and capital of their own. The use of rose-coloured volcanic tuff from local quarries gives Yerevan a distinctive appearance. This great city, having filled the plateau on which it was founded, has ascended the surrounding mountain slopes to such a height that the new quarters are 4,000 feet above the old. The skill of the people is shown in the type of modern industry practised in Yerevan and other Armenian towns: electronics, machine tools, precision instruments, electrical engineering, as well as synthetic rubber and other chemicals.

Baku (1,046,000) is a great oil city, and derricks and complex refinery plant cover extensive districts in and around the city. It also has machine-building, chemical and textile industries. There is an old quarter with palaces and mosques in the eastern style, and on the outskirts, districts made up of modern blocks. It is noteworthy for its racial mixture: besides Russians and Azerbaydzhanis, there are large Georgian, Jewish and Turkish populations. A funicular railway leads from the harbour to the upper part of the town. Other leading Caucasus towns are Grosny (379,000) an old-established oil-town; Ordzhonikidze (287,000), an historic gateway-city where the Terek valley provides a way southwards through the mountains to Tbilisi; and Makhachkala (269,000), an important Caspian port.

The two chief towns of the Crimea are Simferopol (314,000) and Sevastopol (315,000). Simferopol is inland among the northern foothills, and works up agricultural produce, but Sevastopol was founded where the sea enters a cleft in the rugged southwest coast of the peninsula, and soon became Russia's principal Black Sea naval base. The city has been twice destroyed – during the Crimean War siege of 1854–55 (349 days) and during the 1941–42 siege (250 days). It has been rebuilt with neo-classical style buildings in gleaming white, half-concealed amongst the trees and orchards, descending in terraces to the sea.

The leading Uralian towns made dramatic progress in the early Soviet period, when the historic metallurgical industry was renovated and machine-building industries established. The older centres were expanded and new towns built. The 1941–5 war intensified their development, but of late years the growth of many of them has slackened off, it being difficult to attract people to their harsh environment (Table 18).

TABLE 18. *Population and rank of principal Uralian towns (thousands)*

	1926	1939	1959	1981
Sverdlovsk	140 (20th)	426 (14th)	779 (9th)	1,239 (9th)
Chelyabinsk	59 (69th)	273 (25th)	689 (13th)	1,055 (14th)
Magnitogorsk		146 (57th)	311 (41st)	413 (63rd)
Nizhny Tagil	39	160 (51st)	338 (38th)	404 (66th)
Zlatoust	48 (92nd)	99 (85th)	161 (89th)	201 (144th)
Kamensk–Uralsky		51	141 (106th)	191 (151st)
Miass		38	98 (149th)	153 (180th)

Note: Perm and Izhevsk, usually regarded as Ural cities, have here been included in the Forest Belt (see Table 5)

Sverdlovsk (Yekaterinburg) and Nizhny Tagil were founded as iron-working towns by Peter I in the early years of the eighteenth century, but Magnitogorsk is wholly the creation of the past fifty years. Sverdlovsk, an almost entirely wooden town before the Revolution, has been transformed with large austere modern buildings; but several of the magnificent mansions built by prosperous eighteenth-century ironmasters and gold-mine proprietors have been preserved. Even before the Revolution it made steam engines, mining machinery, nails and roofing iron, and is now probably the leading machine-building centre of the Union after Gorky.

Chelyabinsk has its own steelworks and concentrates on the production of large-diameter pipe for the fast-growing pipeline system of the USSR. In Nizhny Tagil (founded 1700), blast furnaces, coke ovens, steel furnaces, all pouring forth smoke and lighting up the night sky with their glow, are a prominent part of the townscape, as they are at Magnitogorsk (founded 1931), site of the Soviet Union's largest steelworks, producing over 16 million tons a year.

In the Tyan Shan Mountains of Central Asia, the only large town is Dushanbe (510,000), capital of the Tadzhik Republic. In 1926 it was a mere village of 6,000 people. It lies in an irrigated cotton-growing valley, and steep mountain sides rise above it. The largest Altay town, Leninogorsk (68,000) serves a non-ferrous mining district, and is distinguished by its lead smelter.

The whole vast eastern mountain area has few cities (Table 19), most of them in valleys along the southernmost margins. Khabarovsk, strategically situated in the marshy flats of the Amur–Ussuri confluence, has expanded in the Soviet period to become the regional centre of the Soviet Far East, with machine building, chemical and wood-working industries. Topographically it is a flat town, whereas Vladivostok is built on a hilly promontory which projects into the fine natural harbour to which it owes its existence, and which is kept open in winter by ice-breakers. Founded in 1860, it grew rapidly as a seaport, industrial town and naval base. It builds and repairs ships and processes fish. On a bay 55 miles to the east, the new port of Nakhodka (139,000) has sprung up since the war. It is built at the foot of the Sikhote Alin range, and forested hills rise steeply in the background. Its new deepwater outport, Port Vostochny, has modern

64. Transbaykalia and the Far East

TABLE 19. *Population and rank of principal towns in the eastern mountain region (thousands)*

	1926	1959	1981
Vladivostok	108 (30th)	291 (46th)	565 (37th)
Khabarovsk	52 (82nd)	323 (40th)	545 (41st)
Chita	62 (68th)	172 (81st)	315 (83rd)
Ulan-Ude	29	174 (80th)	310 (88th)
Komsomolsk-on-Amur		177 (78th)	274 (104th)
Petropavlovsk (Kamchatka)	2	86 (178th)	223 (128th)

export terminals to ship coal and wood products to Japan and to handle containers.

Komsomolsk-on-Amur is the leading steel centre of the Soviet Far East, producing about $1\frac{1}{2}$ million tons a year from imported pig-iron and scrap. Close to Komsomolsk are Amursk, a pulp, paper and wood-chemicals town, built in the late 1960s, and Solnechny, a tin-mining centre. Magadan (128,000), on the bleak north shore of the Sea of Okhotsk, was founded in the 1930s as the base for the exploitation of the Kolyma goldfields, with which it is connected by motor road. At first it was a town of pioneers' tents, then of wooden houses, and now of stone and concrete buildings. Its streets are covered with snow for most of the year.

9
State policy and the environment

In the first years of Soviet power, Lenin's Marxist views on economic development prevailed. These demanded that all regions of the country should be developed according to their natural conditions, and that industry should be located close to energy sources and raw materials. The regions were to be delineated so that each had its own energy supply, and where possible this was to take the form of electric power, generated from coal, lignite, oil, peat or water power, whichever was locally available. Industries were to be varied so as to make the best use, not only of raw materials, but of available labour. And, because of the critical transport situation, inter-regional traffic was to be kept to the minimum.

During the 1930s these principles were increasingly sacrificed to excessive bureaucratic centralization, and decisions came to be made more and more in Moscow, often by Stalin himself, and with a growing disregard for local and natural conditions. There was a greater concern for the fulfilment of an arbitrarily proclaimed plan than for environmental conditions or economic costs. It was suggested that – despite Lenin's views – the state should 'feel quite unrestrained by the territorial distribution of raw materials and energy in deciding the location of an industrial site'.[1] Ambitious schemes were pushed through without any real economic appraisal of their value, diverting enormous amounts of capital from more reasonable but less dramatic use. Examples were the northern sea route and the establishment of local agriculture in the Arctic tundra region.

The imminent threat of war caused a swing of the pendulum back to excessive regional self-sufficiency. The Gosplan (State Planning) regions of 1938–40 were as far as possible to have their own energy, steel, raw material, agricultural and transport bases, so that, if cut off from the rest of the country, they could function as independent economic regions. These ideas, dominated by strategic considerations and transport conditions and conformable with some aspects of Marxist ideology, were continued by Stalin after the war, and they underlay the 1946–50 reconstruction plan and its thirteen Gosplan regions. But ambitious and costly schemes, linked with the personal glorification of Stalin and often without adequate scientific preparation, continued to be proclaimed. Such were the 'Great Stalinist Plans for the Transformation of Nature'. The steppes were to be criss-crossed by tree belts; the Volga was to be converted by hydroelectric dams into a series of great lakes; vast areas of arid land were to be irrigated; the Ob and the Yenisey were to be turned round and sent to water the deserts of Central Asia; nuclear power stations were to heat up the waters of the Arctic; the climate of Siberia was to be changed. The afforestation of the steppes was effected with considerable success; and with the opening of the Cheboksary power station, the Great Volga scheme may be said to have been completed. Irrigation also was successfully expanded. But the other schemes were shelved.

Stalin outdid Canute. Soviet society, provided it was guided by his unique genius, was master of nature. He had but to design a plan for the conquest of some great physical obstacle and, whatever the difficulty, the cost, or the sacrifice involved, Soviet man would fulfil it. Saushkin has written: 'It is difficult to estimate the losses caused to the Soviet economy by voluntarism (i.e. following man's will regardless of natural conditions), including voluntarism in location, but they must have been great.'[2]

Stalin's contempt for nature and his delight in asserting man's ability to conquer it – under his leadership – regardless of the cost and consequences, was linked with his view of the geographical environment as the 'nature that surrounds society'. Nature was to be regarded as static, and society (i.e. Soviet society) as dynamic. They operated according to quite different laws and must therefore be studied separately. As Stalin allowed no views to be expressed that differed from his own, the idea of an integrated geographical environment, consisting of the natural environment as modified by man and influencing as well as influenced by society, could not be voiced. Physical geography and human geography became distinct and separate studies. Stalin could scarcely be blamed for this crude anti-environmentalism, because it was adopted by many in the western world who claimed to be geographers.

Since Stalin's death in 1953 'voluntarism', implying that Soviet society can do as it chooses in defiance of nature, and the geographical anti-environmentalism that went with it, have been officially and academically discredited. The necessity of working with rather than against nature has been recognized. The need for scientifically appraising, not only the economic costs, but also the consequences – both natural and social – of every interference with the geographical environment has been asserted. Regional self-sufficiency is to be balanced by regional specialization, but such specialization must fit into the framework of an industrial complex so as to make the fullest use of the geographical environment and the human resource.

Khrushchev was also criticized for 'wild and harebrained schemes'. In his agricultural policy he continued the Stalinist attitude. In 1965, Anuchin wrote:

A stereotyped approach, caused by the lack of a geographic evaluation of lands (which vary so widely over the territory of our enormous country), has led in the recent past to repeated attempts to impose in all regions a given cropping system or even a particular crop that had suddenly become 'fashionable'. It goes without saying that this had a harmful effect on agricultural production.[3]

Since Khrushchev's departure (1964) the emphasis has been on more local area studies before decisons as to land use are made.

State policy and the landscape

The form and political complexion of government and the nature of society are not without effect upon the landscape. Paris and Petersburg, as residences of absolute monarchs who commanded the wealth of their states and concentrated it in their capitals, outshone London in splendour in the eighteenth century. But the English countryside, with its opulent mansions and well-kept cottages, contrasted with the poverty-stricken rural scene of much of France and Russia. Today Soviet power and Communist ideology also find expression in landscape and townscape alike.

All landscape-affecting activity is controlled by the Communist Party and the various government bodies or agencies which it dominates. Although only about 5 per cent of the population belong to the Party, they consist of the most politically conscious, active and ambitious members of society; candidates for membership undergo a rigorous period of training, probation and examination before being admitted. Members are expected to foster loyalty to the state, efficiency in administration, productivity in industry, honesty and integrity in socialist enterprise, and a high moral standard of behaviour in all aspects of public and family life. Through them the Party is everywhere, advising, supervising, agitating, criticizing, encouraging. Through them it counters the tendency of socialist bureaucracies to be conservative and lethargic.

Government by a single party does not mean that there is no debate about policy. Within the CPSU there is argument, for instance, between those who wish to see most investment go to develop the harsh eastern regions of Siberia, and those who think it wiser to concentrate it in the west, in Russia proper. For many reasons the balance has tilted towards a western policy, although large enterprises continue to be undertaken in the east. Increasing integration with the countries of eastern Europe favours western development, as does the scarcity of labour in the east and the reluctance of people to settle there. Since most of the resources of fuel, power and raw materials are in the east, a western policy is inevitably reflected in more transport. Thus in 1977 a new rail crossing of the Urals was accomplished, enabling steel from Magnitogorsk to move directly westwards. One of the USSR's few modern motorways was built in the 1970s from Chelyabinsk, east of the Urals, to Moscow via Ufa, Kazan and Gorky.

Since 1980 a wide-diameter pipeline has been laid from Surgut in the West Siberian oilfield to the petrochemical town of Polotsk in Belorussia, while six new 56-inch-diameter pipelines make their way westwards from the West Siberian gasfields across the Urals: one to Moscow and the Centre region, then on to Belorussia and Poland; two to the Kursk region at Yelets; one to the Czech frontier at Uzhgorod; one to Petrovsk, between Penza and Saratov in the Volga region; and one to Novopskov in the northwest Ukraine. Another 56-inch-diameter pipeline runs from the Orenburg gasfield, in the southern Urals, to Uzhgorod. From the terminals smaller pipes will distribute the gas to industrial centres. Although mostly underground, these pipelines leave their mark on the landscape at intervals with their compressor stations and the overhead cables which bring them power. During the 1981–85 plan period it is planned to complete the first stage of a 1,500 kV DC transmission line to bring electricity from the Ekibastuz complex of power stations to the Centre region.

State policy has also led recently to movement to the coastal regions. In the prerevolutionary period, industrial growth was largely bound up with overseas trade – in the 1897 census six of the twelve largest cities in Russia were ports. But the new Soviet government, determined upon self-sufficiency, developed the resources of the interior, and the importance of foreign trade sharply declined. In the 1959 census Leningrad was the only seaport among the twelve top towns. However, since the 1960s, growing surpluses of minerals and shortages of foodstuffs, as well as a more liberal attitude to external ties, has led to a striking increase in the participation of the Soviet Union in world trade. In 1982 Soviet trade by value was a tenth the size of the GNP, compared with only a thirtieth in 1960 and 1970 (Table 20). Besides busier seaports, the Soviet coastline, in the last few years, has seen the building of modern export terminals, notably Yuzhny on the Black Sea, Ventspils on the Baltic coast, and Vostochny on the Pacific.

Another aspect of the landscape impact of the concentration of economic power in the hands of the state is 'giantism' – the building of industrial plants on a larger scale than would normally be found elsewhere. Thus, although America still produces more electricity than the USSR, the latter has more very large power stations. Control of capital investment enables the Soviets to build plants of an optimum size for the physical or economic conditions, however large that may be. Private American utility companies cannot afford to do this, and it is noteworthy that the largest American plants, comparable to those of the Soviet Union, are those built by the Federal government (Table 21).

Although it would be wrong to say that public opinion is ignored in the Soviet Union – an important function of the CPSU is to transmit it to the very top – it clearly does not have the same effect upon industrial location as it does in America, where it is impossible to locate an oil refinery, a nuclear power station or a petrochemical works in some districts because of democratically-expressed hostile public opinion. The same state power facilitates a higher degree of capital

TABLE 20. *Foreign trade of the USSR as a percentage of the GNP*

	GNP (billion rubles)	TRADE (billion rubles)	PERCENTAGE
1980	1,072·3	94·1	8·8
1975	862·6	50·7	5·9
1970	643·5	22·1	3·4
1965	420·2	14·6	3·5
1960	304·0	10·1	3·3

Note: In 1980 the foreign trade of USA as a percentage of GNP was 16 per cent.

investment in producers' goods and a lower disposable income for consumers' goods. This lower income finds visible expression in concentrations of large blocks of apartments rather than an urban sprawl of individual houses with gardens, in few cars and fewer roads to carry them, and in a freedom from outside advertising signs and hoardings, though not from political slogans. It is reflected too in far less domestic waste and pollution for there is much less packaging to dispose of.

TABLE 21. *Largest Soviet and American hydroelectric power stations (capacity in MW)*

USSR		USA	
Sayano-Sushensk[1]	6,400	Grand Coulee[5]	6,180
Krasnoyarsk[1]	6,000	John Day[5]	2,160
Bratsk[2]	4,500	Chief Joseph [5]	2,069
Ust-Ilimsk[2]	3,800	Moses [6]	1,950
Nurek[3]	2,700	The Dalles[5]	1,807
Volgograd[4]	2,500	Hoover[7]	1,340

[1]Yenisey river
[2]Angara river
[3]Vakhsh river
[4]Volga river

[5]Columbia river
[6]Niagara river
[7]Colorado river

Economic administration and the landscape

The state finds serious problems in organizing the economy from above. The present organization is basically sectoral – i.e. there is a separate ministry or government department for each and every form of economic activity. The matter is further complicated by the existence of All-Union and Republican ministries, with sometimes one, sometimes the other, and sometimes both responsible for a branch of the economy. Because of their long cumbersome names, contractions are normally used, e.g.:

Mingasprom SSSR – ministry of the gas industry, USSR
Minneftegazstroy SSSR – ministry of oil and gas construction, USSR
Minkhimprom SSSR – ministry of the chemical industry, USSR
Minpromstroy SSSR – ministry of industrial building, USSR
Minavtoprom SSSR – ministry of the automotive industry, USSR
Minstroy SSSR – ministry of construction, USSR
Mintsvetmet SSSR – ministry of non-ferrous metallurgy, USSR
Minavtotrans RSFSR – ministry of motor transport, RSFSR
Minsel'stroy Lit. SSR – ministry of farm construction, Lithuanian SSR

Above the ministries are coordinating state agencies like Gosplan SSSR (the state planning agency), and below them are *glavki* (sectoral, specialized or regional departments). Below the *glavki*, and sometimes directly under the ministries, are the *obyedinyeniye* or *tresty*, the various groupings of enterprises (*predpriyatiye*), which form the bottom tier of the administrative structure.

A modern economy is highly intricate, and does not lend itself to management by separate and independent sectoral bodies pursuing their own priorities. Even with the best will in the world it is difficult to coordinate and synchronize the work of departments having their own programmes and plans. As a result, a striking feature of the Soviet industrial landscape is the number of buildings uncompleted and works standing idle while waiting for some essential supply. Often the problem is solved by the customer ministry attempting itself to do the work of other ministries, although ill fitted to do so, and thereby dislocating its own plan-fulfilment prospects. For example, Minavtoprom SSSR has the greatest difficulty in persuading the ministry of construction to undertake its reconstruction work: 'No. 7 *trest* of Minstroy SSSR practically refused to accept the contract for the reconstruction of the assembly building at the Gorky motor works, and the AvtoGAZ association was compelled to do the work itself.'[4] Minavtotrans RSFSR has a grievance against Minavtoprom, complaining of a shortage of special-purpose vehicles which results in motor-transport undertakings having to assemble their own, 'using parts taken from dismantled vehicles'; not surprisingly, 'such small-scale vehicle building by motor-transport enterprises is very costly and the quality of the vehicles so produced is not high'.[5] In the building of the new railway from Tyumen to Urengoy, 'the ministries of communication and of transport construction "forgot" about laying connecting lines to adjoining factories and works. And now those enterprises themselves, although without experience in such work, are having to build each its own branch line.'[6] Some idea of the administrative complexity can be gauged from these words of the head of Mingazprom:

> We hope that the combined efforts of the ministry of oil and gas construction, the ministry of industrial construction, the ministry of electric power, the ministry of power equipment manufacturing, the ministry of chemical equipment manufacturing, the ministry of shipbuilding, the ministry of instrument manufacturing, and related ministries will help speed the completion of the required gas pipeline systems and supply reliable high-capacity compressor stations.[7]

Sectoral administration of the economy by independent ministries leads to wasteful duplication. To safeguard themselves against the failure of external suppliers they aim for self-sufficiency by building their own facilities such as repair shops and organizing their own services such as motor transport. For instance, if a departmental vehicle breaks down somewhere where the ministry owning it does not have a repair facility, it may have to be 'transported by road or rail enormous distances, through many oblasts and krays, thousands of kilometres' to one of its own garages, even though facilities belonging to another ministry are close at hand.[8] Khrushchev tried to tackle this problem: industrial undertakings, instead of being organized by function under central ministries, were grouped regionally under a regional economic council (*sovnarkhoz*) in the hope that adjacent works within a region would be able the more readily to supply each other, and that they would share common facilities – having, say, one large and efficient machine-tool repair shop between them instead of a dozen small and inefficient ones.

Unfortunately the sovnarkhozy soon gave rise to problems similar to those that had led to the abolition of the ministerial structure. Whereas previously the enterprises in one ministry had found insuperable difficulties in getting satisfactory supplies from the undertakings of another, the enterprises grouped within one sovnarkhoz now began to experience similar difficulties when dealing with those of another. As a result, the sovnarkhozy now also began to strive for self-sufficiency, developing economic functions better discharged elsewhere. Ministry control centralized in Moscow was fully restored in 1965, after Khrushchev's fall, without the problems of interdependence having been solved.

TERRITORIAL PRODUCTION COMPLEXES. Endeavours to secure regional cooperation now focus on the 'territorial production complex' (*territorial'no-proizvodstvennyy kompleks* or TPK), a planned and co-ordinated regional development by several ministries in association. The landscape implications are strong, because a TPK is a large complex of industries requiring a full range of services and one or more large industrial and urban nodes, whereas the same degree of development undertaken by ministries acting independently would have resulted in scattered and unco-ordinated developments, poorly supplied with services and offering only rough accommodation to workers; at best there would be a single-industry-dominated 'company town'. This was the nature of eastern development before the introduction of the TPK.

TPKs are planned by Gosplan. Prerequisites are: a local energy supply and raw materials upon which a complex of industries can be developed; existing or potential transport accessibility; and territory capable of supplying at least some food requirements. Manufacturing activity is concentrated in one or more urban centres known as 'industrial nodes', with employment opportunities for women as well as men, so that a couple's joint income will enable them to afford the amenities offered by a new and well-equipped town. There should be scope for expansion and the employment of what it is hoped – because of acute labour shortage – will be a growing population. Existing developing TPKs are listed below and shown in Fig. 65.

1. KMA, Russia (RSFSR: Belgorod oblast), see p. 106–7.
2. MANGYSHLAK, Kazakhstan (Kazakh SSR: Guryev oblast), see p. 145.
3. LOWER KAMA, Russia (RSFSR: Tatar ASSR), see p. 108.
4. ORENBURG, Russia (RSFSR: Orenburg oblast), see p. 122–3.
5. TIMANO–PECHORA, Russia (RSFSR: Komi ASSR), see p. 52, 72.
6. WEST SIBERIA, Siberia (RSFSR: Tyumen oblast), see p. 75–6.
7. SOUTH TADZHIK, Central Asia (Tadzhik SSR), see p. 164.
8. KARATAU–DZHAMBUL, Kazakhstan (Kazakh SSR: Dzhambul oblast), see p. 143, 145.
9. PAVLODAR–EKIBASTUZ, Kazakhstan (Kazakh SSR: Pavlodar oblast), see p. 124.
10. KANSK–ACHINSK, Siberia (RSFSR: Krasnoyarsk kray), see p. 113.
11. SAYAN, Siberia (RSFSR: Krasnoyarsk kray), see p. 164–5.
12. BRATSK–USTILIMSK, Siberia (RSFSR: Krasnoyarsk kray), see p. 78.
13. SOUTH YAKUTIA, Siberia (RSFSR: Yakut ASSR), see p. 162–3.

The opening of BAM in 1983 is expected to lead to the formation of several more Siberian and Far Eastern TPKs, among which the following have been mentioned: North Baykal (nickel, chromite, molybdenum, asbestos, mercury, polymetallic ores), Upper Lena (lignite, polymetallic ores), North Chita (coking coal, lead–zinc at Ozerny, copper at Udokan), Zeya-Svobodny (hydroelectric power, lignite, iron, cement and glass at Shimanovsk), Komsomolsk.

TPKs do not have a uniform system of administration. The West Siberian is administered by an interdepartmental Gosplan commission based in Tyumen, but the KMA is run by the Party committee (*obkom*) of Belgorod oblast. The Sayan complex, which forms part of Krasnoyarsk kray, is administered by the kray Party committee's planning commission. It remains a problem, however, how to overcome ministerial independence of action, and the theory of the TPK does not always work out too well in practice. To avoid duplication, the planners often give one ministry the task of providing facilities to be shared by others. Thus, according to the chairman of the Sayan TPK's planning commission, Mintsvetmet SSSR, which was put in charge of building the Sayanogorsk town and industrial node, 'has, on various pretexts, delayed for five years building the hot-water plants. It has built one for its own works while disregarding the hot-water needs of the town of Sayanogorsk and the prefabricated-building combine.' Mintsvetmet had also failed to pay its agreed quota of the costs of shared facilities at the Minusinsk industrial node to the ministry responsible for providing them, whereupon that ministry built them for its own needs only. The trouble is that the plans of TPKs are not mandatory upon ministries, and as the chairman says, 'the resolution of this question will not brook delay'.[9]

Even when ministries are persuaded to co-operate with each other within a

65. *Territorial production complexes; the numbers relate to the list of these complexes in the text; no. 13 lies to the east of the area covered by the map*

TPK, it may be difficult to get their subordinate enterprises to give up their independent facilities. Thus, in Kazakhstan,

> an unresolved problem remains the co-operation and specialization of the subsidiary enterprises. In practically all TPKs small foundry shops work side by side – these and other services are not centralized. All this leads to dearer production.[10]

It cost, for instance, twice as much to make castings at the Dzhambul works of Minkhimprom as at a nearby foundry belonging to another ministry. This duplication is wasteful of scarce labour as well as of finance.

Soviet roads and the landscape

Although the USSR has seen a remarkable upsurge of economic activity, this has been restricted to relatively few areas and zones by the sheer inaccessibility of so much of its territory. Unlike other advanced countries it does not have an all-pervasive system of roads and railways. The USA has on average 0.58 km of road or rail for every km^2 of its territory (including Alaska), whereas the figure for the USSR is only 0.04 km per km^2. This means that whereas almost all of America is open to exploitation, only a relatively small and discrete part of the Soviet Union is readily available for development. The disparity with the countries of western Europe is much greater even than that with the USA. In these countries one is seldom without the sight of a road or the sound of traffic. But in the Soviet Union vast expanses, including settled regions, are far removed from road and rail and have to rely on sledges in winter and on streams in summer for transport. The small-river department of the ministry of the river fleet RSFSR transports about 18 million tons of goods a year to otherwise wholly isolated settlements.[11]

There are about 450,000 miles of hard-surfaced road in the USSR, under half of which have a concrete or tarmacadam surface. Often only a narrow strip is tarred and one vehicle has to turn aside if it meets another. Russian motor roads are not only relatively few, but usually in a bad condition, to which both geology and climate contribute. There is a lack of readily available road-building material: the northern parts of the country are covered with glacial drift, while alluvial and aeolian deposits, notably the fine-grained powdery loess, are extensive over the south, and in neither case can a firm road bed be made with local resources. Although much of the country is fairly uniform in relief, this apparent advantage is offset by its extrememly dense drainage network, necessitating the provision of an extraordinarily large number of bridges and culverts. Rivers, streams and rivulets are a problem not merely because of their excessive numbers, but also because of their seasonal behaviour: although frozen in winter and shallow in late summer and autumn, they swell in spring to many times their normal size, and the speed and volume of their waters, reinforced by masses of ice during the thaw, threaten bridges with damage or destruction.

Even more forbidding are the problems presented to the road-builders by climate. The extremely low winter temperatures experienced over most of the country reduce the productivity of labour because of the need to work heavily gloved and clothed; they lessen the productivity of machines because of lubrication problems, the brittleness of steel at very low temperatures, and the wear of working with frozen-hard ground. Summer conditions are little better: over very large areas the firm surface of the frozen ground gives way to swamp which may make overland movement impossible, so that heavy machinery and materials have to be carried by air. And over this ill-drained land the summer heat draws forth clouds of tormenting flies and mosquitoes; these reduce the productivity of road-building labour in some regions by between 30 and 50 per cent. Drier southern areas are much better off, but even here heat and dust are drawbacks.

Nevertheless in the 1970s the Soviet Union embarked upon a modern motorway programme. Its main achievement was the completion in 1976 of the newly-aligned Moscow–Volgograd road. This modern multi-lane highway is almost 625 miles long, and avoids populated areas with which it is linked by approach roads and flyover intersections; the road has sixty-four bridges and innumerable culverts with a total length of 19,281 yards. Once roads are built, however, their maintenance poses an acute problem. It is, in fact, a sisyphean task to attempt to build up a Russian road network, for as fast as new roads are created, existing ones are destroyed. Frost-heaving in winter opens up cracks and distorts horizontal and vertical profiles; the freeze–thaw alternation which characterizes early spring and late autumn, breaks up surfaces; the floods and torrents that stem from the headlong thaw may wash roads away or encumber them with unwelcome deposits of mud and other debris. In the more arid regions, the extreme diurnal range of temperature subjects road-building materials to stresses which weaken them and hasten their disintegration. Tarmacadam surfaces melt in great heat while concrete surfaces are damaged by the salts necessitated to counter winter icing.

The country's poor roads helped to save it during the German onslaught of 1941. The Germans, whose armoured might had raced over the good highways of western Europe, were soon frustrated by Russia's roads. In the summer months they found rutted dusty tracks whose loose grit wrought havoc with their engines: the 10th Panzer division lost most of its heavy tanks from this cause. With the coming of the autumn rains, these same roads became ribbons of churned-up mud. The speed of the advance on Moscow, which had averaged 28 miles a day in the summer, had by mid-October dropped to barely a mile, and was never more than three.[12]

The absence of good roads leads to encroachment on farmland. To avoid the ruts and boulders, the potholes and the mud, drivers depart from the original track on to untravelled ground, progressively widening the road. A dirt road, originally 12 feet wide, may finish up as a broad swathe of 60 or 70 yards. In the more arid parts, unsurfaced roads and tracks produce dust which, blown over the adjoining fields, damages crops over wide areas. On the roads themselves thick accumulations of dust often occur; when it rains, as it does from time to time even in these dry lands, the dust is rapidly converted into mud so sticky that not even cross-country vehicles can operate on it.

Environmental pollution

The transformation of the countryside that takes place especially in TPKs is not limited to the usual forms of growing economic activity – roads and railways, plant and buildings, stimulated agricultural exploitation. There is an even more pervasive if less obtrusive impact upon the total environment over a large area, and since the effect of this is inevitably to lessen the purity of air and water and to damage the organisms of the biosphere it is widely known as environmental pollution.

Highly industrialized and urbanized areas discharge enormous quantities of smoke and dust, and of carbonic, nitric and sulphuric gases. The still atmosphere of much of the continental USSR fails to disperse these pollutants which hang as cloud, fog or discoloured haze, eventually to fall as acid rain with deleterious effects not only upon the plant life of the countryside but also upon the limestone façades of buildings in the towns. The oil- and gas-refining, petrochemical, metallurgical, non-ferrous-smelting and wood-chemical industries are the worst atmospheric polluters, along with thermal power stations, despite the adoption of costly protective measures: filters trap ash and the larger dust particles, but the smaller particles and the gases escape. Dust is also blown off spoil heaps, and from ploughed fields in semi-arid areas. These problems are not, of course, peculiar to the Soviet Union, and automotive pollution is less than in the West; not only are there fewer cars, but most petrol is lead-free and much public transport is electric.

Water is affected, indirectly by rain bringing down atmospheric pollution, and directly by the discharge into it of industrial effluent, urban sewage and the run-off from fields treated with agrochemicals. Many rivers have thus developed high concentrations of nitrates, phosphates, sulphates, hydrocarbons, phenols and metallic pollutants; fish and other beneficent organisms can no longer survive in them; furthermore, they carry their poisons down to the seas which are almost or wholly closed. Where there is high evaporation, as in the southern seas, pure water is lost while polluted water is gained, and water quality deteriorates pro-gressively. Northern rivers and streams, such as those polluted by effluents from the West Siberian oil- and gasfields, have weak self-purification capability: they have slight gradient, little velocity and volume, and low temperatures. Many of those in the south are in regions of internal drainage and cannot carry their offensive load away to any sea. The problem is recognized and much is being done to improve matters, especially by substituting air-cooling for water-cooling wherever possible and by recycling water: in the tenth plan period (1976–80) the water requirement of the chemical industry was not expected to rise above its level in the ninth, despite a rise in output of 60 per cent.[13]

Much concern has been felt for Lake Baykal because it is unique. Occupying a deep crack in the earth's surface, it holds the largest volume of fresh water of any lake in the world. Until recently this water was exceptionally pure and gave life to a remarkably rich and varied fauna with rare species unable to live in less pure waters elsewhere. The Soviet period has brought economic development to its shores in the form of logging and the building of two pulp mills intended to produce cellulose cord for heavy bomber tyres by a process for which pure water was essential, but which returned that water heavily polluted. Despite an unparalleled outcry, both scientific and public, the building and operation of the plants went ahead as being essential for national defence. Ironically, the cellulose cord they were to make was soon superseded by nylon cord. The effluent now undergoes costly cleansing treatment, but the water returned to the lake is still impure, and the equipment often functions inadequately or breaks down altogether. The logging of the surrounding slopes exposes the ground to erosion and this results in the washing of silt into the lake. The logs are rafted across the lake, but the bark gives off toxic wastes, and stray logs decay, consuming vital oxygen, and interfering with fish-breeding. Since the building of BAM began, the lake has become an important highway – for freighters in summer and trucks on its frozen surface in winter; this traffic has led to spillages of diesel fuel, oil and grease. Its main tributary, the Selenga, receives effluent and sewage from Ulan Ude. All this bodes tragedy for the lake, in many parts of which the minute plankton which constitute the first link in the food chain, are becoming extinct. The catch of its chief commercial fish, the choice omul, fell from some 10,000 tons in 1945 to 800 tons in 1968. Fishing has since been prohibited and there has been some recovery.

Pollution of the land surface takes many forms, the most unsightly being the industrial waste around factories and works, domestic garbage around urban centres, and the spoil heaps from mines. Open mining is expanding at an alarming pace; billions of tons of overburden are stripped off, together with soil and vegetation; it is dumped over further extensive areas, obliterating their soil and vegetation, and disrupting the natural drainage. From these vast dumps the wind blows the lighter material over wide areas, while the rain washes out gulleys, overloading streams and forming stagnant pools. In the northern lands low temperatures, low precipitation and the impermeable permafrost arrest the decay of sewage and lead to the formation of foul-smelling fly-ridden swamps. In the arid lands of the south, dustbowls and badlands follow all too easily from injudicious ploughing, while lands down-wind are coated with dust. In 1960 the USSR produced less mineral fertilizer than France or Germany and about a quarter as much as USA; in 1980 she produced more than USA, and this, along with growing quantities of herbicides and pesticides, is spread and sprayed upon the land with unknown long-term effects. Land reclamation, both as irrigation and drainage, has also had deleterious effects where it has not been properly managed.

The effect of all this upon the biosphere cannot be assessed, although it is known that the forest dies off around many forms of economic activity, where air, water and soil are all polluted. In the tundra the lichens upon which reindeer feed, are killed off by the growing amount of sulphur dioxide and other gases given off by the gas industry. The destructive effect of fire is felt wherever there is human settlement, and this destroys not only the forest but the mosses of the newly-invaded tundra. Unsympathetic lumbering, despite protective legislation, has also led to widespread deforestation. Wild life is likewise a victim of economic progress.

The Soviet Union leads the world in its official and national attitude to environmental pollution, and it proclaims its stand in the Constitution (Article 18), which also lays upon citizens the duty to protect and conserve nature (Article 67). It is an active supporter of and participator in the work of the International Union for the Conservation of Nature. It has set up numerous nature reserves, wild-life refuges, national parks and game reserves. It had protective legislation in the 1950s, long before the West had awoken to the environmental crisis. The maximum concentrations of toxic substances legally permitted in the atmosphere are lower than elsewhere. The five-year plans enjoin upon ministries and enterprises the need to take protective or remedial measures against pollution; vast sums are set aside for such purposes. Numerous scientists are employed in studying the possible environmental effect of projects under consideration. Societies to promote and agencies to organize nature protection abound and a sympathetic outlook is fostered in the schools. Green belts surround the larger towns, and every works or plant which may give offence is separated from residential areas by minimum distances fixed according to the nature of the operation. Ethyl petrol with added lead is little used and banned in several cities, while buses are run on gas to lessen urban pollution; electric transport is encouraged in urban and suburban areas, where 42 per cent of all public-transport passengers used it in 1980. No less a person than the Commander of the Strategic Missile Forces is said to have been fined 18,000 rubles for shooting polar bear in 1976: his adjutant, who actually did the shooting, lost his commission and was expelled from the Party.[14]

Yet in no country is economic growth more gloried in and nowhere is the goal of rapid industrialization more fervently pursued. To fulfil the plan, at almost whatever cost, is the ambition universally inculcated by the Party. The old ideas of Soviet technology and Communist resolution triumphing over an obstinate and difficult nature, resulting in its transformation into a more amenable environment, persist. The humiliating failure of Soviet agriculture to overcome an impossibly hostile environment has impelled the country into the greatest polluting campaign of all, the chemicalization of agriculture. Thus a strong awareness of the threat to the natural environment and a readiness to fight it, is in conflict with an even stronger determination to advance the economic development of the country. Also the Soviet Union is locked in an arms race with America, and this enables the producers of military ware to claim that nothing, not even nature protection, must stand in the way of national security.

Consequently reality falls short in many respects of the ideals. Environmental protection laws are a Republican function and the Republic of Estonia was the first to pass an atmospheric protection law in 1957 (all Republics had them by 1963). The urgency in Estonia was caused by massive pollution from the oil-shale power stations of Kokhtla Yarve; but the Moscow-based All-Union ministry responsible was not subject to Republican law and is said to have ignored it. Inspection of factories and works is inadequate and unpopular in a society where it is in everyone's interest to fulfil the plan. Small fines or suspended sentences are the commonest punishment, and it is said that enterprises even set sums aside for such fines in their financial plans. It may pay an individual manager to incur a low fine if it means winning a big bonus for being on target with production. The Marxist theory of value, whereby cost or price is assessed according to the amount of labour invested, has meant that land, water and air have been virtually free, with no economic incentive to conserve them.

Although there is informed discussion of most forms of pollution, there is no public debate about the dangers of nuclear power, and the Soviet public must take upon trust official assurances that its nuclear plants are clean and safe.

The 128 nature reserves are extremely difficult to protect.[15] Those in the more populous areas are under pressure from surrounding farmers and from tourists, while those in the more sparsely-peopled parts of Siberia and Central Asia are invaded by hunters, fishers and poachers. A Russian geographer[16] who made a cycle tour in south Russia and the Ukraine found much that was disquieting. Some reserves were 'literally overwhelmed by waves of human interference'; in others the managers were 'struggling to maintain the protected status of the areas entrusted to them', and getting little help from the local authorities. Nevertheless, the situation does not seem to be worse than elsewhere in the industrial world and may well be better. If it seems worse it is because it gets more publicity abroad and at home. It is certainly untrue that 'since 1975 you will not find a single reference to pollution of the air, the water, or the soil even in special articles'.[17] Soviet geographers, unlike their Western counter-parts, who are mostly geomorphologists, economic historians or social scientists, show a lively interest in what is happening to the natural environment, and they do not hide their concern. The leading journals have published many special articles on the subject since 1975, several of which have been translated into English in *Soviet Geography*.[18]

Water engineering

Interference with the natural flow of surface water – thereby indirectly affecting the rest of the hydrological cycle – is probably the most powerful way in which the Soviet state has altered the natural environment, and with it the landscape. Canals, for both irrigation and navigation, have been cut, and 'cascades' or hydroelectric dams and power stations built on many rivers, converting long stretches into reservoir lakes, thus altering the appearance of even a small-scale atlas map.

The Volga–Kama cascade (Table 22), planned by Stalin, will be accomplished with the completion of the Lower Kama station now under construction. It has a total capacity of nearly 11,000 MW, and its reservoir lakes, which together hold 22 cubic miles of water, have a combined area of 970 square miles. The more southerly of these reservoirs are used to supply water to badly-needed irrigation systems in the drought-stricken areas of southern Russia, but they themselves have flooded much agricultural land and there are many who argue that the environmental losses outweigh the economic gain. The Dnieper cascade, although its stations are of a relatively modest capacity, has converted that river also into a string of lakes, with similar advantages and disadvantages.

The greatest cascade of all is that of the Yenisey and its main tributary, the Angara (Table 23). This system has a potential capacity of 32,000 MW. Those stations already built or building are in the south where these rivers flow in deep narrow valleys, and reservoir construction requires high dams but not the wide inundations found on the Volga and Dnieper. It was at one time planned to build

TABLE 22. *The Volga–Kama cascade*

RIVER VOLGA		RIVER KAMA	
	(capacity MW)		(capacity MW)
Gorky	520	Perm (Kamskaya)	500
Cheboksary	1,400	Votkinsk	1,000
Kuybyshev	2,300	Lower Kama*	1,248
Saratov	1,400		
Volgograd	2,500		

*At Naberezhnye Chelny
Note: There are also older smaller stations on the Upper Volga, e.g. Rybinsk.

a cascade on the lower Ob involving extensive flooding of the swamp tayga, but these plans were dropped when the region was found to be rich in oil and gas. There are also large developments in Central Asia on the Naryn and Vakhsh, and cascades of small-capacity stations on many of the rivers of northwest Russia and the Caucasus region.

TABLE 23. *The Yenisey–Angara cascade*

RIVER YENISEY		RIVER ANGARA	
	(capacity MW)		(capacity MW)
Sayano–Shushensk	6,400	Irkutsk	400
Maynsk	320	Bratsk	4,500
Krasnoyarsk	6,000	Ust Ilimsk	3,800
(Mid-Yenisey	7,000)†	Boguchansk	3,000*

*Under construction   † Planned

The advocates of giant hydroelectric schemes have been able, in every five-year plan, to obtain the investment required for huge capital constructions, despite strong competing claims for funds, and the objections of other powerful interests, such as agriculture, fishing, forestry and mining; these interests do not wish to see land inundated which they hope themselves to exploit. It has been said that the power of the hydrological planning agency dates from the time when it was a branch of the NKVD, the police body which organized forced labour for Stalin's first five-year plans: as the cutting of canals and construction of hydroelectric stations was the use to which conscript labour was to be put, the NKVD needed an organization to plan and administer the work.[19] The prestige and power of the agency were enhanced because it combined electrification, which Lenin had enthusiastically advocated, with Stalin's predilection for canals, dams and reservoirs, and because it produced rapid and visible evidence of Soviet man's ability to conquer and transform nature.

A major achievement of the hydrological agency while a branch of the NKVD was the Baltic–White Sea canal (see pp. 71–72). The Moscow canal, linking the capital with the Volga waterway, followed. Later, in the 1950s, the Volga–Don canal was cut; associated with it is a hydroelectric station and a large reservoir-lake, the Tsimlyansk Sea. Subsequent work has improved the Russian network of rivers and waterways to such an extent that specially-built river–sea vessels are able to penetrate to inland industrial centres of Russia from Mediterranean, Channel and North Sea ports as well as from the Baltic and Black Seas.

Apart from the continuing hydroelectric programmes, the main concern of the water engineers in the 1980s is the planning and designing of water-transfer projects. As the northern part of the country is afflicted by a surplus of water, expressed in the form of extensive swamps, whereas the southern parts suffer from aridity, schemes to transfer water from one to the other are attractive. The urgency of such a transfer has been increased by two factors. One is the USSR's desire to feed its growing population from its own territory, a strategic necessity in a landlocked state subject to blockade; the agricultural productivity of the southern arid lands could be vastly increased if more water were made available. The other is the rapid growth of population in Soviet Central Asia: here people are reluctant to work in factories and unwilling to migrate, but would welcome employment on new irrigated farms. These two compelling reasons make the adoption of some sort of transfer scheme essential and inevitable. The 25th Party Congress in 1976 called for feasibility studies and research into possible environmental impact, and these have since been arranged by the research institute *Soyuzgiprovodkhoz*.

The various water transfers under consideration include those from the Sukhona and Onega rivers to the Volga at Rybinsk, from the Pechora and Vychegda to the Kama, from the lower Ob across the Urals to the Kama, and from the Ob and Irtysh to the Aral via the Turgay gap. The latter is the most important because it would supply Central Asia where water is most badly needed. The favourite plans calls for a dam on the Ob just below the mouth of the Irtysh, with water pumped back along the Irtysh to a reservoir-lake at Tobolsk; hence a canal would carry it through the Turgay gap into the Aral basin. Alarmist reports put about in the West that catastrophic climatic and sea-level changes would follow from the lessening of freshwater input into the Arctic Sea can be disregarded. The water to be diverted is surplus water that at present feeds the swamps of the West Siberian tayga. The amount proposed for withdrawal will help drain the swamps without greatly affecting flow into the Arctic. Geographers from the Universities of Moscow and Tashkent who have been commissioned to study the environmental effects of the scheme report that they will be 'fairly well localized'.[20] Other suggested transfers are from the lower Danube river to the southern Ukraine and from the Dnieper to the Donbass, the latter of which has been put into effect.

Settlement and the environment

The Soviet state has a pronounced impact on the landscape through its population and settlement policy. Although the various settlement forms which make up the 'residential' landscape are to some extent inherited from the past, the traditional forms were largely dislocated, damaged or destroyed in western regions by the war. The facts that during the Soviet period agriculture has been completely reorganized, that rural population has declined by 35 million, that urban population has risen by nearly 150 million, and that over 1,200 new towns have been founded, mean that the present pattern and morphology of settlement has been greatly affected by Soviet policies.

Traditionally the villages of the Soviet countryside had a distinctive appearance according to region. The Russian village of log houses, with carved and painted window frames, was found not only in old Muscovy but in all those areas colonized by Russians. Villages and hamlets had these izbas lined along a main street with perhaps a few along tracks leading off at right angles. A plainer cruder version of the izba, with less carving or none at all, was found in the poverty-stricken villages of Belorussia. The *khata*, a cottage mainly of clay, reeds and thatch, with a minimum of wood, characterized the Ukrainian village of the treeless steppe. Many of the nomadic peoples of the Central Asian and south Siberian steppe lived in round skin tents or *yurts*. Much village architecture in the Baltic Republics was reminiscent of German forms.

During the collectivization of agriculture in the late 1920s and early 1930s, the smallholdings attached to several villages were amalgamated into one large collective farm or *kolkhoz*. Subsequently collective farms were expanded or amalgamated, so that they are now huge units. One of the many villages embraced within these vast estates becomes the farm centre and is transformed as it develops administrative buildings, storage, maintenance and repair facilities, social and political organizations, services such as schools, etc. All the other villages tend to decline or decay. Generally state policy favours the building up of the farm centre into an *agrogorodok* or 'agrotown', and the concentration of population within it. This facilitates the provision of a range of services impossible to supply to widely scattered villages. Besides the usual collective farm–centre buildings, the agrogorodok will have small blocks of modern flats, a hospital, schools, kindergarten, cinema, clubs, shops, etc. It will have electricity and possibly gas, as well as piped water and mains drainage, none of which are available in the villages. It will also have some light industry, food-processing or textiles perhaps. This enables the workforce to be usefully and gainfully employed in the winter months when farming activity ceases, and may retain surplus population which would otherwise leave. On the whole, younger people welcome the move to the agrotown because of the improved standard of living, but older people prefer to stay in the old village despite such hardships as having to fetch water from the pump.

Official approval of the agrogorodok is not universal. Rural housing is a Republican function, and in Lithuania, for instance, the ministry responsible, Minsel'stroy, favours a scattered form of rural settlement. Soviet collective farmers are entitled to allotments on which they can raise their own food, selling the surplus to friends and relatives or in the market of a nearby town. Although at one time the authorities were hostile to these private farms as distracting the peasants from working for the collective, they are now encouraged because they increase the total food supply. When workers leave the village for the agrogorodok, although they do not lose their right to a private plot, it is located at an inconvenient distance and the former interest in private farming is lost in urban surroundings. Lithuania's Minsel'stroy advocates building individual family houses on the private plots of collective farmers.[21] Thus the settlement landscape can change according to the Republic one is in.

The enormous increase in the urban population during the Soviet period has gone in the main to expand existing towns, but new Soviet towns account for 14 million people. Many of them have grown into large cities (Table 24). The eight fastest-growing towns in the 1970–79 intercensal (Chelny, Nizhnevartovsk, Surgut, Nizhnekamsk, Stary Oskol, Tolyatti, Shevchenko and Zelenograd) were all new towns.

TABLE 24. *Population (1981) of the larger new towns founded in the Soviet period (thousands)*

Karaganda	583	Sumgait	201
Novokuznetsk	551	Norilsk	184
Tolyatti	533	Nizhnekamsk	143
Dushanbe	510	Salavat	142
Kemerovo	486	Surgut	137
Magnitogorsk	413	Zelenograd	135
Naberezhnye Chelny	346	Rustavi	134
Angarsk	245	Nizhnevartovsk	134
Bratsk	222	Volgodonsk	126
Volzhsky	220	Shevchenko	122
Temirtau	217	Nukus	119*

*Centre for newly irrigated land in the Amu delta in Soviet Central Asia

Soviet towns of old foundation have not always expanded in area as they have grown in population, and when they have done so, the expansion has been disproportionately small. The old Russian town was a great sprawl of individual wooden houses, just as the traditional Central Asian city was a vast extent of adobe huts. The Soviet period has seen their replacement by ever larger blocks of flats, concentrating a much denser population in a much smaller area. Thus although Moscow and Chicago hold similar numbers, the American city, with its vast residential and suburban areas of one- and two-storey wood-framed houses, is many times as large as the compact, concentrated, high-built Soviet capital.

There are in fact noteworthy contrasts between Soviet and Western towns. Apart from Moscow and Leningrad, with their distinctive historical roles, the central area of the typical Russian town tends to be rather drab, with the two-storey painted stucco buildings of the late tsarist period predominating. As one moves away from the old centre the first Soviet blocks of flats appear, modest in height and undistinguished in architecture. And the farther one goes out, the newer and taller these blocks become, with veritable skyscrapers on the periphery. This is quite different from the American town, with its concentrated central business district characterized by tall blocks, and with a progressive diminution in the average height of buildings outwards until the low and individual 'ranch-style' dwellings of the newest and most select residential areas are found on the fringe. This contrast is rooted in the different economic systems. Private business develops the central areas of large American cities. But in Russia, where economic administration is headquartered in Moscow, there is little need for office space in the normal large Soviet city. The exceptions, apart from the obvious one of Moscow itself, are the republican and oblast capitals, which have central administrative blocks. Republican capitals have also the governmental, cultural and educational buildings for their peoples and these often give them impressive city centres with imposing modern edifices.

It is the private automobile that has enabled Western cities to sprawl over vast expanses of urban–rural fringe land. When the Western city is approached there is normally a gradual transition from country to town as buildings, traffic and people increase in density. The beginning of a modern Soviet town is sharply announced and defined by its outermost tall cliff-like twenty- and twenty-five-storey apartment blocks. Once it has reached its limits, it may not intrude into its green belt; in any case it cannot practically grow beyond the size that can be served by public transport, as only a tiny proportion of its population have cars. Instead, a satellite town will grow up at the next station along the railway line, allowing its inhabitants to commute by train into the big city. Zelenograd (Table 24) is a satellite town of Moscow. Nowhere is the impact of a distinctive political, social and economic system portrayed more strikingly than in the Soviet townscape.

References

Chapter 1 (pages 1–12)

1. Carl O. Sauer, 'The morphology of landscape', *University of California Publications in Geography*, **2** (1925), 39.
2. L. S. Berg, *Die Geographischen Zonen der Sowjetunion*, Leipzig, 1958, vol. 1, p. 12.

Chapter 2 (pages 13–29)

1. W. Coxe, *Travels into Poland, Russia, etc.*, London, 1784, vol. 1, p. 254.
2. S. H. Cross and O. P. Sherbowitz-Wetzor, *The Russian Primary Chronicle: Laurentian text*, Cambridge, Mass., The Medieval Academy of America, 1953, p. 139.
3. P. H. Bruce, *Memoirs*, London, 1782, pp. 103–4.
4. Constantine Porphyrogenitus, *c.* A.D. 950, IX.15.
5. P. J. Strahlenberg, *Das Nord und Ostliche Theil von Europa und Asia*, Stockholm, 1730, p. 408.
6. *Ibid.*, p. 348.
7. Coxe, *op. cit.*, vol. 1, p. 253.
8. G. Fletcher, 'Of the Russe Commonwealth', in *Russia at the Close of the Sixteenth Century*, ed. E. H. Bond, London, Hakluyt Society, 1856, p. 26.
9. Fletcher, *op. cit.*, p. 63.
10. Coxe, op. cit., vol. 2, p. 181.
11. *Ibid.*, vol. 1, pp. 421–2.
12. G. T. Robinson, *Rural Russia under the Old Régime*, New York, Macmillan, 1932, p. 53.
13. Herodotus, trans. J. E. Powell, Oxford, Clarendon Press, 1949, IV.46.
14. E. D. Clarke, *Travels in Various Countries*, London, 1810, vol. 1, pp. 274–99.
15. M. Holderness, *New Russia: A Journey from Riga to the Crimea*, London, 1823, pp. 160–1.
16. *Ibid.*, p. 147.
17. Clarke, *op. cit.*, vol. 1, pp. 309–12.
18. Holderness, *op. çit.*, p. 96.
19. M. Guthrie, *A Tour Performed in the Years 1795–96 through the Tauride, etc.*, London, 1802, p. 25.

20. R. A. Lewis, 'Early Irrigation in West Turkestan', *Annals of the Association of American Geographers*, **56** (1966), 467.
21. Herodotus, trans. J. E. Powell, III.116–17.
22. R. Lyall, *Travels in Russia, the Krimea, the Caucasus and Georgia*, London, 1825, vol. 1, pp. 260–1.
23. *Ibid.*, p. 316.
24. *Ibid.*, p. 361.
25. H. D. Seymour, *Russia on the Black Sea and Sea of Azov*, London, 1855, p. 211.

Chapter 4 (pages 42–56)

1. F. N. Mil'kov and N. A. Gvozdetskiy, *Fisicheskaya Geografiya SSSR*, Moscow, 1958, pp. 163–4.
2. F. Nansen, *Through Siberia, the Land of the Future*, trans. A. G. Chater, Heinemann, 1914, p. 150.

Chapter 5 (pages 57–92)

1. J. Stadling, *Through Siberia*, ed. F. H. H. Guillemard, Constable, 1901, p. 45.
2. *Ibid.*, p. 74.
3. C. Le Brun, *Travels*, London, 1759, p. 20.
4. Giles Fletcher, 'Of the Russe Commonwealth', in *Russia at the Close of the Sixteenth Century*, ed. E. H. Bond, London, Hakluyt Society, 1856, pp. 13–14.
5. E. Felinska, *Revelations of Siberia*, London, 1852, vol. 1, pp. 67, 86.
6. F. Nansen, *Through Siberia, the land of the Future*, trans. A. G. Chater, Heinemann, 1914, p. 254.
7. P. J. Strahlenberg, *Das Nord und Ostliche Theil von Europa und Asia*, Stockholm 1730, pp. 376–8.
8. Stadling, *op. cit.*, p. 68.
9. I. P. Gerasimov, ed., *Srednyaya Polosa Yevropeyskoy Chasti SSSR*, Moscow, Academy of Sciences, USSR, Institute of Geography, 1967, p. 383.

Chapter 6 (pages 93–124)

1. F. N. Mil'kov and N. A. Gvozdetskiy, *Fisicheskaya Geografiya SSSR*, Moscow, 1958, p. 195.
2. L. S. Berg, *Die Geographischen Zonen der Sowjetunion*, Leipzig, 1958, vol. 1, p. 357–8
3. H. D. Seymour, *Russia on the Black Sea*, London, Murray, 1855, p. 294.
4. I. P. Gerasimov, ed., *Srednyaya Polosa Yevropeyskoy Chasti SSSR*, Moscow, Academy of Sciences, USSR, Institute of Geography, 1967, p. 383.

5. *Ekonomicheskaya Gazeta*, 1981 (30), 6.
6. *Ibid.*, 1979, (20), 16.
7. C. H. Cottrell, *Recollections of Siberia*, London, 1842, pp. 199–200.
8. Clarke, *op. cit.*, p. 306.

Chapter 7 (pages 125–146)

1. M. P. Petrov, *Pustyni SSSR i ikh osvoyeniye*, Moscow, 1964, p. 23.
2. For a more detailed treatment of Central Asian irrigation problems, see P. P. Micklin, 'Irrigation development in the USSR during the 10th five-year plan (1976–80)', *Soviet Geography*, **19** (1) (Jan. 1978), 1–24.

Chapter 8 (pages 147–171)

1. L. S. Berg, *Die geographischen Zonen der Sowjetunion*, Leipzig, Teubner, 1959, vol. **2**, p. 445.
2. N. A. Gvozdetsky and N. I. Mikhaylov, *Fisicheskaya geografiya SSSR, aziatskaya chast'*, Moscow, 1963, p. 513; Berg, *op. cit.*, vol. 2, p. 501.
3. I. P. Gerasimov *et al.*, *Ural i Priural'e*, Moscow, 1968, p. 350.

Chapter 9 (pages 172–192)

1. I. T. Smilga (1932), quoted in Y. G. Saushkin, 'A history of Soviet economic geography', *Soviet Geography*, **7**, (8) (Oct. 1966), 31.
2. Saushkin, *op. cit.*, 45.
3. V. A. Anuchin, 'A sad tale about geography', *Soviet Geography*, **6**, (7) (Sept. 1965), 31.
4. *Ekonomicheskaya Gazeta*, 1978, (27), 2.
5. *Ibid.*, 1974, (47), 8.
6. *Ibid.*, 1981, (30), 6.
7. *Soviet Geography*, **22** (10) (Dec. 1981), 538.
8. *Ekonomicheskaya Gazeta*, 1974, (47), 8.
9. *Ibid.*, 1981, (50), 10.
10. *Ibid.*, (45), 8.
11. *Soviet Weekly*, 17 May 1969.
12. P. Carell, *Hitler's war on Russia*, trans. E. Ossers, London, Harrap, 1964, p. 149.
13. *Soviet Geography*, **20** (1), (Jan. 1979), 4.
14. B. Komarov, *The destruction of nature in the Soviet Union*, London, Pluto, 1980, p. 90.
15. A comprehensive account is D. Fischer, 'Nature reserves of the Soviet Union: an inventory', *Soviet Geography*, **22** (10) (Dec. 1981), 500–22.
16. Yu. A. Mekayev, 'Nature reserves in the southern European USSR, their condition and future prospects', *Soviet Geography*, **22** (10) (Dec. 1981), 523–28.

17. Komarov, *op. cit.*, 16.
18. For example, **19** (1) (Jan. 1978), 25; **20** (2) (Feb. 1979), 97; **20** (10) (Dec. 1979), 496; **21** (6) (June 1980), 377; **22** (2) (Feb. 1981), 67; **22** (4) (April 1981), 217; **22** (5) (May 1981), 325.
19. Komarov, *op. cit.*, 59–61.
20. *Soviet Geography*, **22** (6) (June 1981), 365.
21. *Ekonomicheskaya Gazeta*, 1981 (50), 18.

Further reading

Soviet Geography, published monthly (not July and August) by Scripta, Washington DC, is by far the best source in English of articles on the Soviet landscape and other matters geographical; its 'News Notes', compiled by the editor, T. Shabad, offer a unique opportunity to keep abreast of developments in Soviet economic geography. Useful books on various aspects of Soviet geography include:

BATER, J. H. *The Soviet city: ideal and reality*, Arnold, London, 1980.

BERG, L. S. *Natural regions of the U.S.S.R.*, Macmillan, New York, 1950.

BORISOV, A. A. *Climates of the U.S.S.R.*, C. A. Halstead (ed.), trans. R. A Ledward. Oliver and Boyd, Edinburgh, 1966.

DEMKO, G. J. and FUCHS, R. J. *Geographical perspectives in the Soviet Union*, Ohio State University Press, Columbus, Ohio, 1974.

DEWDNEY, J. C. *The USSR*, Hutchinson, London, 1978.

GOLDMAN, I. *The spoils of progress: environmental pollution in the Soviet Union*, MIT, Cambridge, Mass., 1972.

GREGORY, J. S. *The geography of the USSR: an introductory survey*, Novosti, Moscow, 1975.

MATHIESON, R. S. *The Soviet Union: an economic geography*, Heinemann, London, 1975.

MELLOR, R. E. H. *The Soviet Union and its geographical problems*, Macmillan, London, 1982.

PALLOT, J. and SHAW, D. J. B. *Planning in the Soviet Union*, Croom Helm, London, 1981.

PARKER, W. H. *An historical geography of Russia*, University of London Press, London, 1968.

SHABAD, T. and MOTE, V.L. *Gateway to Siberian resources: the BAM*, Scripta, Washington DC, 1977.

SINGLETON, F. (ed.) *Environmental misuse in the Soviet Union*, Praeger, New York, 1976.

Society and the environment: a Soviet view, Progress, Moscow, 1977.

SYMONS, L. *Russian agriculture: a geographic survey*, Bell, London, 1972.

SYMONS, L. and WHITE, C. (eds) *Russian transport*, Bell, London, 1975.

Index

Brezhnev, *see* Naberezhnye Chelny
Bryansk, 85
Bukhara, 27–8, 144
buran, 139

Calligonum caput-medusae, 132
canals, 35, 39, 71–2, 83, 86, 92, 117,
    140–1, 187, 188
capital investment, 174–5
Carpathians, 148, 156, 160
Caspian fishery, 144–5
Catherine II, 119
Caucasus Mountains: glaciation, 152;
    hydroelectricity, 163; karstic
    features, 154, 155; maps, 152, 162;
    minerals, 161; relief, 155; resorts,
    165; valleys, 166; vegetation, 148–9,
    151, 153
cement manufacture, 38, 107, 110
Central Asian Mountains, 149, 152, 153,
    154, 162, 163, 166
Central Russian Heights, 95
Cheboksary, 92; power station at, 92
Cheleken peninsula, 142
Chelyabinsk, 169–70, 174
chemical industry, 35, 85, 88, 184
Cheremkhovo, 78
Cherepovets, 74, 107
Cherkassk, 24
Chernobyl nuclear power station, 85
Chernogorsk, 164–5
Chersonesus, 23
Chimkent, 144
Chirchik, 144
Chita, 171, 179
Chukotka peninsula, 54
Chusavaya valley, 158
citrus fruit, 165–6
climate: Amur valley, 158–9; desert,
    127–8; effect of, 21; mixed forest,
    65–6; mountain belt, 147–8, 151,
    154; and roads, 181–3; semi-desert,
    126; steppe, 93–5; tayga, 59, 60–1,
    62–3; tundra, 44 coalfields:
    Cheremkhovo, 78; Donbass, 115,

117–18; Ekibastuz, 124; Kansk-
    Achinsk, 113; Karaganda, 115;
    Kuzbass, 113; Neryungri, 161–3;
    Pechora, 52; Ural, 160
collectivization of agriculture, 36–7,
    104–5, 116, 190
Communist party (CPSU), 174–5
copper mining and smelting, 73, 142,
    160, 161, 179
Cossacks, 23–4, 75
cotton growing, 141, 165
Crimean Mountains, 148, 154–5, 165,
    169
Crimean Tartars, 28–9
Crimean War, 23
cultural landscapes, 6

Dahurian (Dauric) larch, 62, 150
desert gopher, 129
desert lily, 132
determinism, 30–1
diamonds, 78, 79
direct reduction steelworks, 107
Dneprodzerzhinsk, 119
Dnepropetrovsk, 119
Dneprorudny, 119
Dnieper rapids, 35, 101
Donbass (Donets) coalfields, 115, 117–18
Donets Heights, 100–1
Donetsk, 118
dry rain, 128
Dudinka, 50, 56
dunes, 131–2, 141
Dushanbe, 163, 170, 191
Dzerzhinsk, 88
Dzhambul, 144, 181

earthquakes, 138, 143, 155
East Siberian Mountains, 161–2
East Slavs, 13, 16
eastern development, 174–5, 178–9
Ekibastuz lignite field, 38, 124, 179
electrification, 34, 38, 175; *see also*
    hydroelectricity

irrigation, 26–7, 39, 117, 121–3, 138–41, 146–7, 163, 166–7
Ishim steppe, 98
Ivan III, 21
Ivan IV, 17, 20
Ivano-Frankovsk, 160
Ivanovo, 87, 88
Ixiolirion tataricum, 129
izbas, 13–14, 84, 113, 190
Izhevsk, 73, 74

jerboa, 129
Juniperus semiglobosa, 149

Kachkanar, 161
Kakhovka irrigational canal, 39, 117
Kakhovka reservoir, 117
Kalinin, 21, 83, 87, 88
Kaliningrad, 82, 83
Kaluga, 87
Kama motor works (KamAZ), 39, 108
Kama river, 108, 160, 187
Kamchatka, 155, 167
Kamchatka Mountains, 150
Kamyshin, 120
Kandalaksha, 74
Kansk-Achinsk coalfield, 38, 113, 179
Kara-bogaz-gol, 142, 145
Karaganda, 123, 124, 191
Kara-Kum canal, 39, 140, 143
Kara-Kum desert, 131, 138
Karatau-Dzhambul complex, 144, 179
Karelia, 59–60
karstic features, 64, 154–5
Kaunas, 82, 83
Kazakh folded upland, 102, 127
Kazakhstan, 123
Kazan, 91–2
Kemerovo, 113, 191
Khabarovsk, 170, 171
Kharkov, 109–10
khatas, 25, 105, 116, 190
Khibin Mountains, 60
Khiva, 144

Khorezm, 27
Khrushchev, 173–4, 178
Kiev, 108–9, 110
Kievan Russia, 23
Kineshma, 88
Kirov (Vyatka), 74
Kirovsk, 74
Kishinev, 110, 111
Kochia prostrata, 100
Kokhtla Yarve, 83, 186
Kola nuclear power station, 53
Kola peninsula, 59–60, 73
Kolkhid lowland, 149, 166
kolkhozi, 190
kolki, 98
Komi ASSR, 72, 74
Komsomolsk, 171, 179
Konstantinovka, 118; nuclear power station at, 118
Kostroma, 87–8; power station at, 88
Krasnodar, 117
Krasnovodsk, 145
Krasnoyarsk, 111, 112, 114–15; power station at, 38, 114–15, 176, 188
Kremenchug, 118, 119
Krivoy Rog, 118, 119
Kuban, 117
Kulunda steppe, 102, 121
Kura river, 163, 168
Kurgan, 114
kurgans, 22
Kursk magnetic anomaly (KMA), 39, 106–7, 179
Kursk nuclear power station, 106, 107
Kuybyshev, 103, 110; power station, at, 107, 108, 110
Kuzbass, 78, 113
Kyzyl-Kum desert, 131, 132, 142

Lake Balkhash, 146
Lake Baskunchak, 127, 141
Lake Baykal, 158, 165, 184
Lake Elton, 127
Lake Issyk-Kul, 158
Lake Karakul, 157

Vladimir I, 18, 23, 109
Vladivostok, 170, 171
volcanoes, 155–6
Volga-Baltic canal, 39, 72
Volga delta, 135
Volga-Don canal, 39, 117
Volga-Kama waterway, 108
Volga-Ural oilfield, 92, 107–8, 110
Volgodonsk, 120, 191
Volgograd (Stalingrad), 39, 120; power
   station at, 120, 176, 187
Vologda, 70, 74
Volsk, 110
Volynian-Podolian upland, 96
Volzhsky, 120, 191
Vorkuta, 56
Vorkutugol, 54
Voronezh, 103, 110
Voronezh nuclear power station, 106,
   107, 110
Voroshilovgrad, 118

War of 1941–45, 37, 45, 105, 109, 116,
   182, 82
water resources, 146, 163, 187–9
West Siberian complex, 53, 75–6, 179
West Siberian railway, 39, 75–6, 177–8
wheat cultivation, 120–3
whistling mouse, 129
White Russia (Belorussia), 84–5, 190
wood chemicals, 39, 78, 171
wood culture, 13–16, 67
woodworking, 73, 160, 170

wormwood (*Artemisia*), 126, 129, 131,
   134

xerophytes, 128

Yakutia, 76–9, 167, 179
Yakuts, 76–7
Yakutsk, 63, 77, 79
Yalta, 29
Yamal peninsula, 49
Yamburg gasfield, 53
Yaroslavl, 86, 87, 88
yary, 95, 100
yasak, 76
Yavan, 163, 167
yayly, 154–5
Yenieseysk, 75
Yerevan, 168
Yergeni Hills, 127
yurts, 190
Yuzhny, 119, 175

Zainsk power station, 108
Zaporozhe, 118, 119
Zeravshan valley, 26, 140–1
Zeya power station, 165, 179
Zhdanov, 119
Zheleznogorsk, 107
Zhiguli Mountains, 95
Zhitomir, 106
Zhlobin, 85
Zlatoust, 169